NIGHT OF THE LIVING CAT

Story by HAWKMAN   **Art by MECHA-ROOTS**

2

CONTENTS

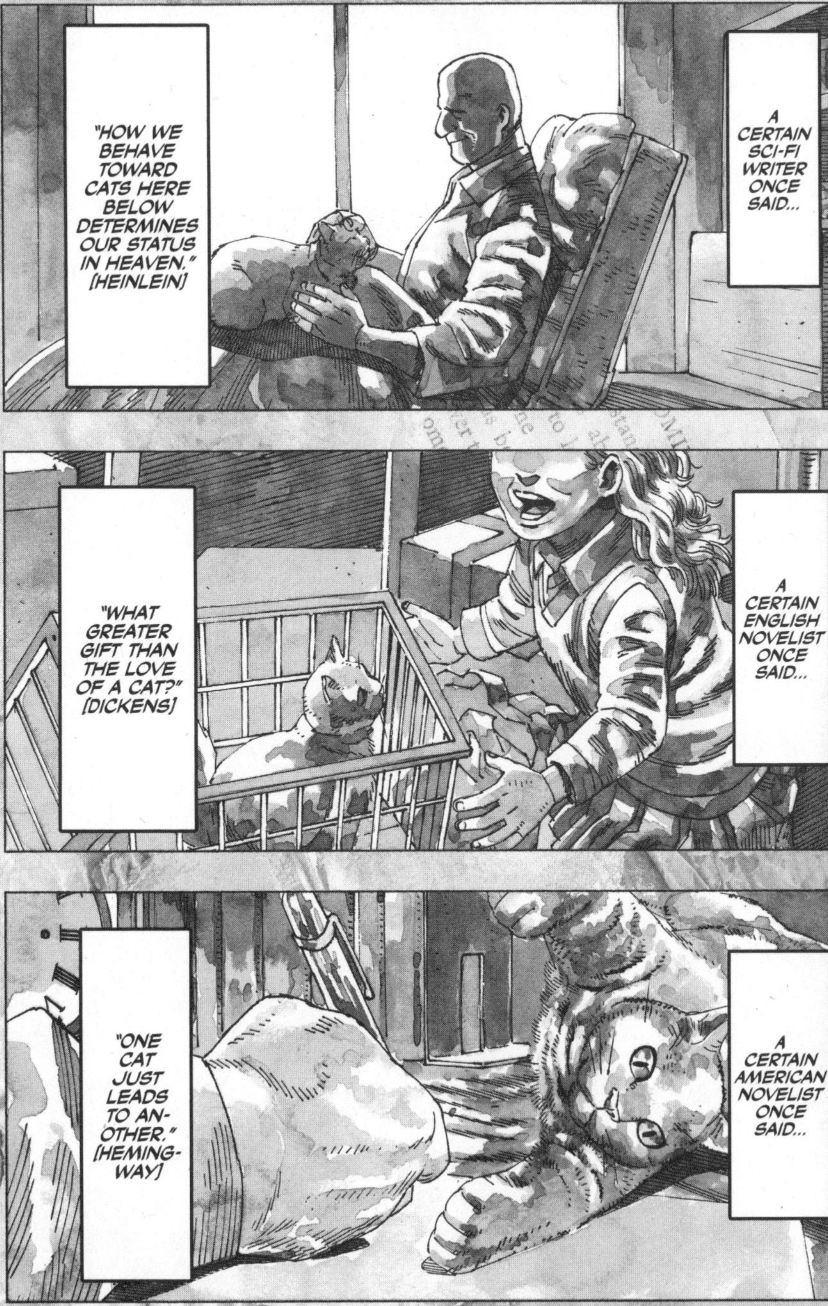
A CERTAIN SCI-FI WRITER ONCE SAID...
"HOW WE BEHAVE TOWARD CATS HERE BELOW DETERMINES OUR STATUS IN HEAVEN." [HEINLEIN]
A CERTAIN ENGLISH NOVELIST ONCE SAID...
"WHAT GREATER GIFT THAN THE LOVE OF A CAT?" [DICKENS]
A CERTAIN AMERICAN NOVELIST ONCE SAID...
"ONE CAT JUST LEADS TO AN-OTHER." [HEMING-WAY]

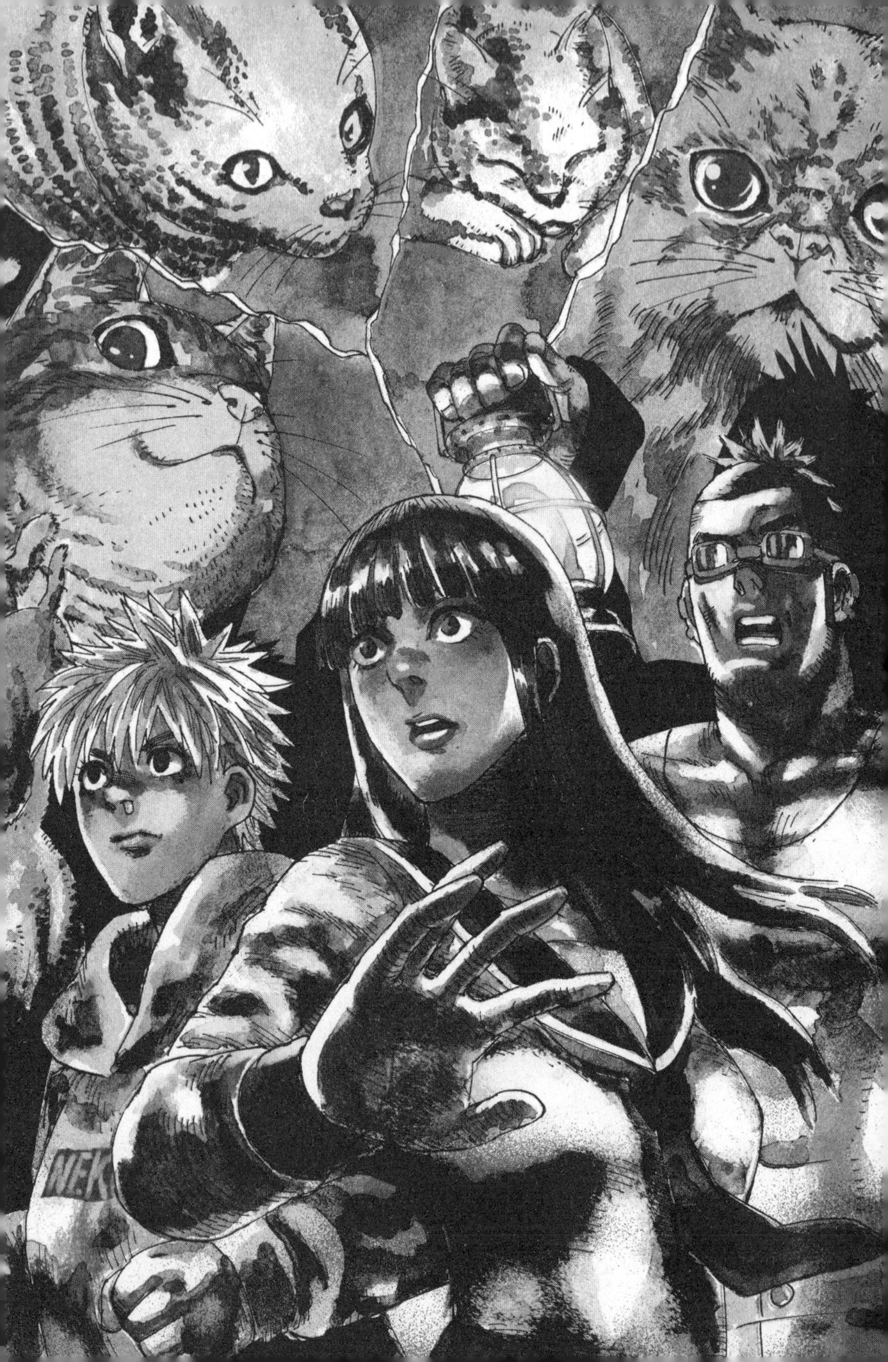

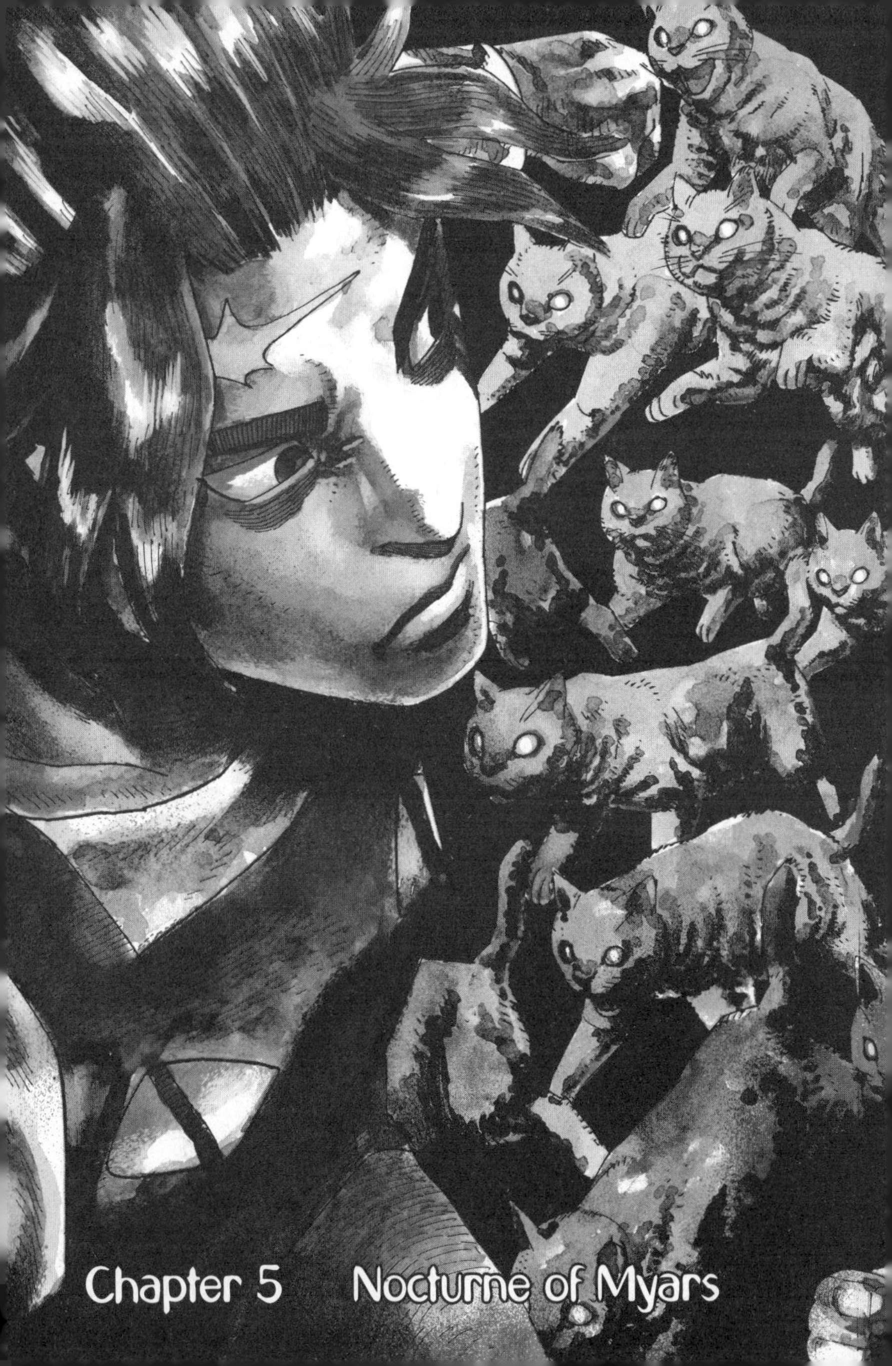
Chapter 5 Nocturne of Myars

NYAIGHT
OF THE
LIVING
CAT
2

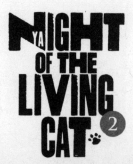

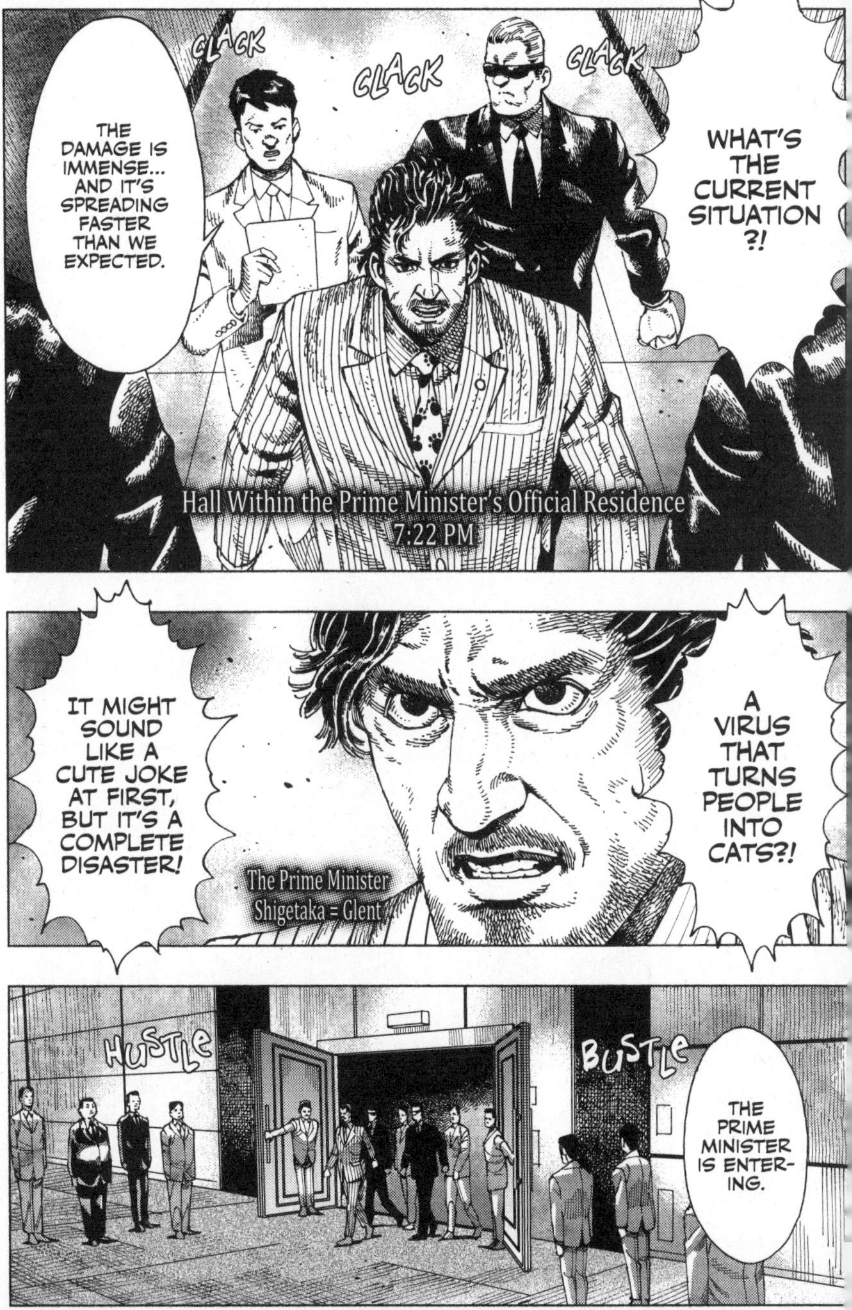
WHAT'S THE CURRENT SITUATION?!
CLACK
CLACK
CLACK
THE DAMAGE IS IMMENSE... AND IT'S SPREADING FASTER THAN WE EXPECTED.
Hall Within the Prime Minister's Official Residence
7:22 PM
A VIRUS THAT TURNS PEOPLE INTO CATS?!
The Prime Minister
Shigetaka = Glent
IT MIGHT SOUND LIKE A CUTE JOKE AT FIRST, BUT IT'S A COMPLETE DISASTER!
BUSTLE
HUSTLE
THE PRIME MINISTER IS ENTER-ING.

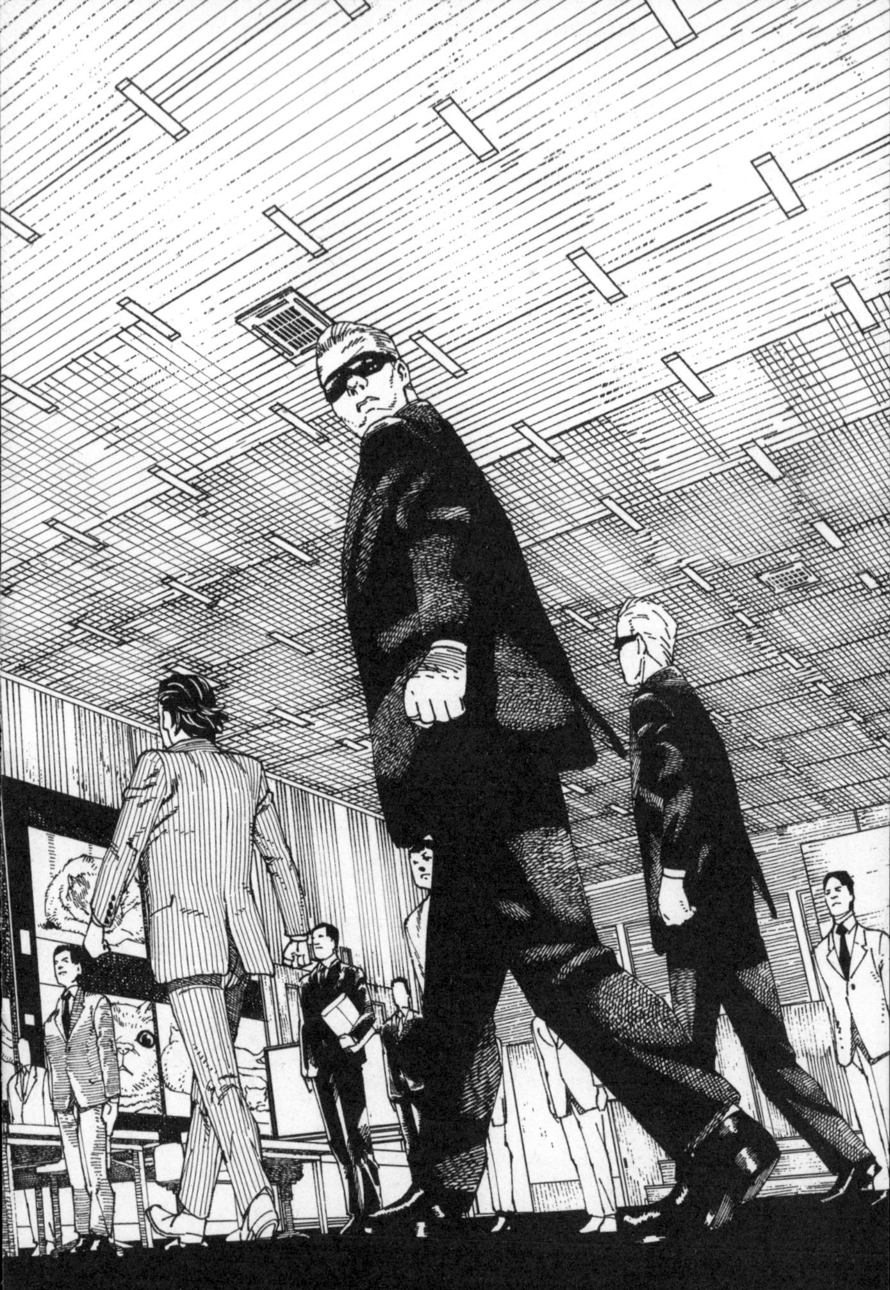

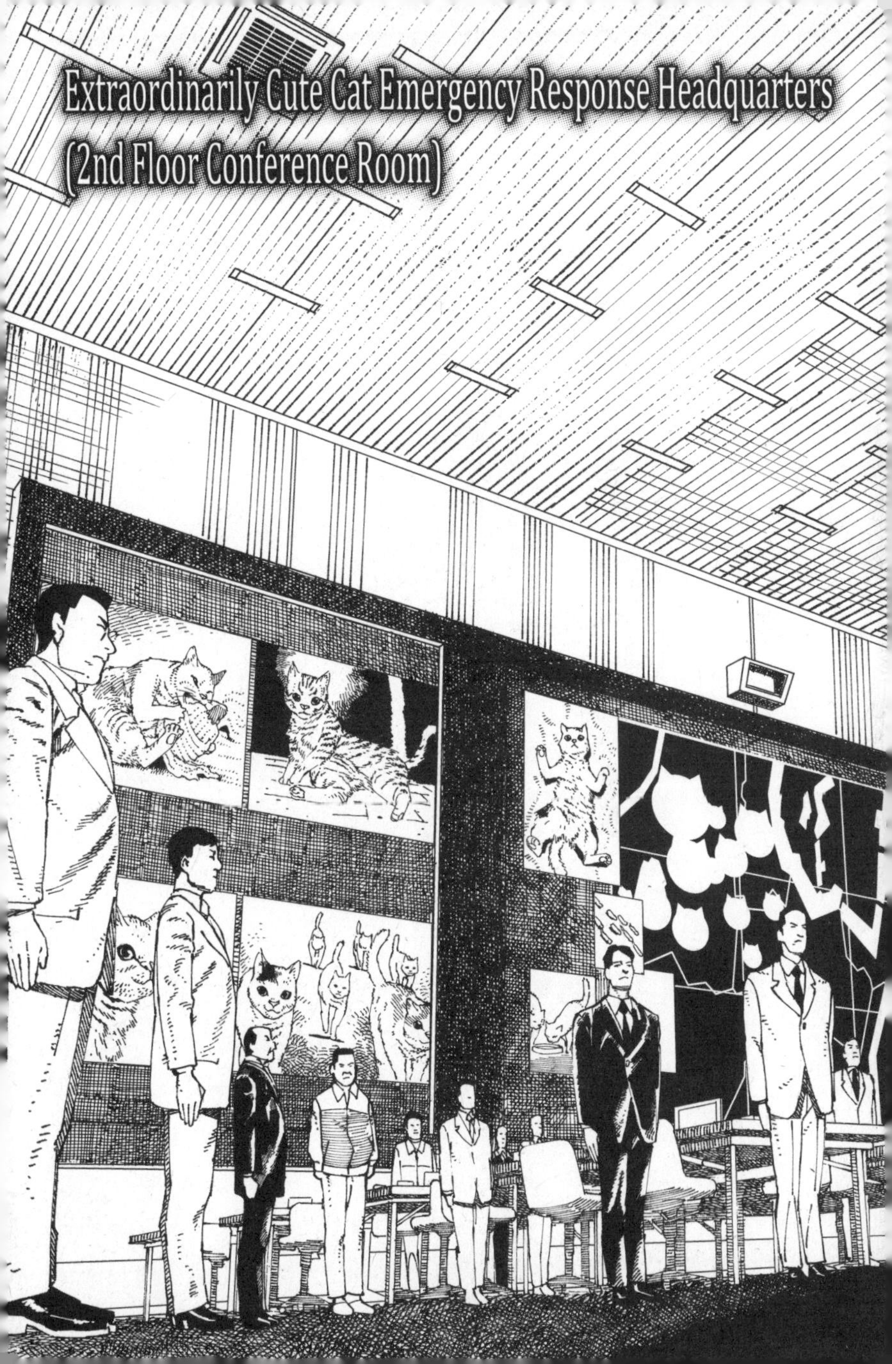
Extraordinarily Cute Cat Emergency Response Headquarters
(2nd Floor Conference Room)

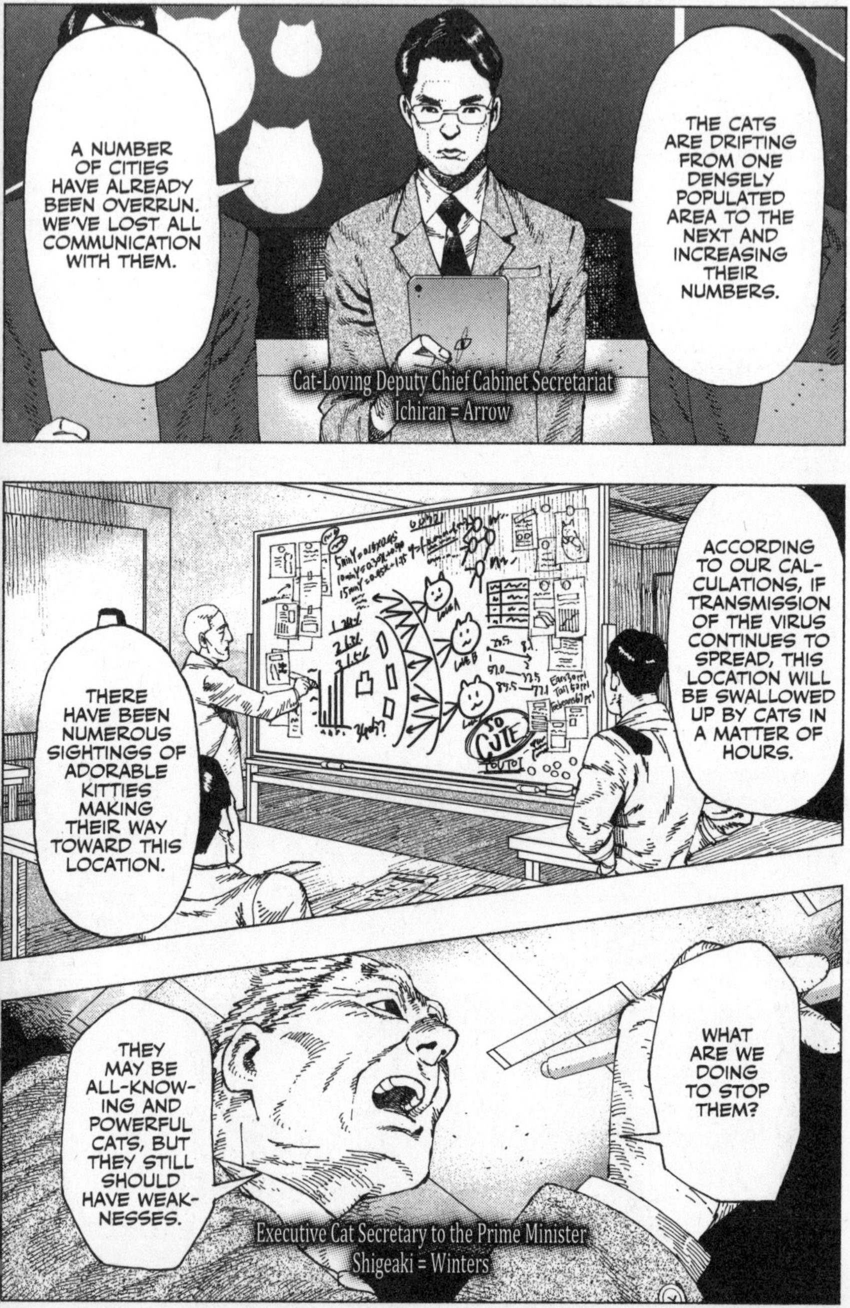
THE CATS ARE DRIFTING FROM ONE DENSELY POPULATED AREA TO THE NEXT AND INCREASING THEIR NUMBERS.
A NUMBER OF CITIES HAVE ALREADY BEEN OVERRUN. WE'VE LOST ALL COMMUNICATION WITH THEM.
Cat-Loving Deputy Chief Cabinet Secretariat
Ichiran = Arrow
ACCORDING TO OUR CALCULATIONS, IF TRANSMISSION OF THE VIRUS CONTINUES TO SPREAD, THIS LOCATION WILL BE SWALLOWED UP BY CATS IN A MATTER OF HOURS.
SO CUTE
THERE HAVE BEEN NUMEROUS SIGHTINGS OF ADORABLE KITTIES MAKING THEIR WAY TOWARD THIS LOCATION.
WHAT ARE WE DOING TO STOP THEM?
THEY MAY BE ALL-KNOWING AND POWERFUL CATS, BUT THEY STILL SHOULD HAVE WEAKNESSES.
Executive Cat Secretary to the Prime Minister
Shigeaki = Winters

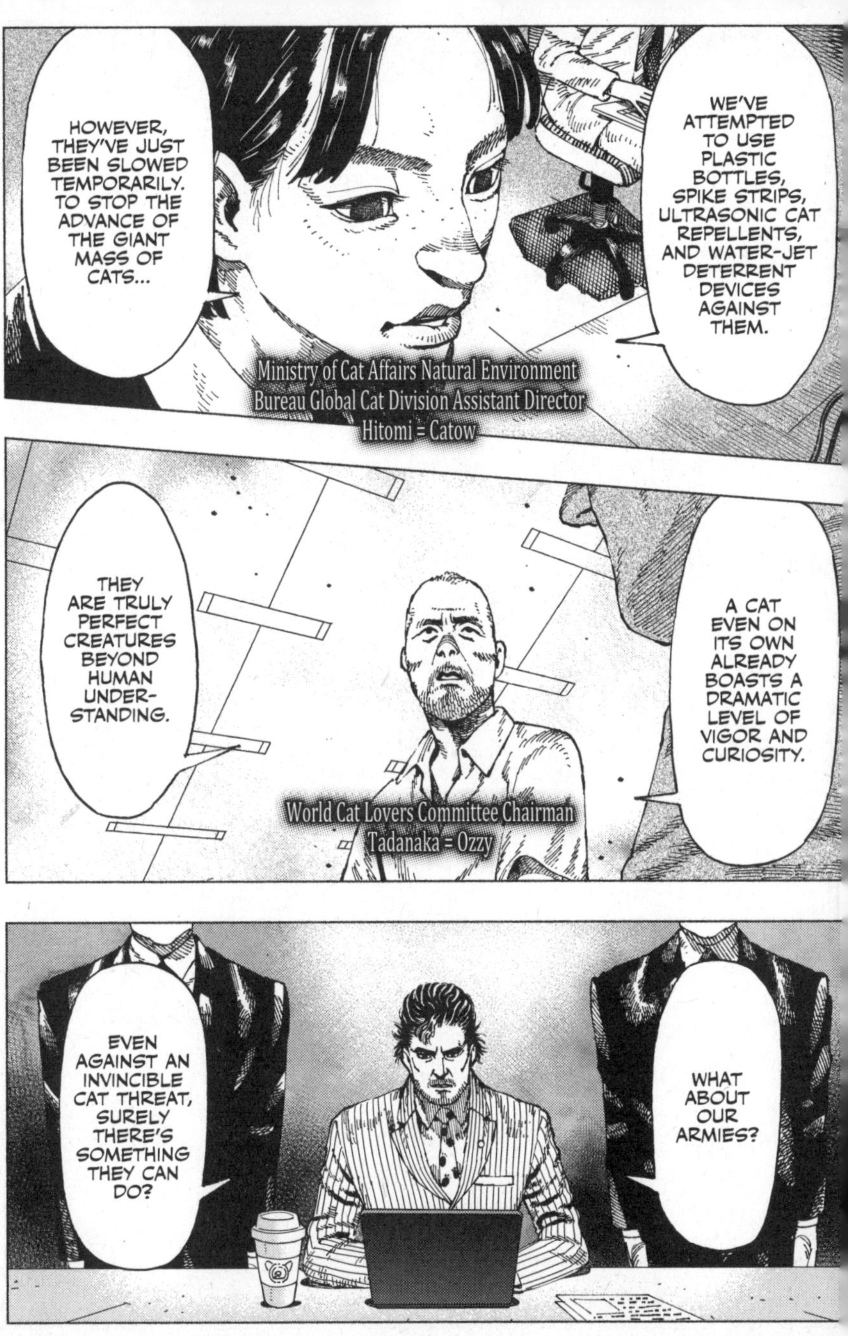
WE'VE ATTEMPTED TO USE PLASTIC BOTTLES, SPIKE STRIPS, ULTRASONIC CAT REPELLENTS, AND WATER-JET DETERRENT DEVICES AGAINST THEM.
HOWEVER, THEY'VE JUST BEEN SLOWED TEMPORARILY. TO STOP THE ADVANCE OF THE GIANT MASS OF CATS...
Ministry of Cat Affairs Natural Environment Bureau Global Cat Division Assistant Director Hitomi = Catow
A CAT EVEN ON ITS OWN ALREADY BOASTS A DRAMATIC LEVEL OF VIGOR AND CURIOSITY.
THEY ARE TRULY PERFECT CREATURES BEYOND HUMAN UNDER-STANDING.
World Cat Lovers Committee Chairman Tadanaka = Ozzy
WHAT ABOUT OUR ARMIES?
EVEN AGAINST AN INVINCIBLE CAT THREAT, SURELY THERE'S SOMETHING THEY CAN DO?

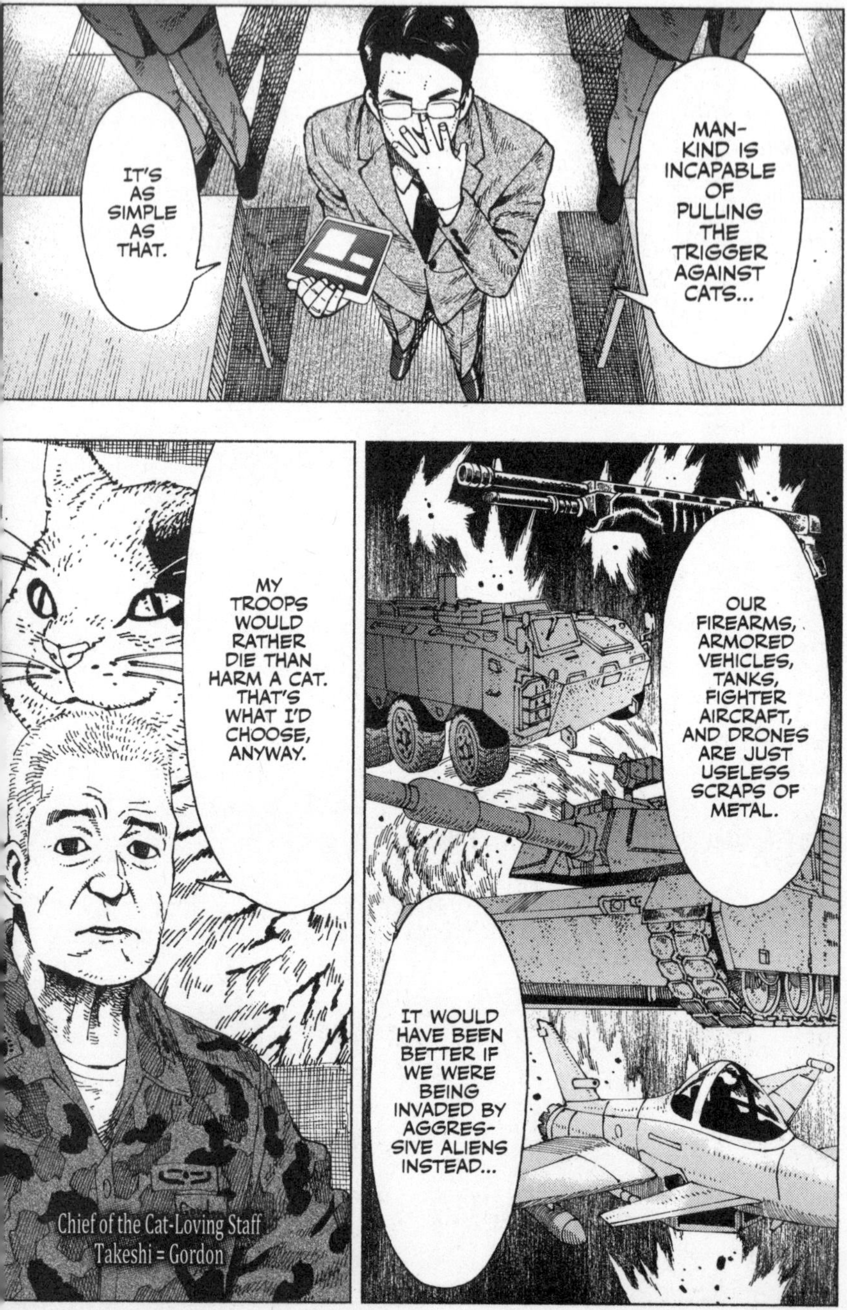
MAN-KIND IS INCAPABLE OF PULLING THE TRIGGER AGAINST CATS...
IT'S AS SIMPLE AS THAT.
OUR FIREARMS, ARMORED VEHICLES, TANKS, FIGHTER AIRCRAFT, AND DRONES ARE JUST USELESS SCRAPS OF METAL.
IT WOULD HAVE BEEN BETTER IF WE WERE BEING INVADED BY AGGRES-SIVE ALIENS INSTEAD...
MY TROOPS WOULD RATHER DIE THAN HARM A CAT. THAT'S WHAT I'D CHOOSE, ANYWAY.
Chief of the Cat-Loving Staff
Takeshi = Gordon

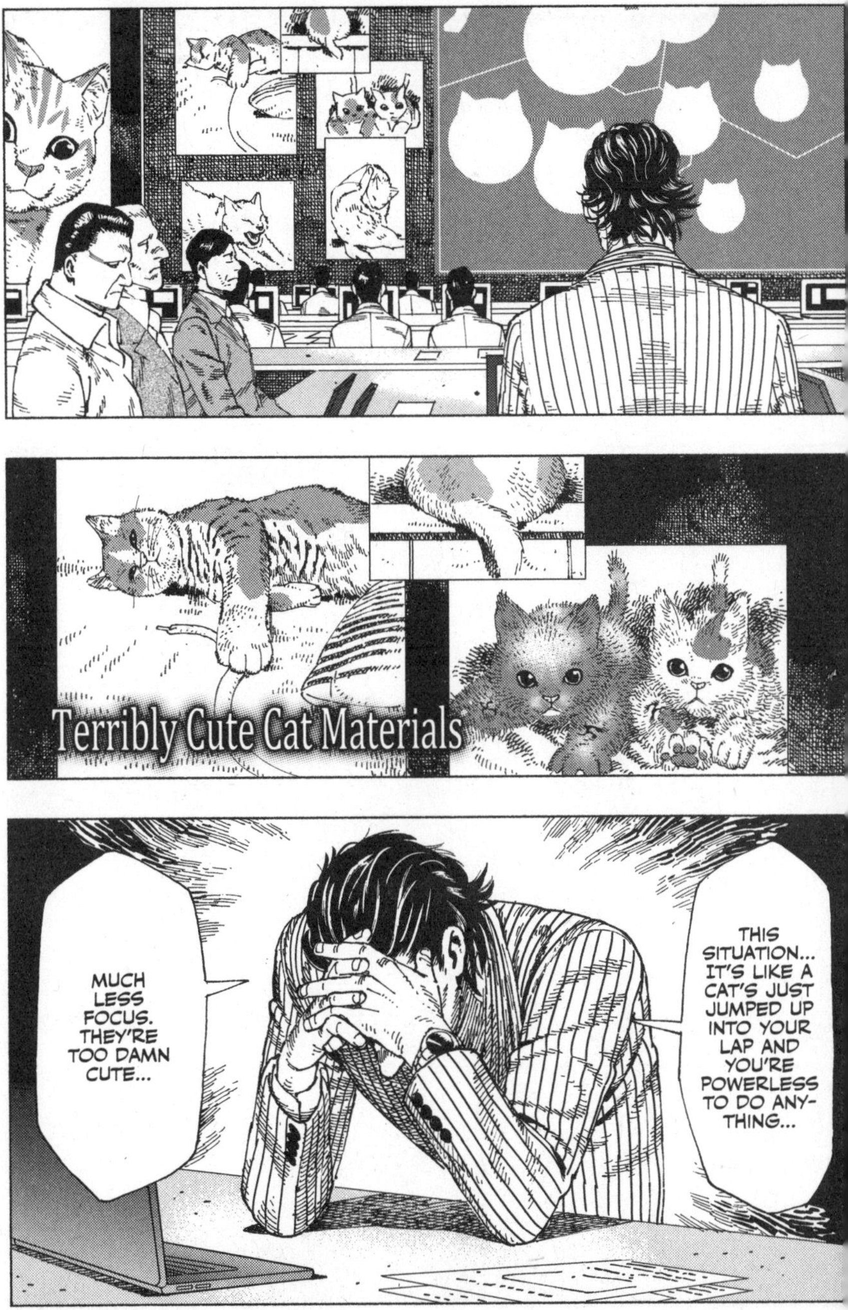
Terribly Cute Cat Materials
THIS SITUATION... IT'S LIKE A CAT'S JUST JUMPED UP INTO YOUR LAP AND YOU'RE POWERLESS TO DO ANY-THING...
MUCH LESS FOCUS. THEY'RE TOO DAMN CUTE...

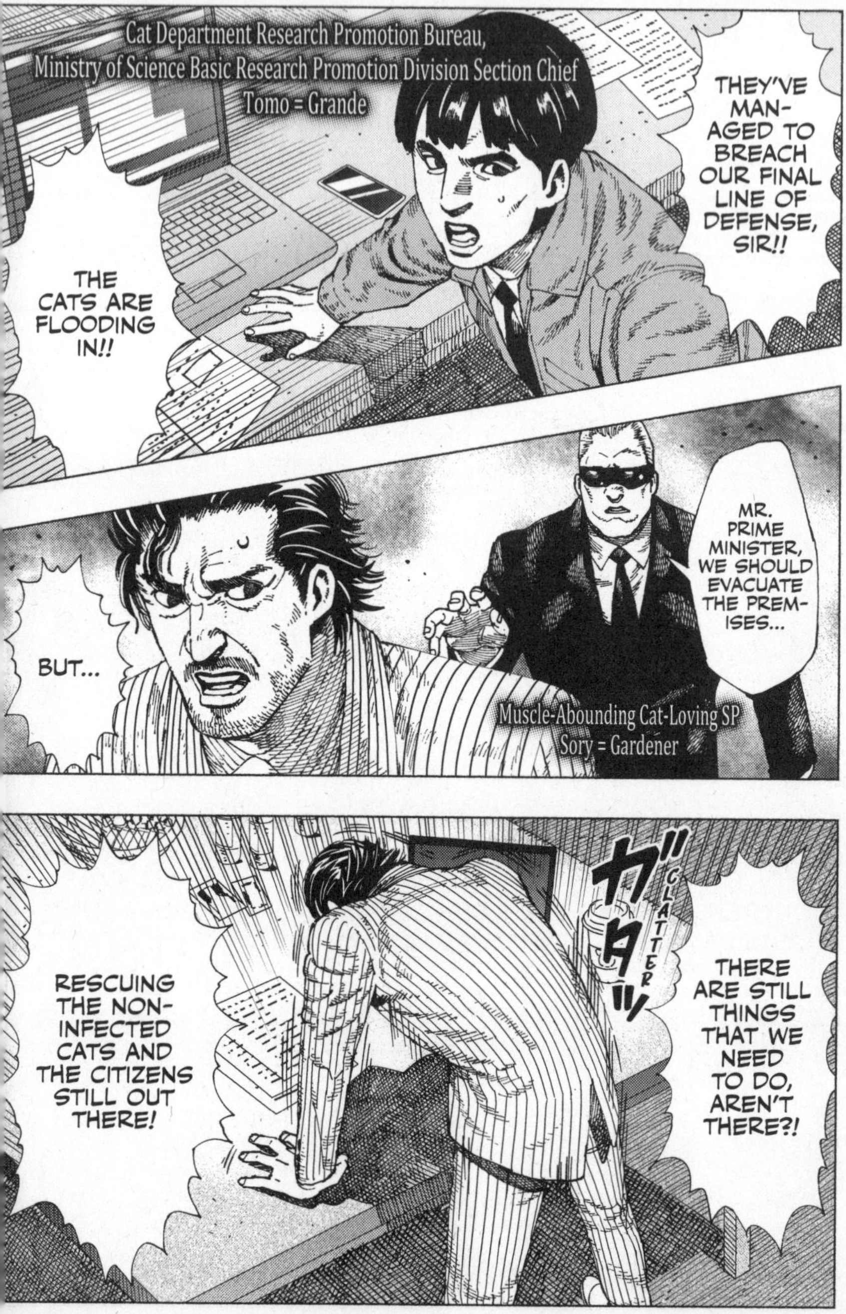
Cat Department Research Promotion Bureau,
Ministry of Science Basic Research Promotion Division Section Chief
Tomo = Grande
THEY'VE MAN-AGED TO BREACH OUR FINAL LINE OF DEFENSE, SIR!!
THE CATS ARE FLOODING IN!!
MR. PRIME MINISTER, WE SHOULD EVACUATE THE PREM-ISES...
Muscle-Abounding Cat-Loving SP
Sory = Gardener
BUT...
CLATTER
THERE ARE STILL THINGS THAT WE NEED TO DO, AREN'T THERE?!
RESCUING THE NON-INFECTED CATS AND THE CITIZENS STILL OUT THERE!

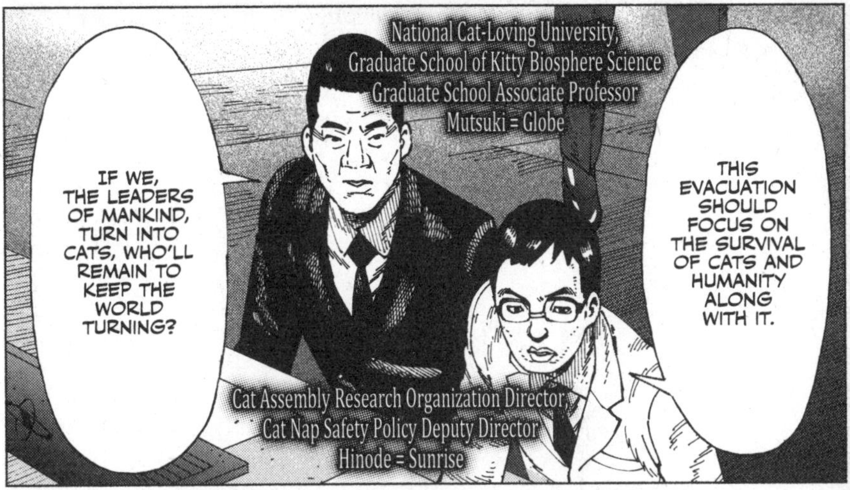
National Cat-Loving University, Graduate School of Kitty Biosphere Science Graduate School Associate Professor Mutsuki = Globe
THIS EVACUATION SHOULD FOCUS ON THE SURVIVAL OF CATS AND HUMANITY ALONG WITH IT.
IF WE, THE LEADERS OF MANKIND, TURN INTO CATS, WHO'LL REMAIN TO KEEP THE WORLD TURNING?
Cat Assembly Research Organization Director, Cat Nap Safety Policy Deputy Director Hinode = Sunrise
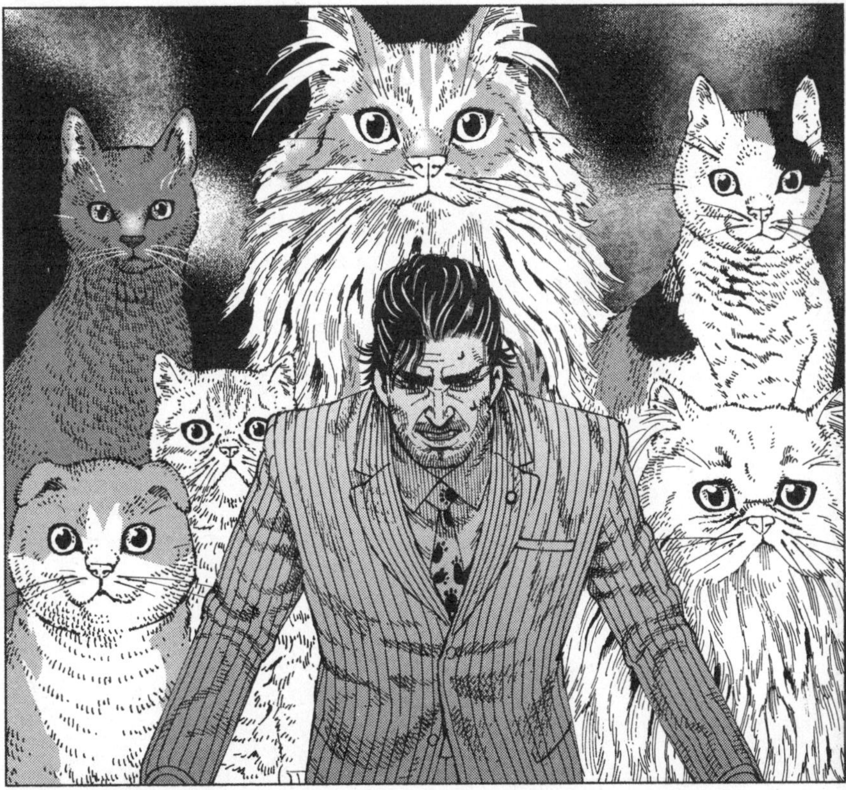

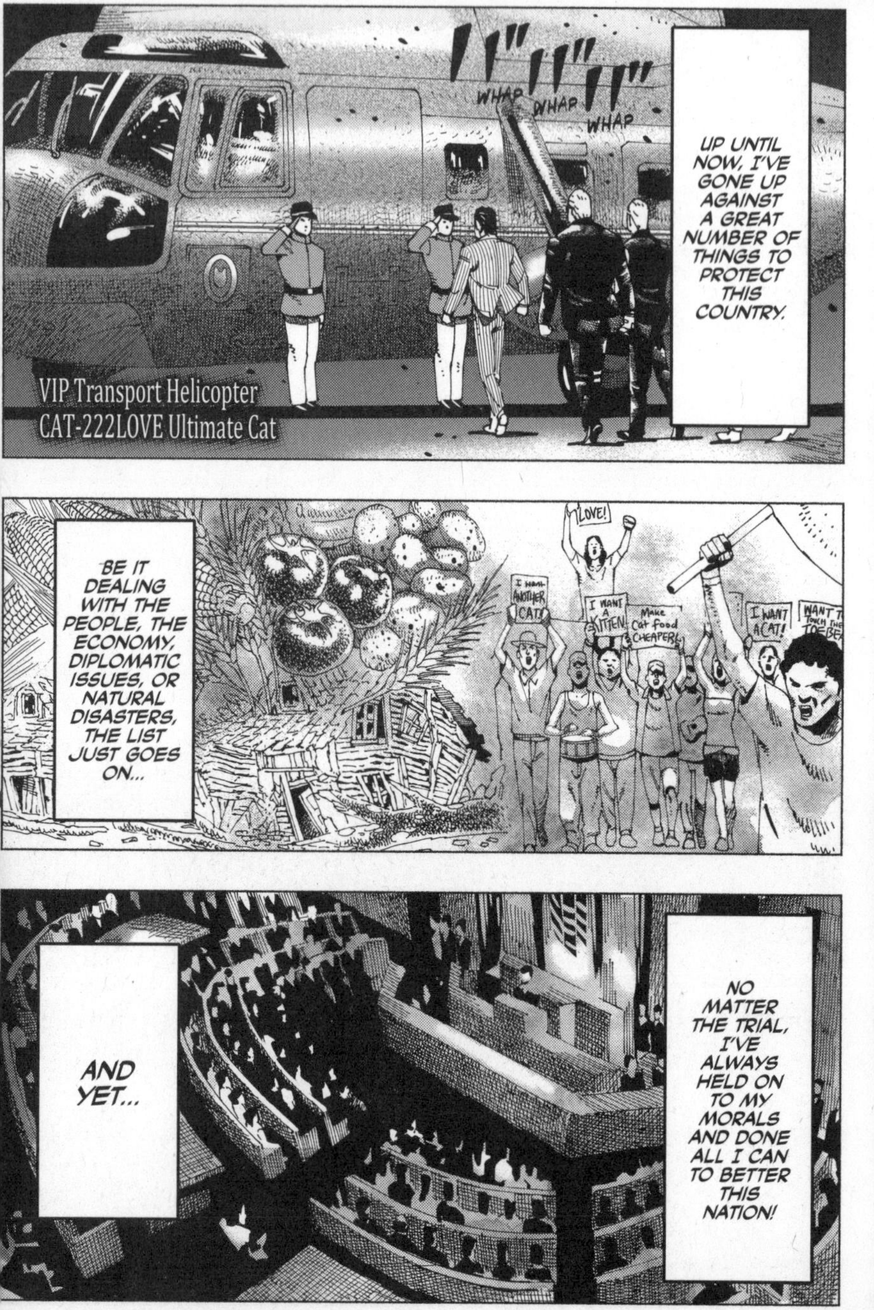
UP UNTIL NOW, I'VE GONE UP AGAINST A GREAT NUMBER OF THINGS TO PROTECT THIS COUNTRY.
WHAP
WHAP
WHAP
VIP Transport Helicopter CAT-222LOVE Ultimate Cat
I WANT A CAT!
Make Cat food CHEAPER!
I WANT A KITTEN
LOVE!
I WANT ANOTHER CAT!
BE IT DEALING WITH THE PEOPLE, THE ECONOMY, DIPLOMATIC ISSUES, OR NATURAL DISASTERS, THE LIST JUST GOES ON...
NO MATTER THE TRIAL, I'VE ALWAYS HELD ON TO MY MORALS AND DONE ALL I CAN TO BETTER THIS NATION!
AND YET...

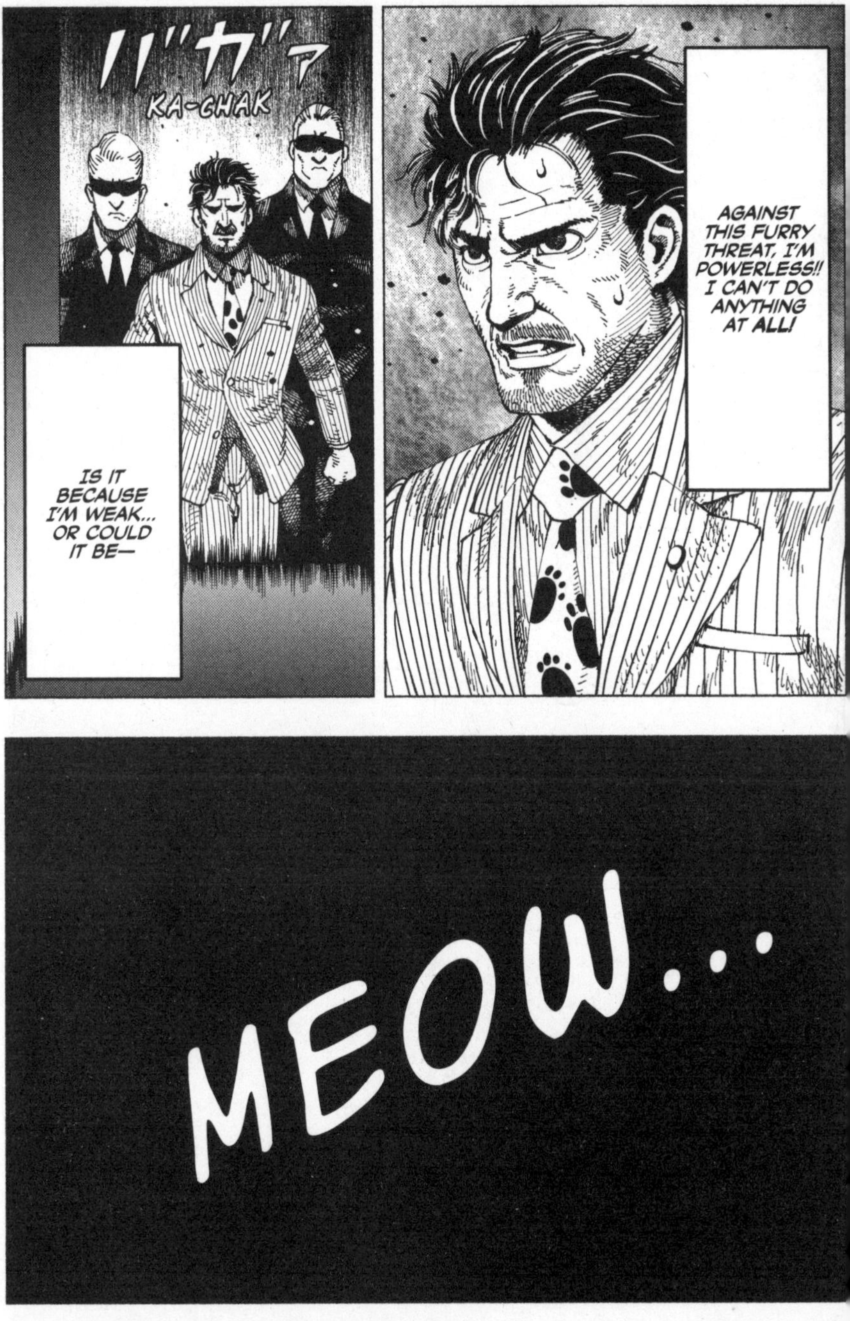
AGAINST THIS FURRY THREAT, I'M POWERLESS!! I CAN'T DO ANYTHING AT ALL!
バガァ
KA-CHAK
IS IT BECAUSE I'M WEAK... OR COULD IT BE—
MEOW...

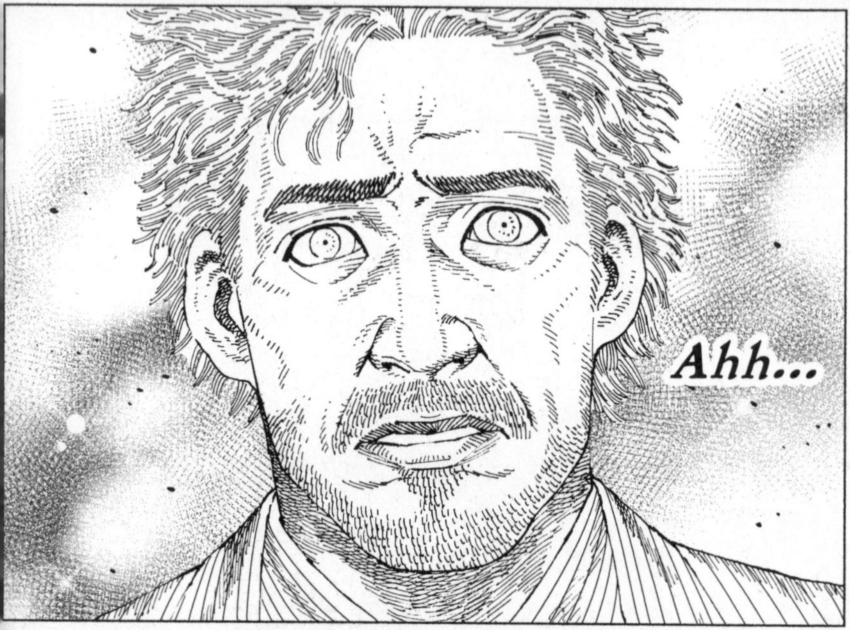
Ahh...

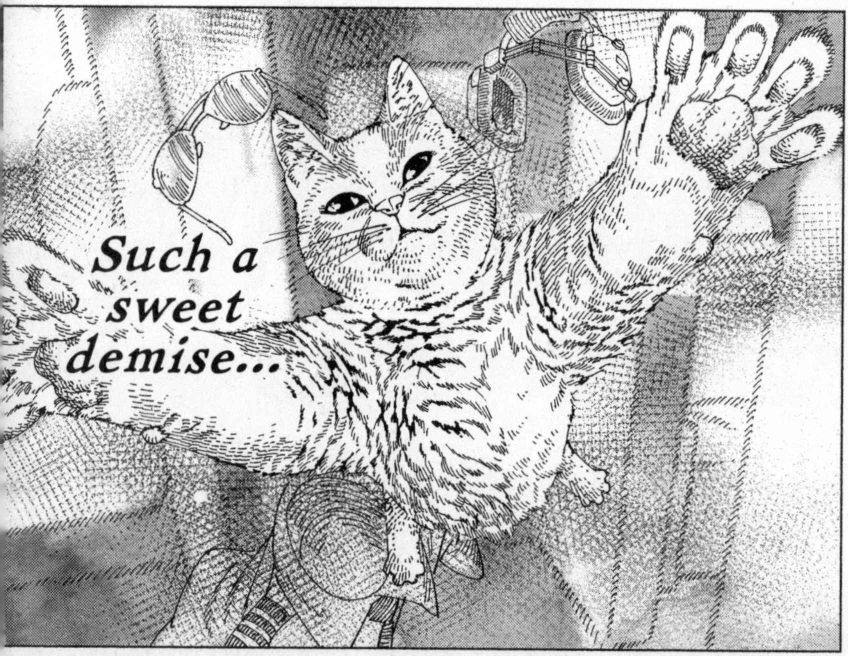
Such a sweet demise...

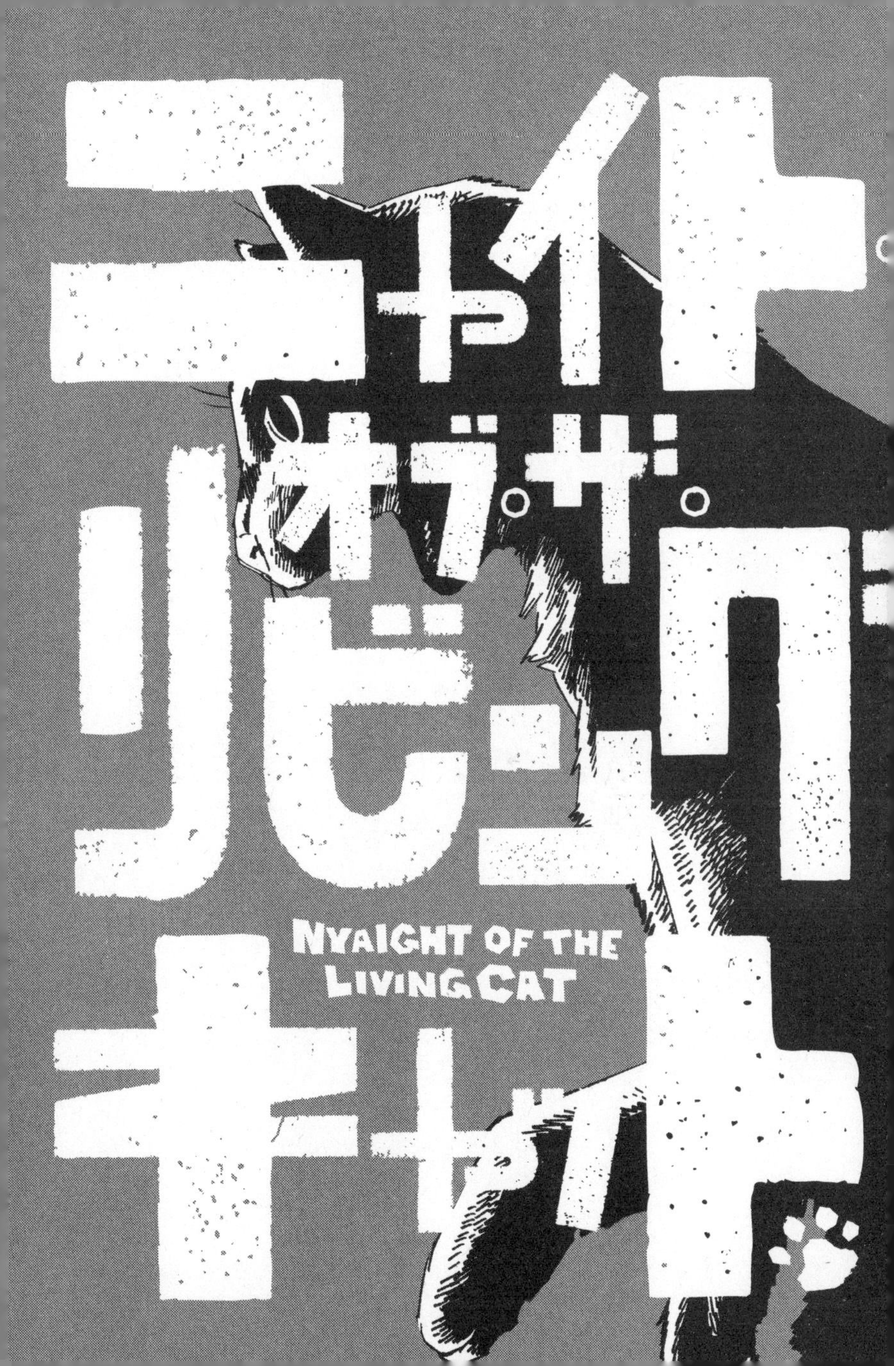
ナイト・オブ・ザ・リビングキャット
NYAIGHT OF THE
LIVING CAT

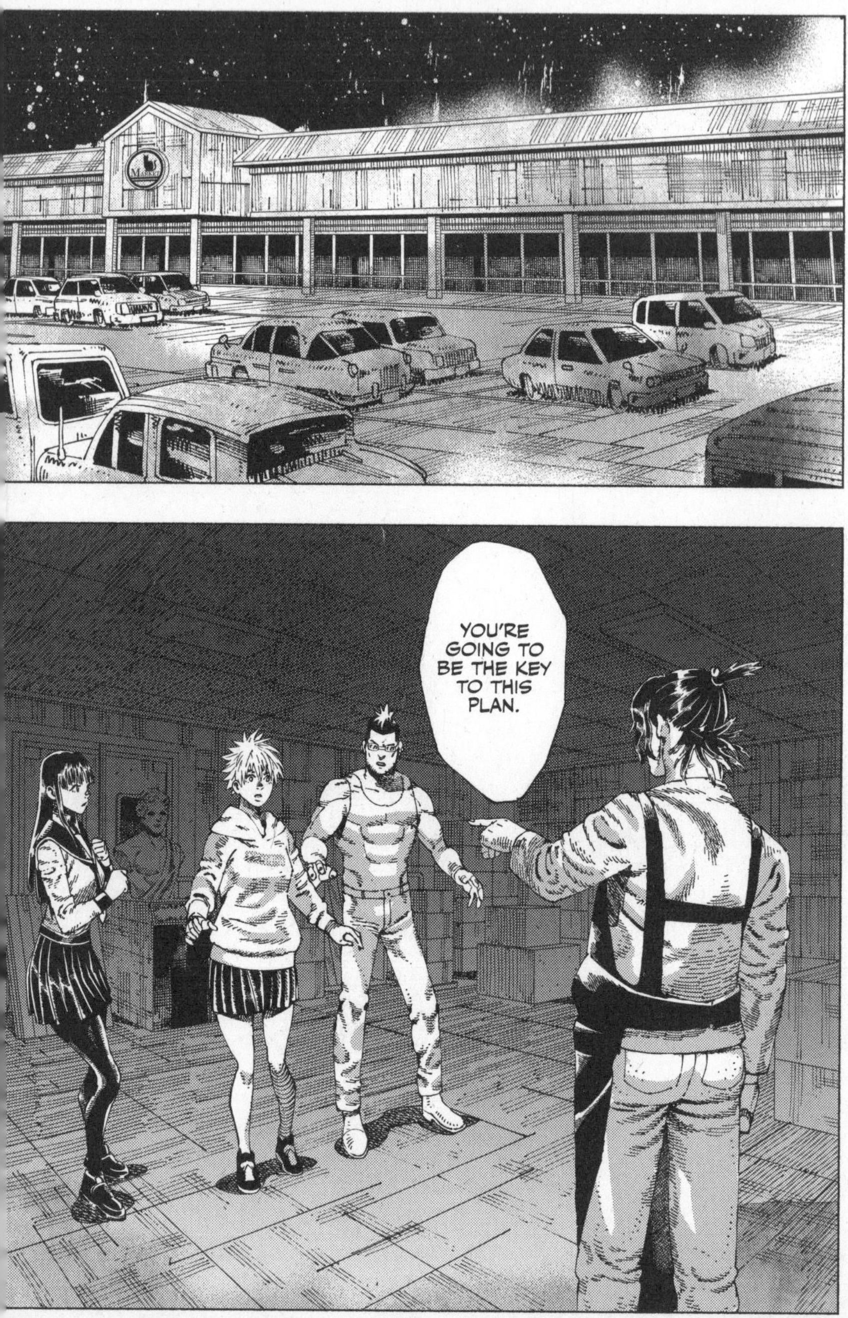
YOU'RE GOING TO BE THE KEY TO THIS PLAN.

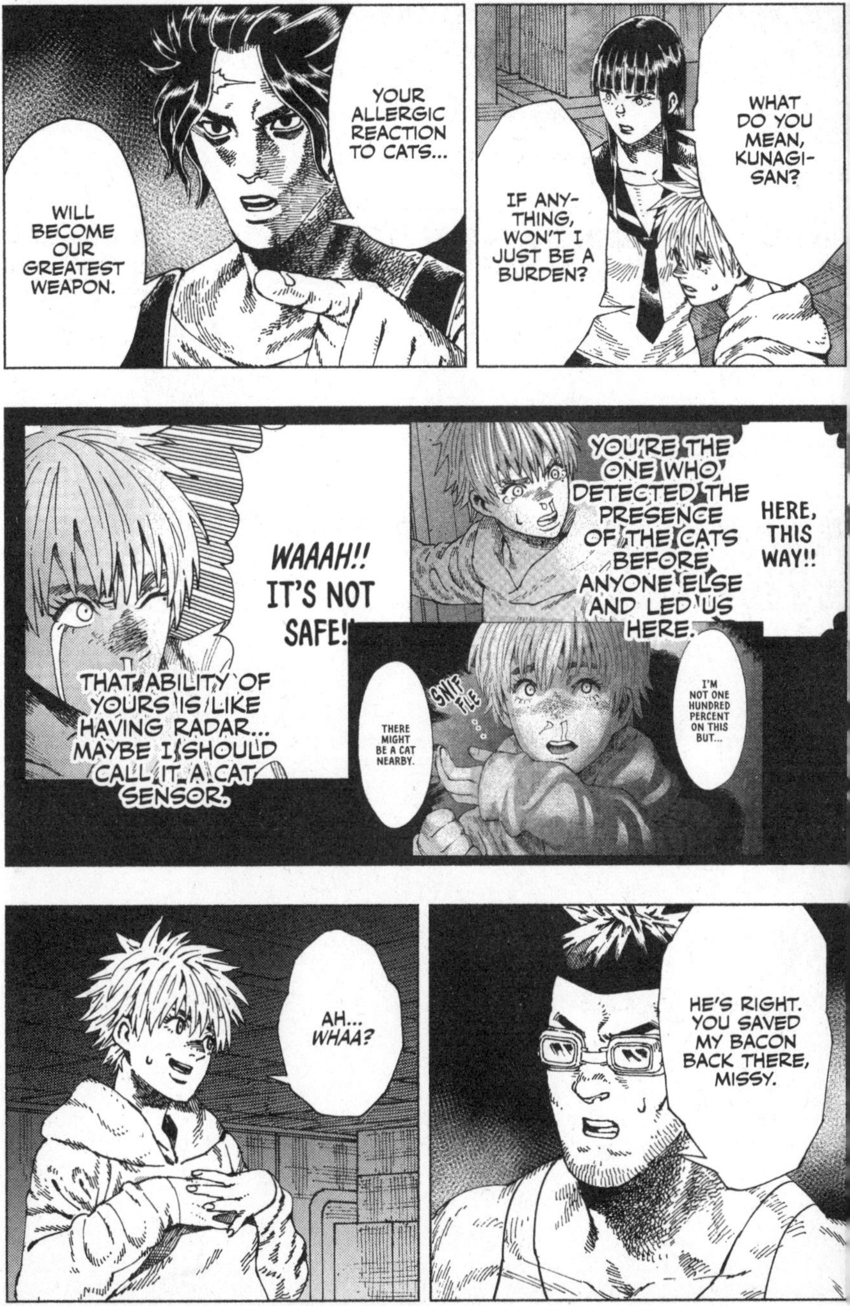

WHAT DO YOU MEAN, KUNAGI-SAN?
IF ANYTHING, WON'T I JUST BE A BURDEN?
YOUR ALLERGIC REACTION TO CATS...
WILL BECOME OUR GREATEST WEAPON.
HERE, THIS WAY!!
YOU'RE THE ONE WHO DETECTED THE PRESENCE OF THE CATS BEFORE ANYONE ELSE AND LED US HERE.
I'M NOT ONE HUNDRED PERCENT ON THIS BUT...
SNIFFLE
THERE MIGHT BE A CAT NEARBY.
WAAAH!! IT'S NOT SAFE!!
THAT ABILITY OF YOURS IS LIKE HAVING RADAR... MAYBE I SHOULD CALL IT A CAT SENSOR.
HE'S RIGHT. YOU SAVED MY BACON BACK THERE, MISSY.
AH... WHAA?

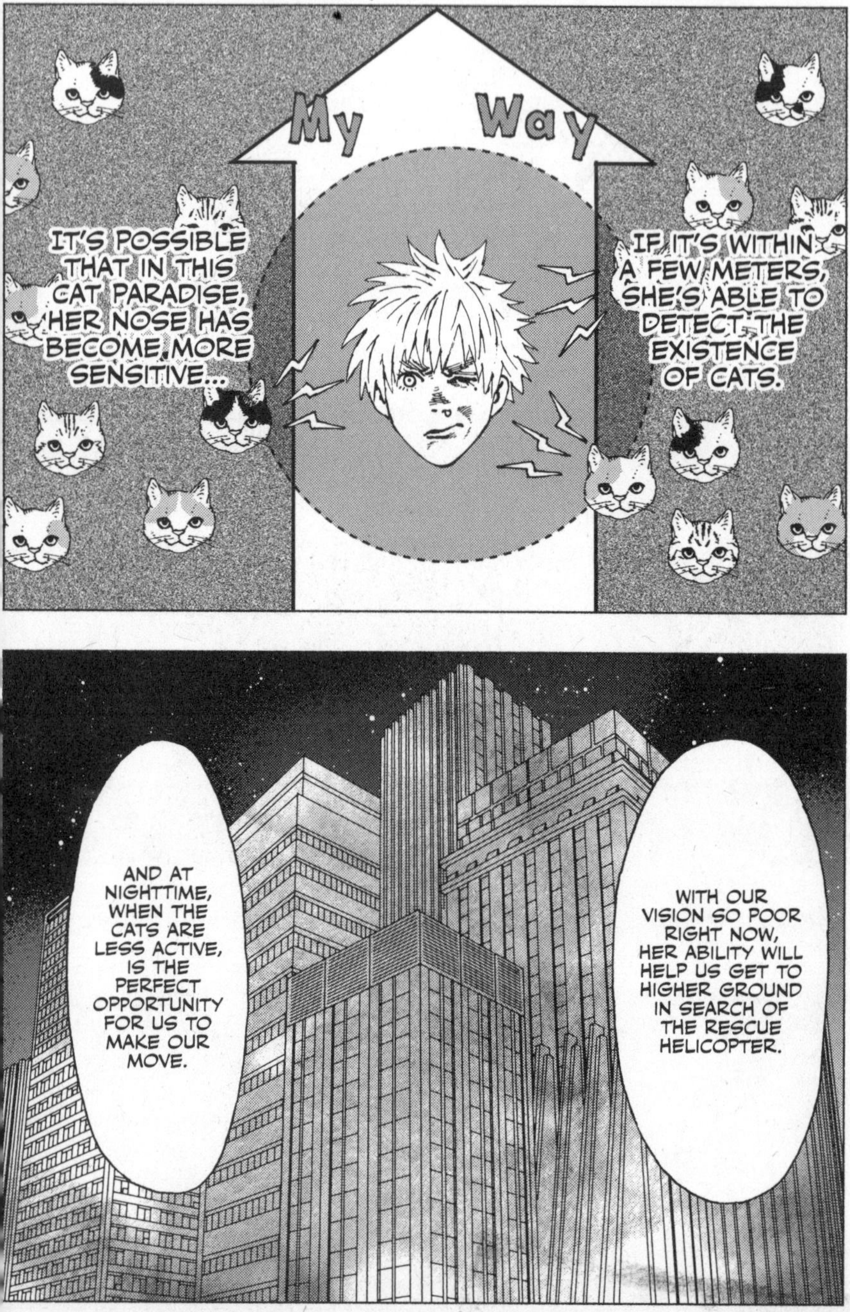
My Way
IF IT'S WITHIN A FEW METERS, SHE'S ABLE TO DETECT THE EXISTENCE OF CATS.
IT'S POSSIBLE THAT IN THIS CAT PARADISE, HER NOSE HAS BECOME MORE SENSITIVE...
WITH OUR VISION SO POOR RIGHT NOW, HER ABILITY WILL HELP US GET TO HIGHER GROUND IN SEARCH OF THE RESCUE HELICOPTER.
AND AT NIGHTTIME, WHEN THE CATS ARE LESS ACTIVE, IS THE PERFECT OPPORTUNITY FOR US TO MAKE OUR MOVE.

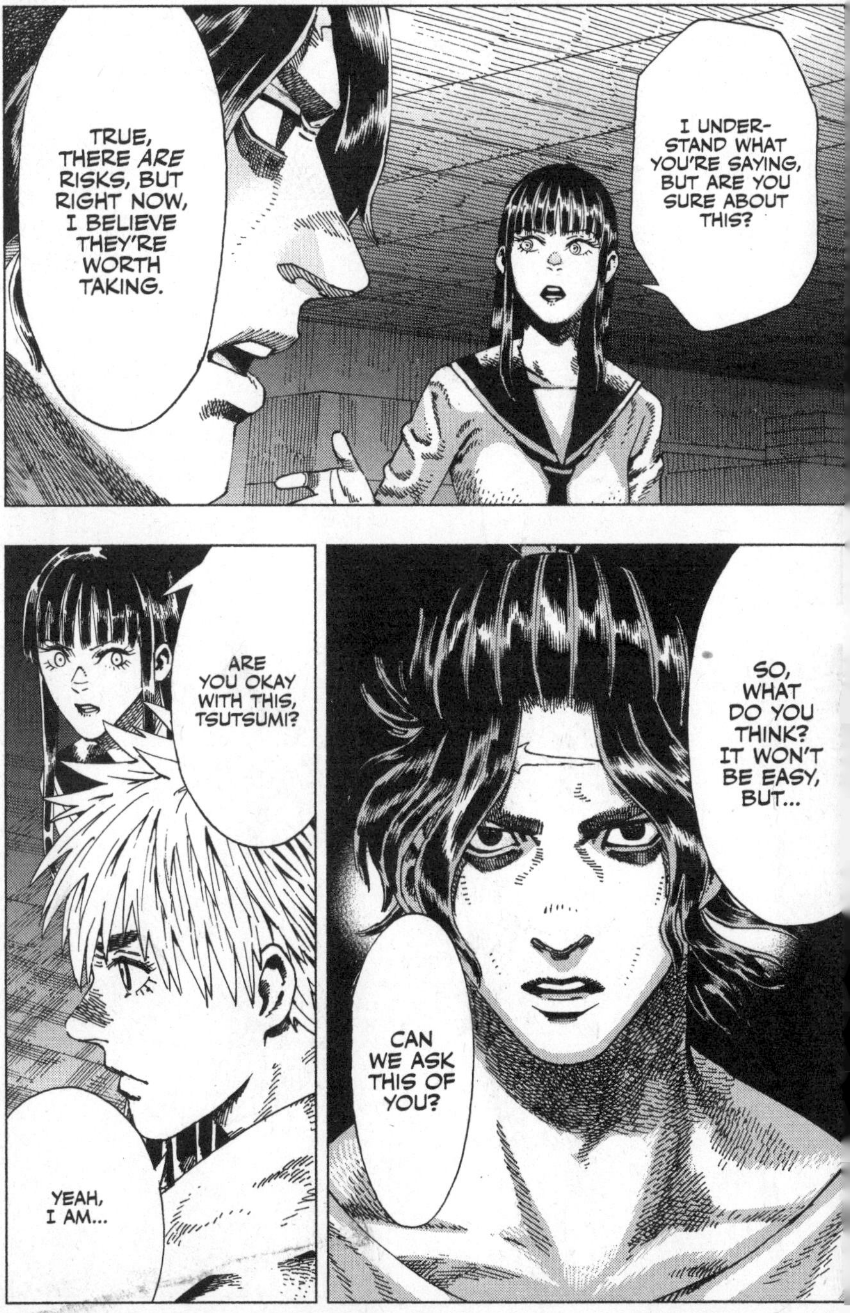
I UNDERSTAND WHAT YOU'RE SAYING, BUT ARE YOU SURE ABOUT THIS?
TRUE, THERE *ARE* RISKS, BUT RIGHT NOW, I BELIEVE THEY'RE WORTH TAKING.
SO, WHAT DO YOU THINK? IT WON'T BE EASY, BUT...
CAN WE ASK THIS OF YOU?
ARE YOU OKAY WITH THIS, TSUTSUMI?
YEAH, I AM...

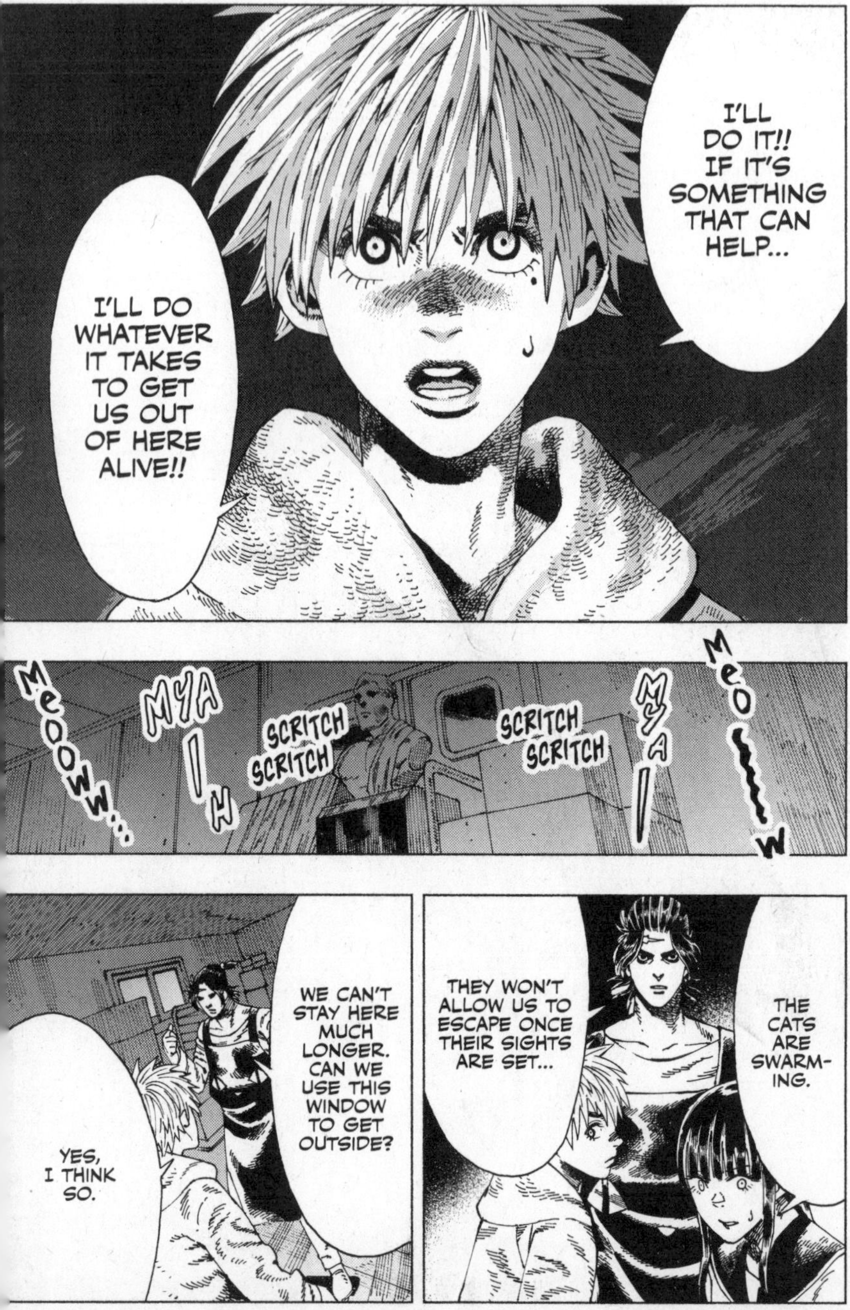
I'LL DO IT!! IF IT'S SOMETHING THAT CAN HELP...
I'LL DO WHATEVER IT TAKES TO GET US OUT OF HERE ALIVE!!
Meo~w
MYA~
SCRITCH SCRITCH
SCRITCH SCRITCH
MYA~H
MeOOWW...
THE CATS ARE SWARM-ING.
THEY WON'T ALLOW US TO ESCAPE ONCE THEIR SIGHTS ARE SET...
WE CAN'T STAY HERE MUCH LONGER. CAN WE USE THIS WINDOW TO GET OUTSIDE?
YES, I THINK SO.

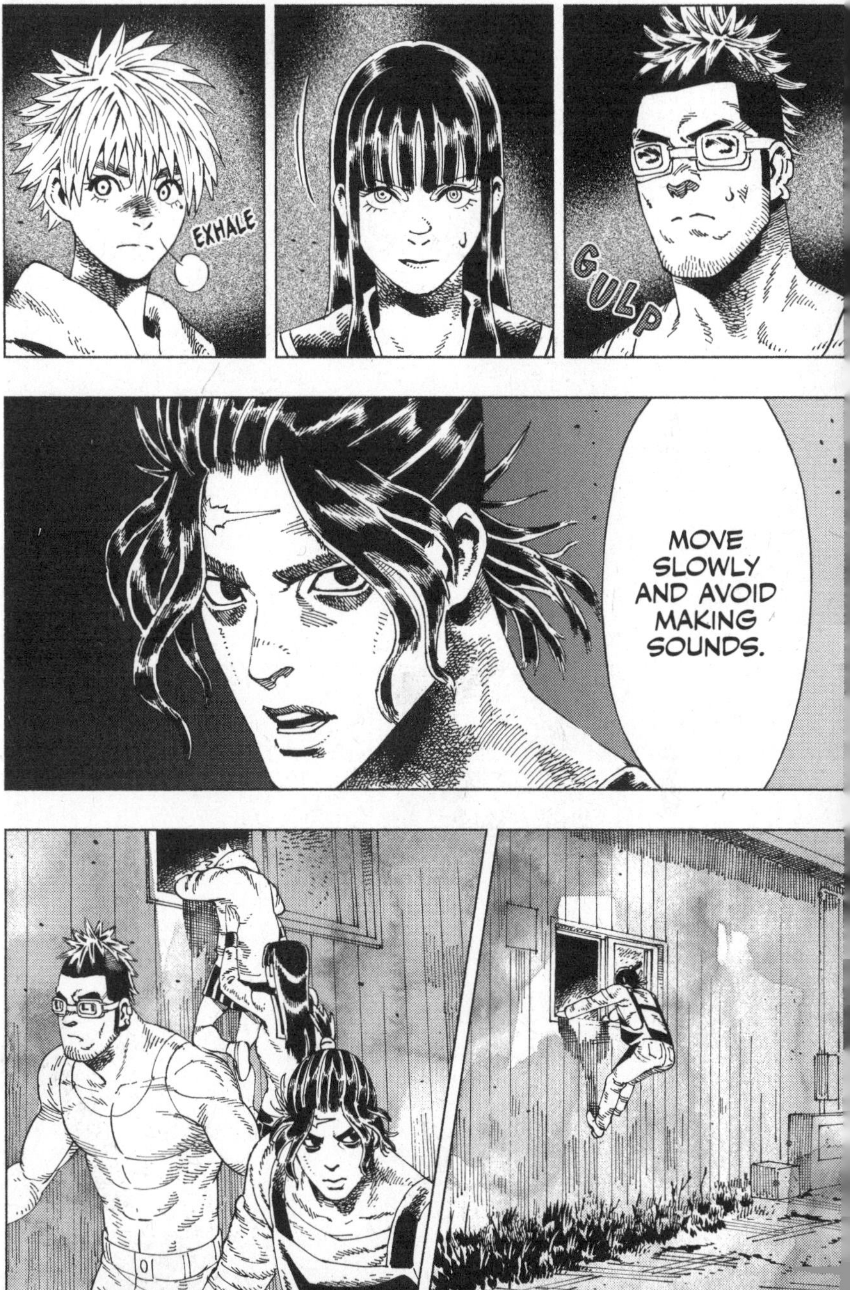
GULP
EXHALE
MOVE SLOWLY AND AVOID MAKING SOUNDS.

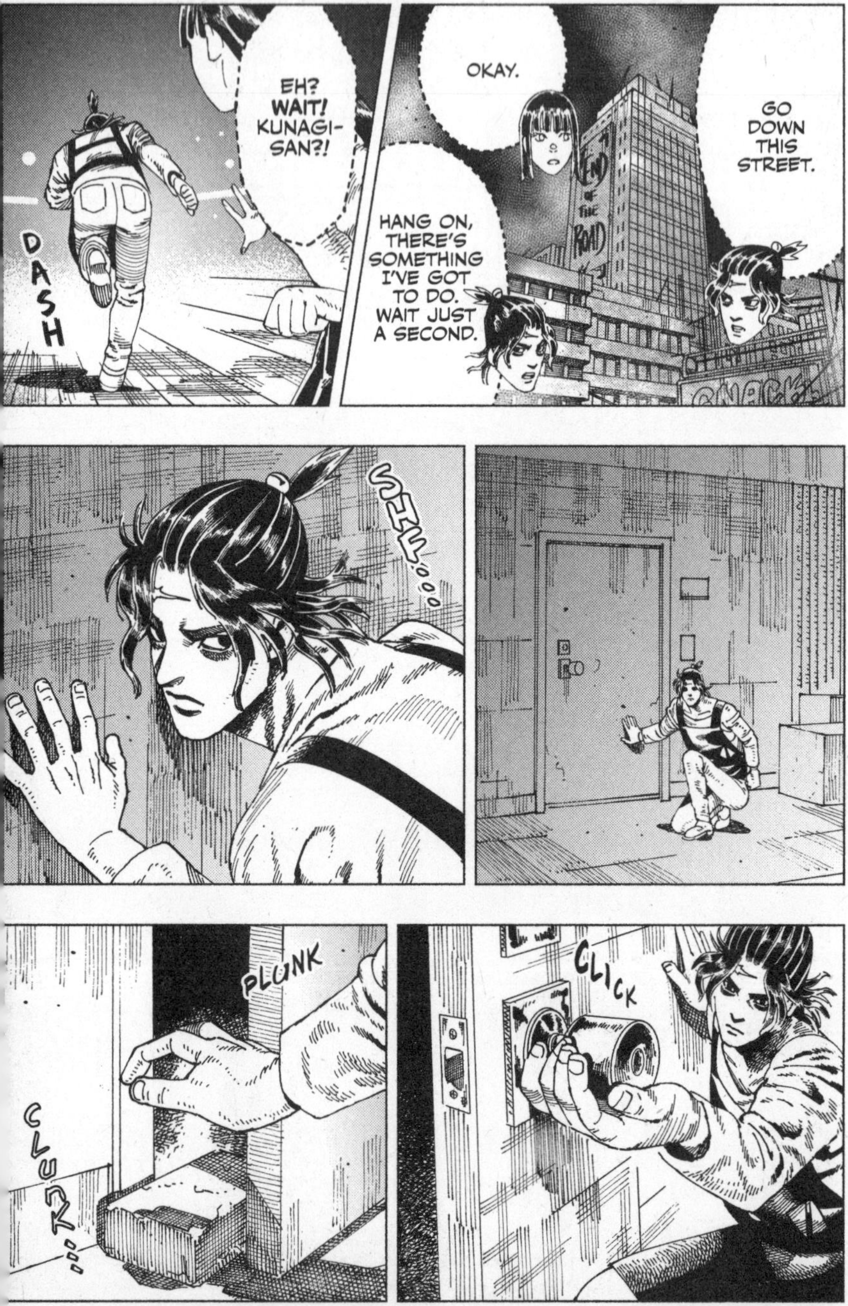
GO DOWN THIS STREET.
OKAY.
HANG ON, THERE'S SOMETHING I'VE GOT TO DO. WAIT JUST A SECOND.
END OF THE ROAD
EH? WAIT! KUNAGI-SAN?!
DASH
SHF...
CLICK
PLUNK
CLUNK...

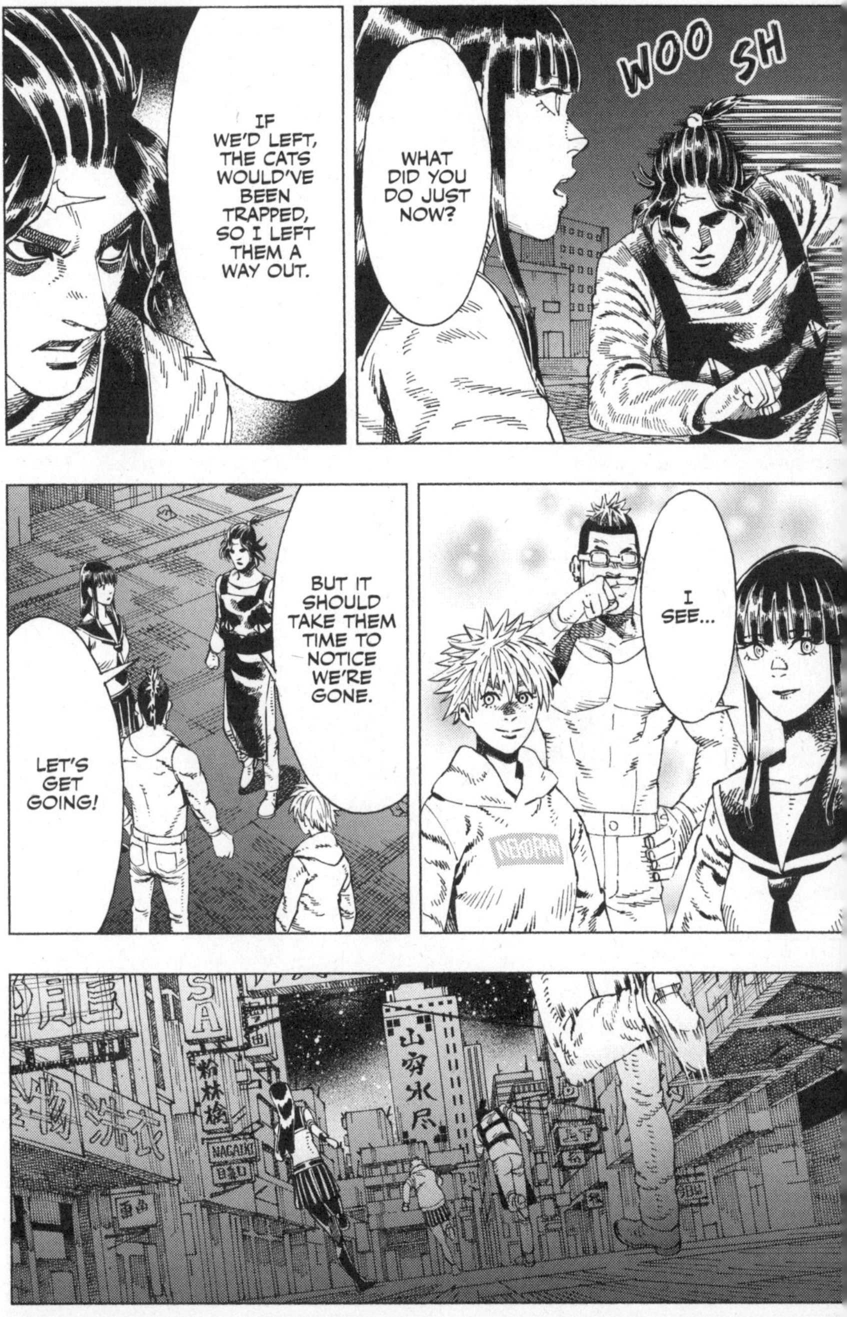
WOO SH
WHAT DID YOU DO JUST NOW?
IF WE'D LEFT, THE CATS WOULD'VE BEEN TRAPPED, SO I LEFT THEM A WAY OUT.
I SEE...
BUT IT SHOULD TAKE THEM TIME TO NOTICE WE'RE GONE.
LET'S GET GOING!
NAGAIKI

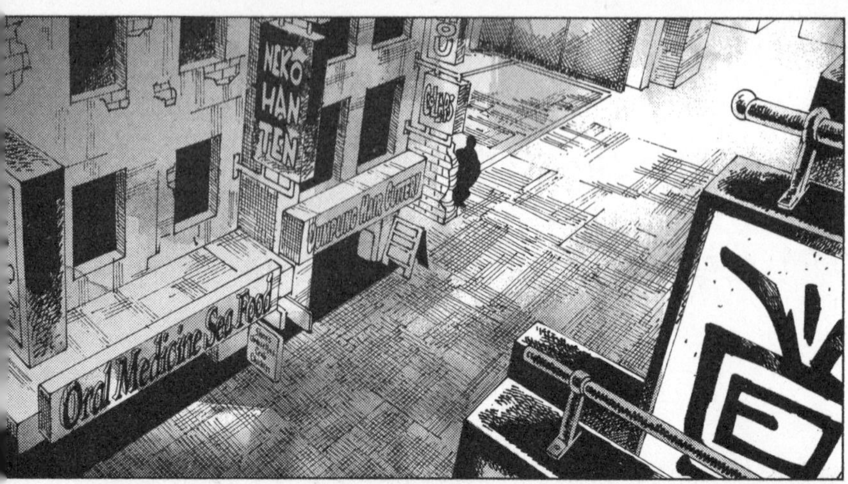
NEKO HAN TEN
Oral Medicine Sea Food

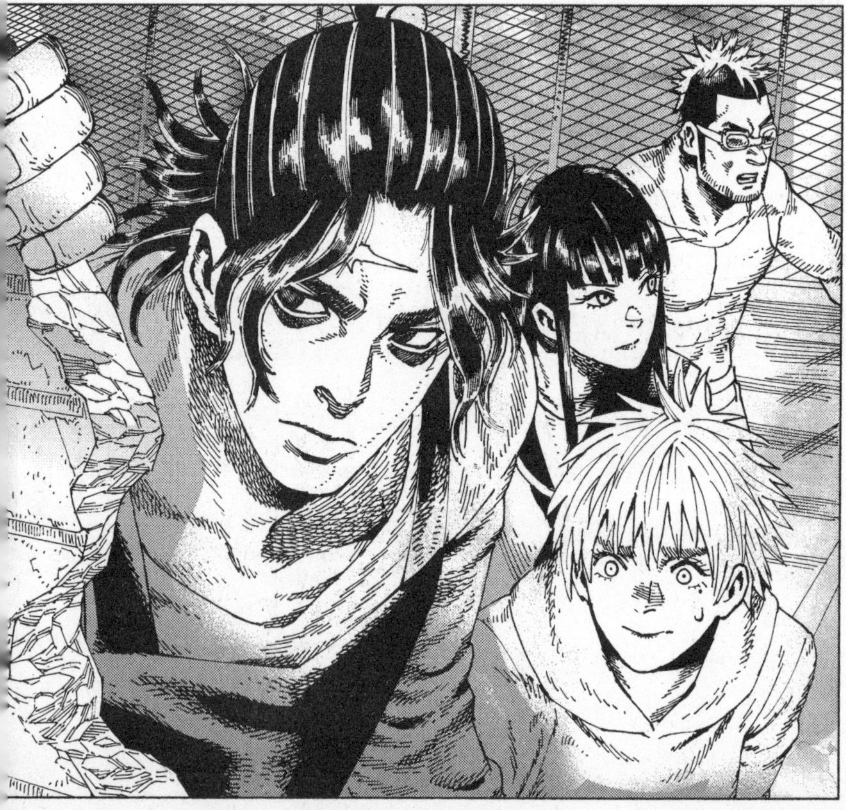

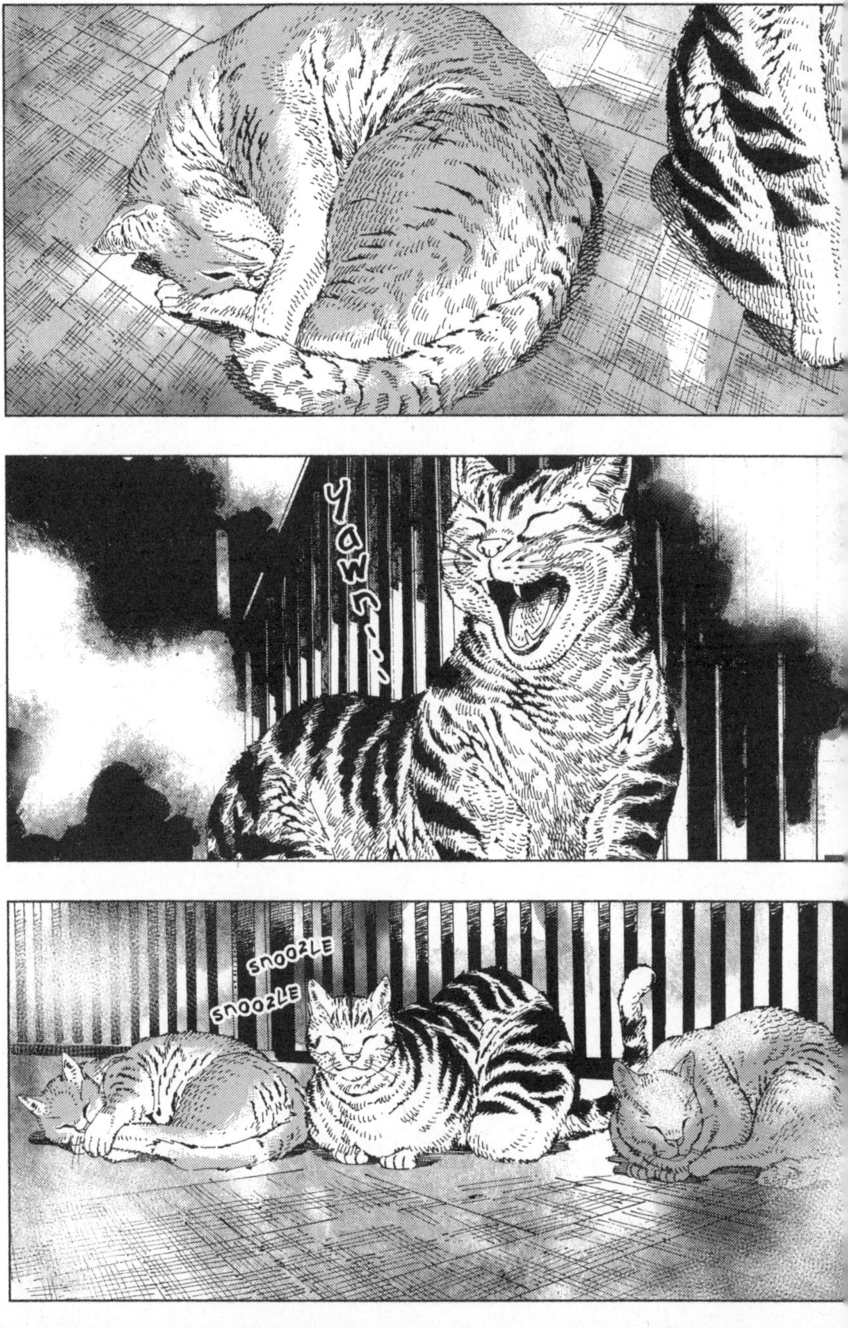
YAWN...
SNOOZLE
SNOOZLE

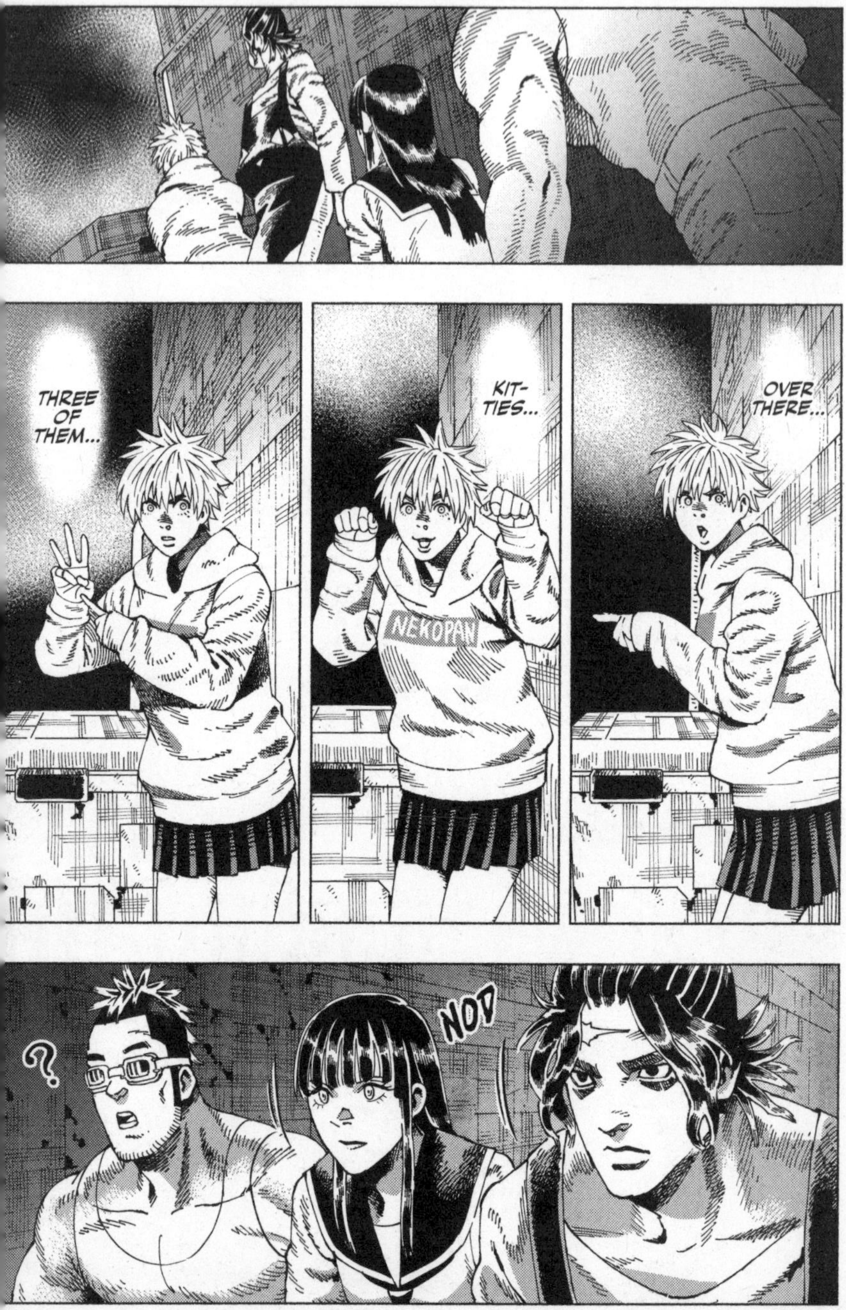
OVER THERE...
KIT-TIES...
THREE OF THEM...
NEKOPAN
NOD
?

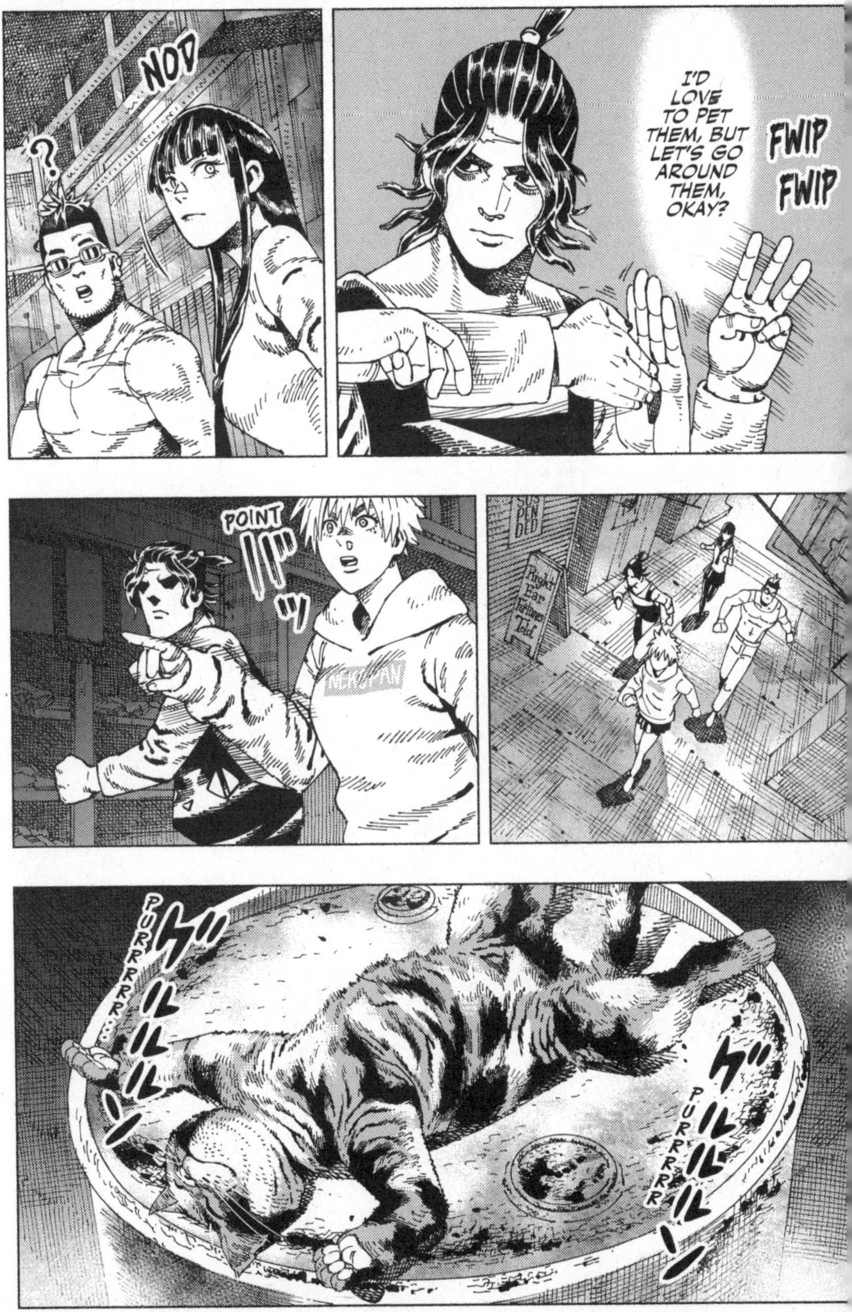
I'D LOVE TO PET THEM, BUT LET'S GO AROUND THEM, OKAY?
FWIP FWIP
NOD
?
Right Ear Fortunes Told
POINT
NEKOPAN
PURRRRR...
PURRRRR

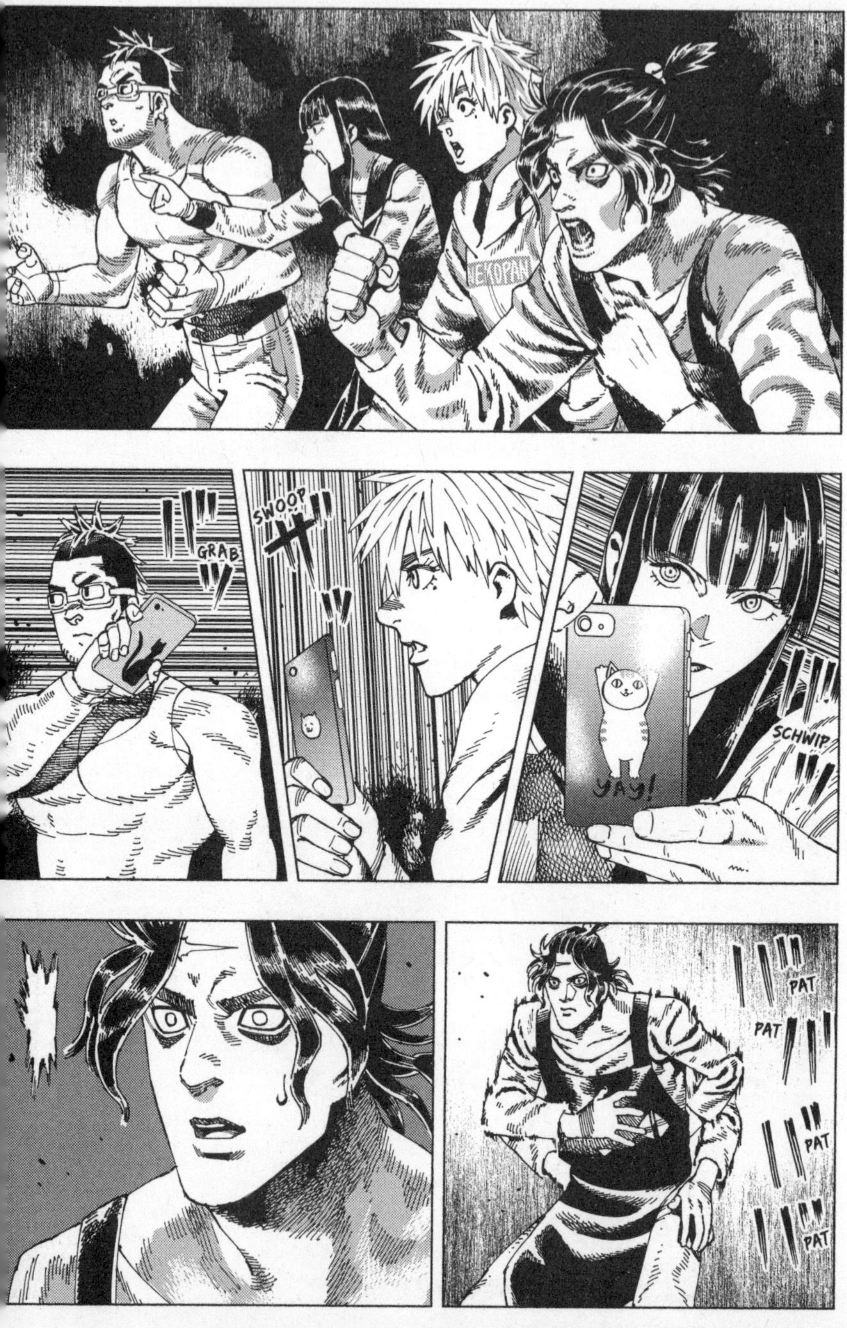
YAY!
SCHWIP
SWOOP
GRAB
PAT
PAT
PAT
PAT

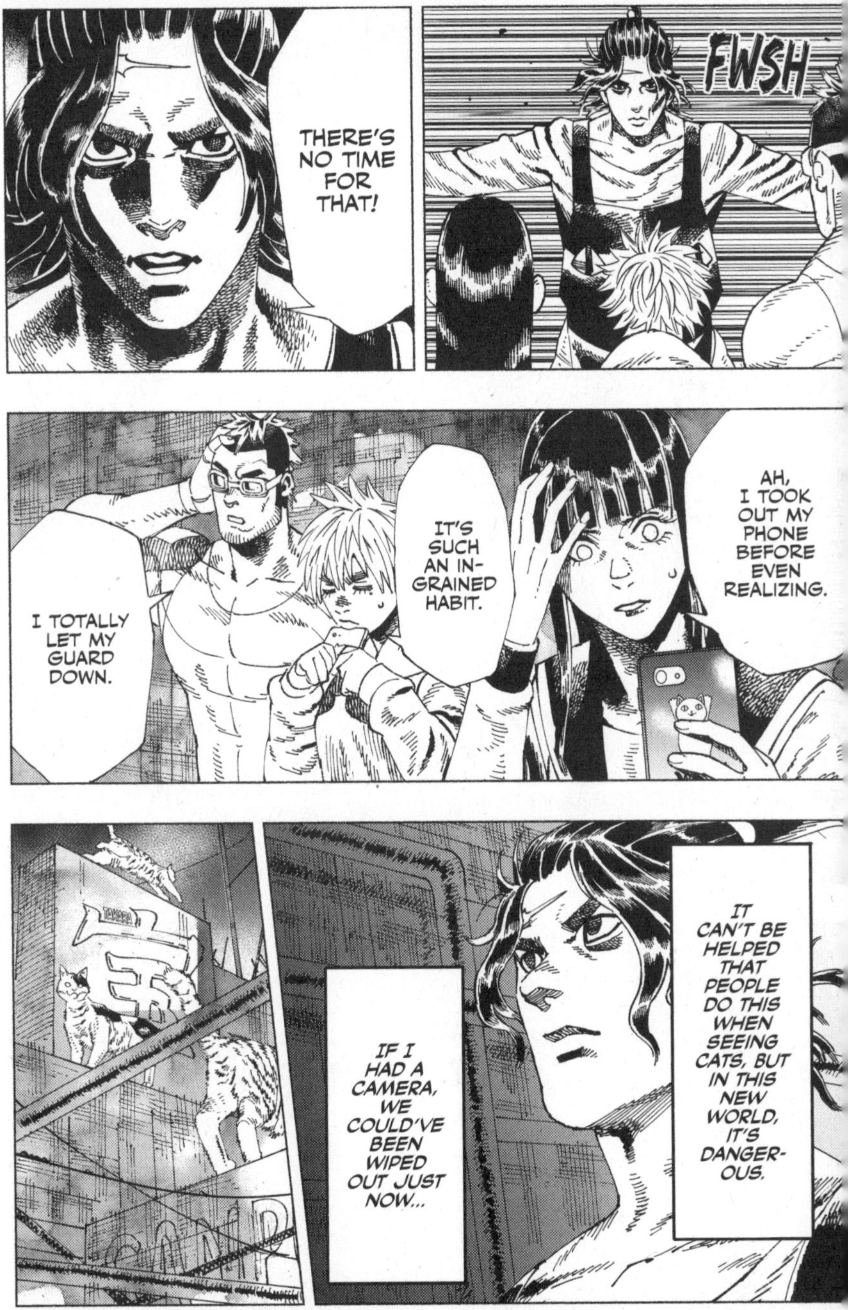
FWSH
THERE'S NO TIME FOR THAT!
AH, I TOOK OUT MY PHONE BEFORE EVEN REALIZING.
IT'S SUCH AN IN-GRAINED HABIT.
I TOTALLY LET MY GUARD DOWN.
IT CAN'T BE HELPED THAT PEOPLE DO THIS WHEN SEEING CATS, BUT IN THIS NEW WORLD, IT'S DANGER-OUS.
IF I HAD A CAMERA, WE COULD'VE BEEN WIPED OUT JUST NOW...

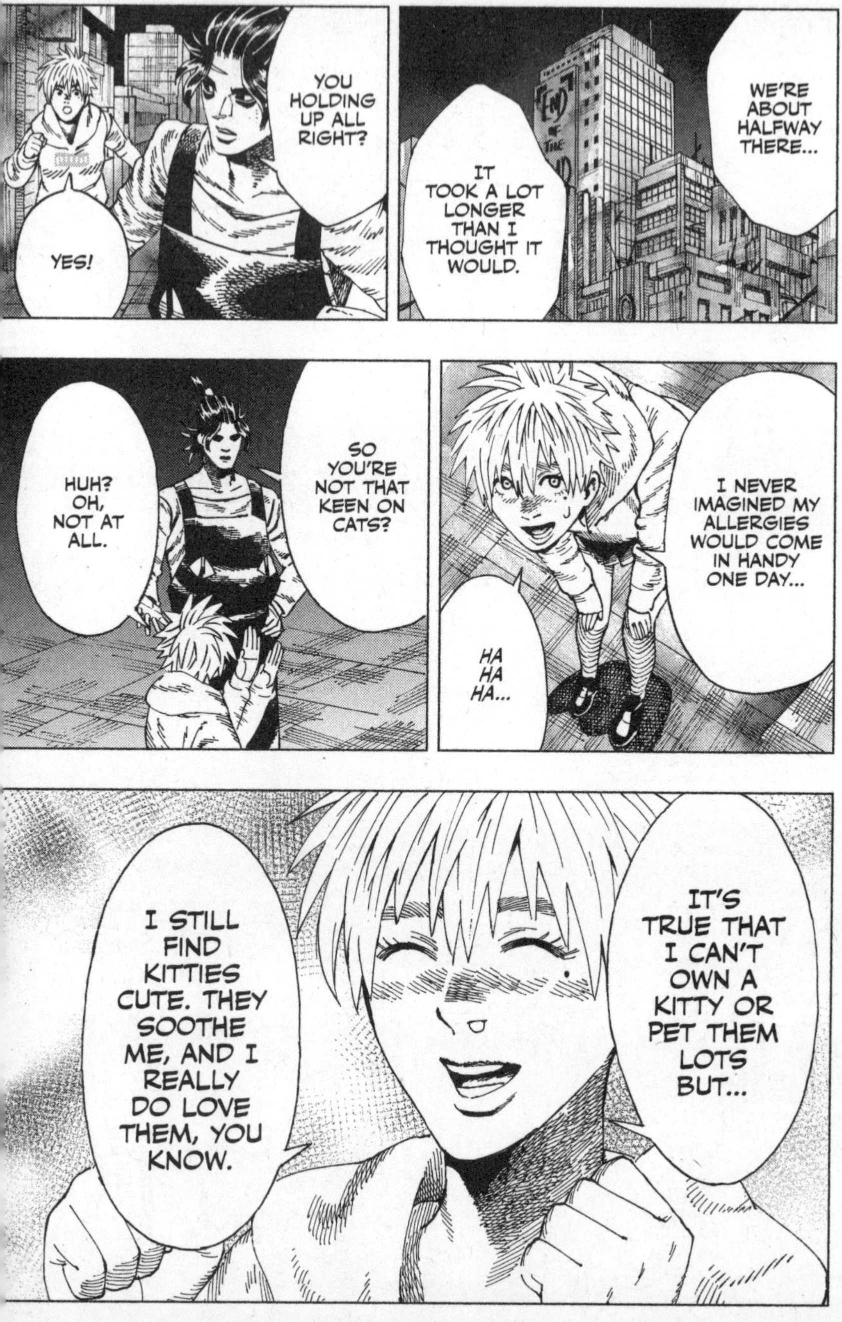
WE'RE ABOUT HALFWAY THERE...
IT TOOK A LOT LONGER THAN I THOUGHT IT WOULD.
YOU HOLDING UP ALL RIGHT?
YES!
I NEVER IMAGINED MY ALLERGIES WOULD COME IN HANDY ONE DAY...
HA HA HA...
SO YOU'RE NOT THAT KEEN ON CATS?
HUH? OH, NOT AT ALL.
IT'S TRUE THAT I CAN'T OWN A KITTY OR PET THEM LOTS BUT...
I STILL FIND KITTIES CUTE. THEY SOOTHE ME, AND I REALLY DO LOVE THEM, YOU KNOW.

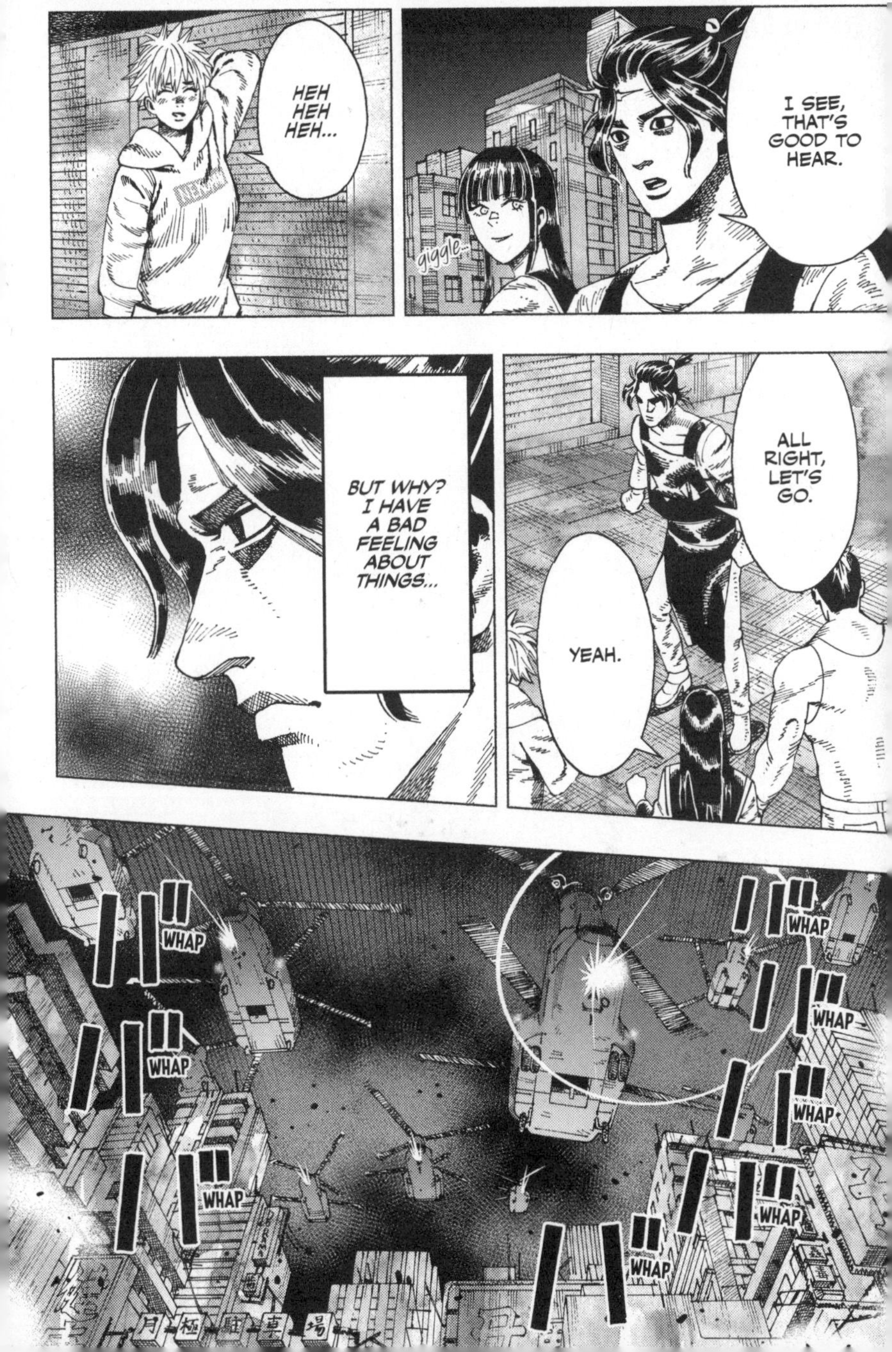
I SEE, THAT'S GOOD TO HEAR.
giggle...
HEH HEH HEH...
ALL RIGHT, LET'S GO.
YEAH.
BUT WHY? I HAVE A BAD FEELING ABOUT THINGS...
WHAP
WHAP
WHAP
WHAP
WHAP
WHAP
WHAP
WHAP
月極駐車場

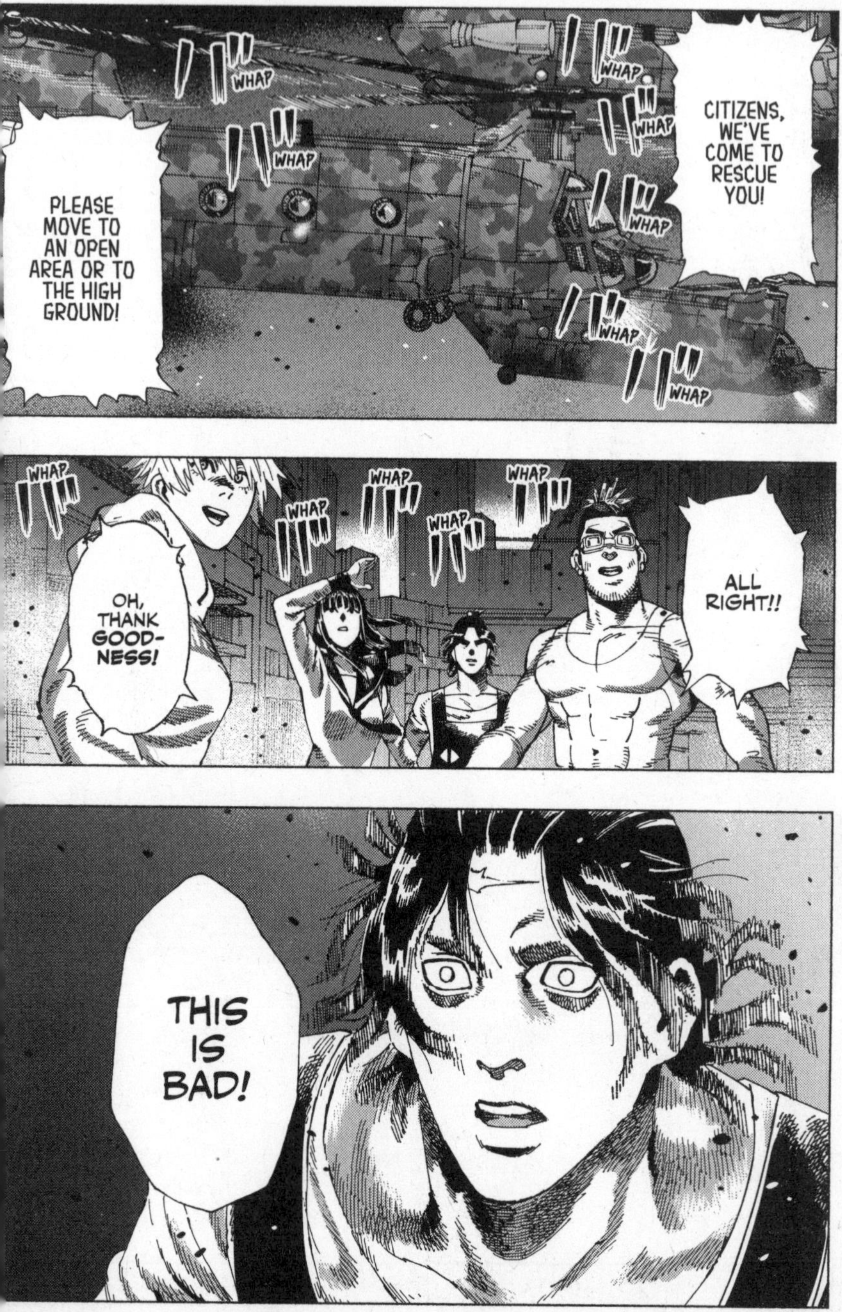
CITIZENS, WE'VE COME TO RESCUE YOU!
WHAP
WHAP
WHAP
WHAP
WHAP
WHAP
WHAP
PLEASE MOVE TO AN OPEN AREA OR TO THE HIGH GROUND!
WHAP
ALL RIGHT!!
WHAP
WHAP
WHAP
WHAP
OH, THANK GOODNESS!
THIS IS BAD!

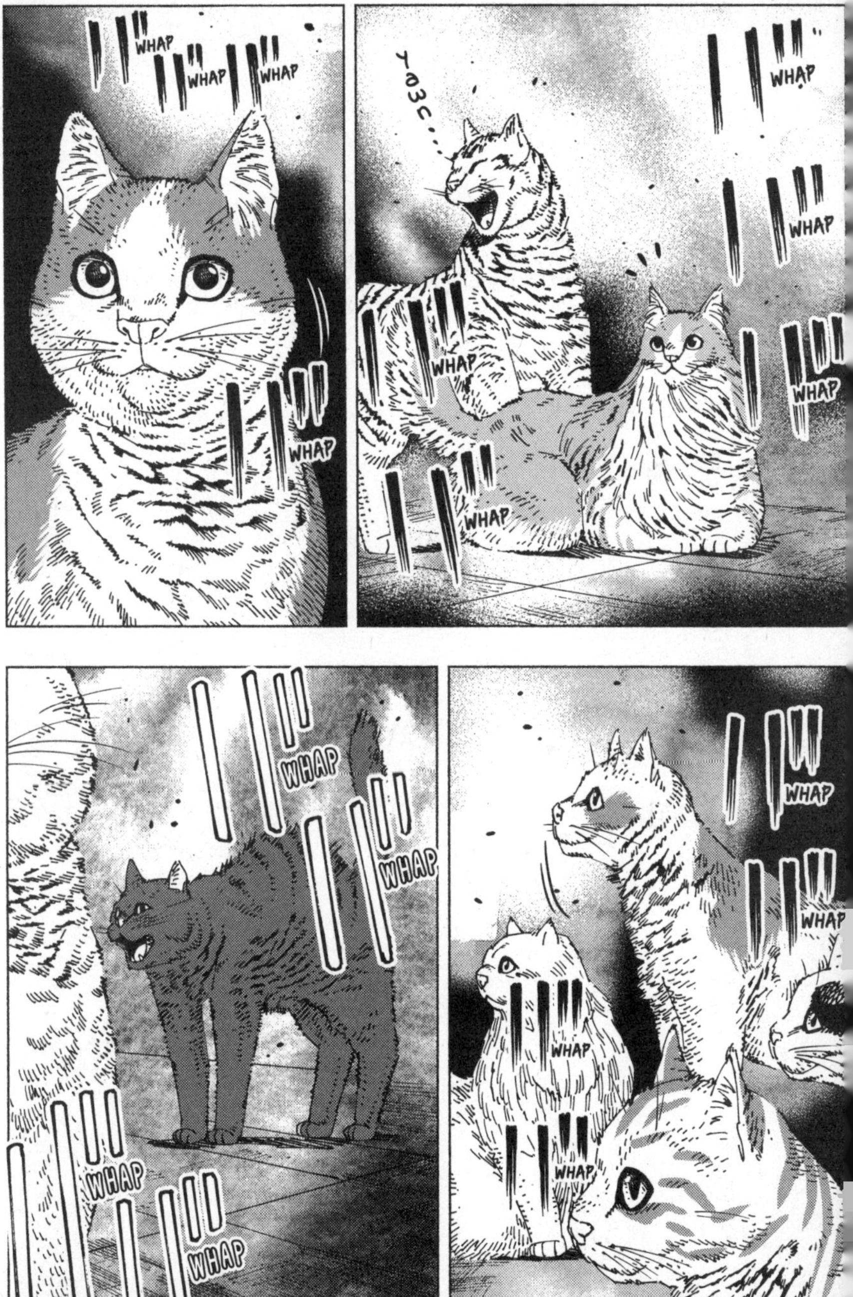
WHAP
WHAP
YAWN...
WHAP
WHAP
WHAP
WHAP
WHAP
WHAP
WHAP
WHAP
WHAP
WHAP
WHAP
WHAP
WHAP
WHAP
WHAP
WHAP

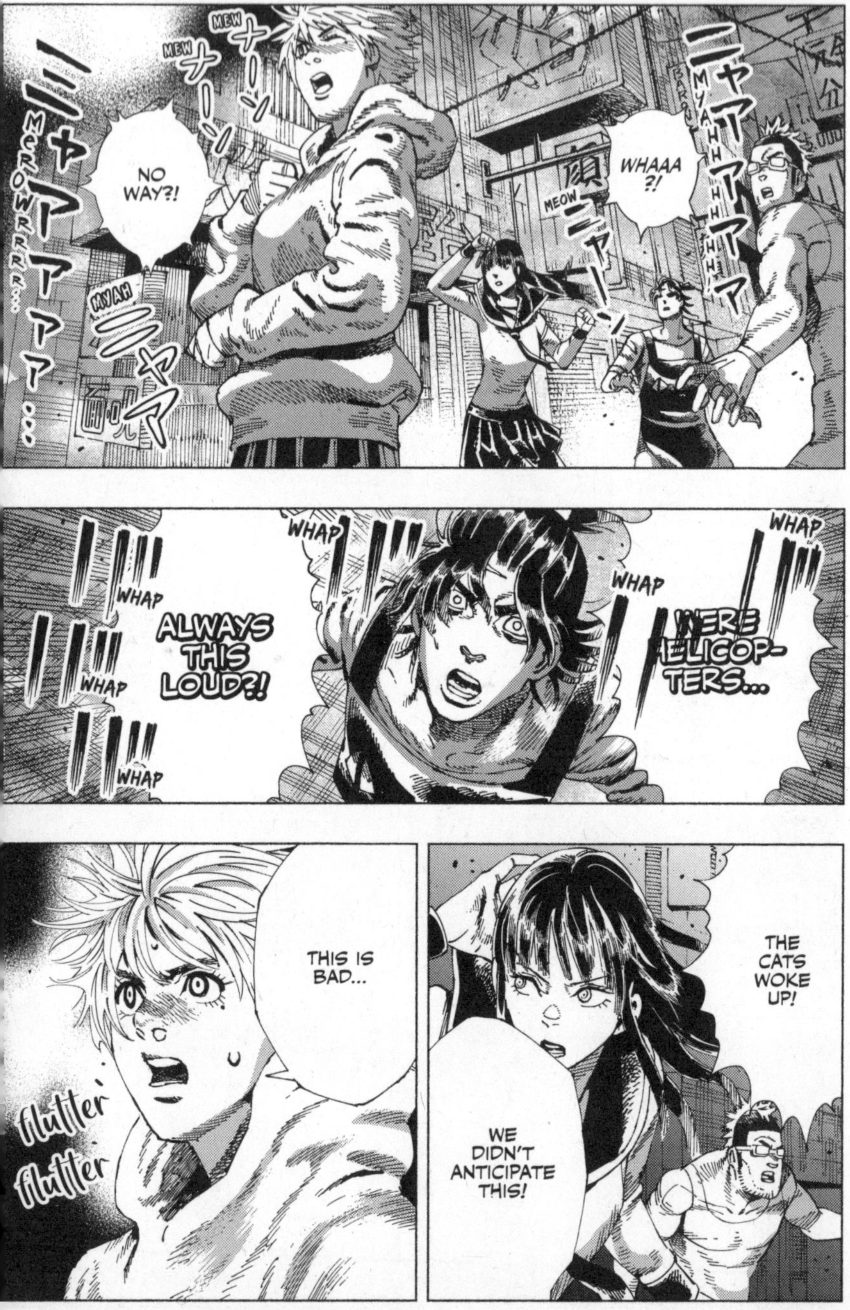

ニャアアアア
MYAHHHHHH!
WHAAA?!
MEOW ニャーー
NO WAY?!
MEW ナーーン
MEW ナーーン
MYAH ミャア
ミャアアアア...
MEROWRRRR...
WHAP
WHAP
WERE HELICOPTERS...
WHAP
ALWAYS THIS LOUD?!
WHAP
WHAP
WHAP
THE CATS WOKE UP!
WE DIDN'T ANTICIPATE THIS!
THIS IS BAD...
flutter flutter

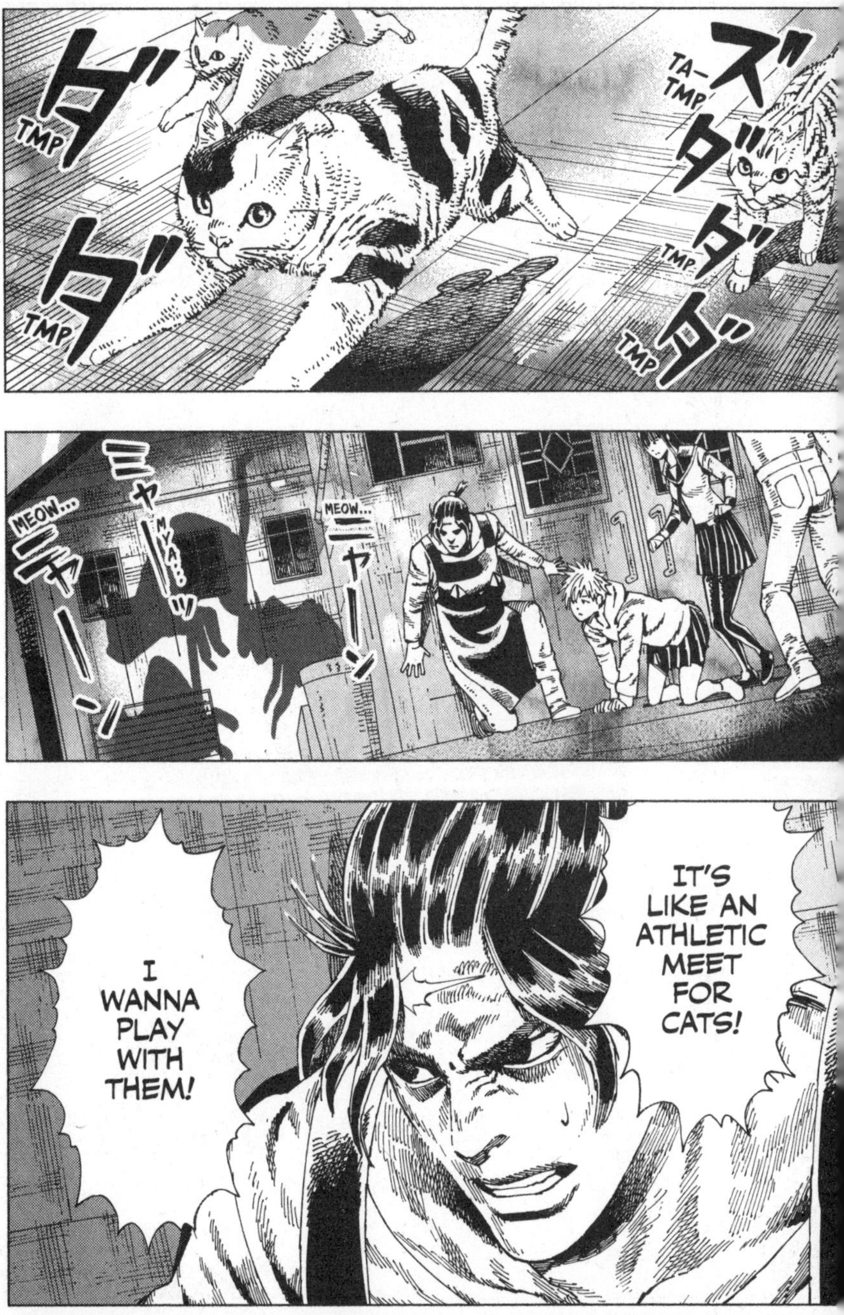
TA-TMP
TMP
TMP
TMP
TMP
MEOW...
MYA...
MEOW...
IT'S LIKE AN ATHLETIC MEET FOR CATS!
I WANNA PLAY WITH THEM!

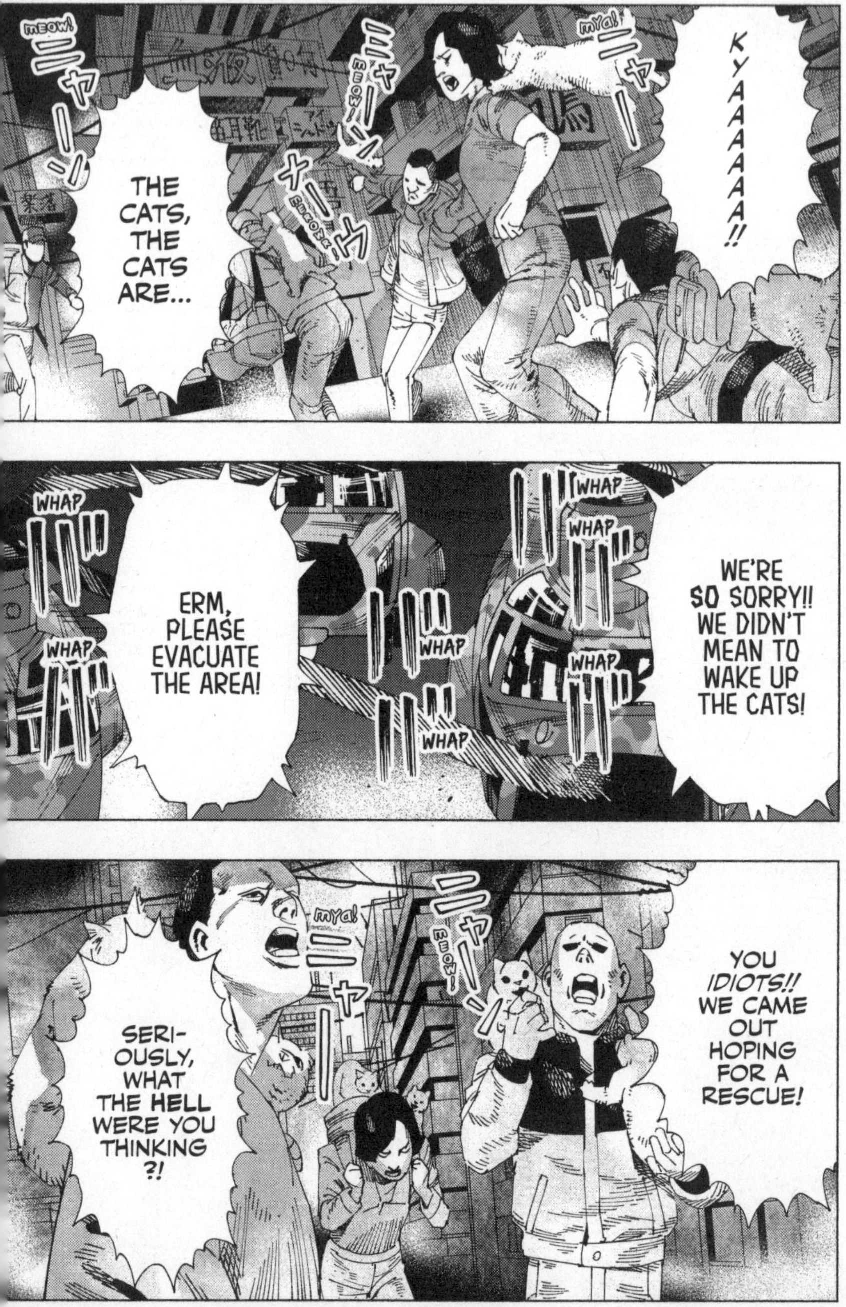
KYAAAAAAA!!
mYa!
MEOW!
BEROWR!
THE CATS, THE CATS ARE...
MEOW!
WHAP
WHAP
WE'RE SO SORRY!! WE DIDN'T MEAN TO WAKE UP THE CATS!
WHAP
WHAP
WHAP
ERM, PLEASE EVACUATE THE AREA!
WHAP
WHAP
YOU IDIOTS!! WE CAME OUT HOPING FOR A RESCUE!
MEOW!
mYa!
SERI-OUSLY, WHAT THE HELL WERE YOU THINKING ?!

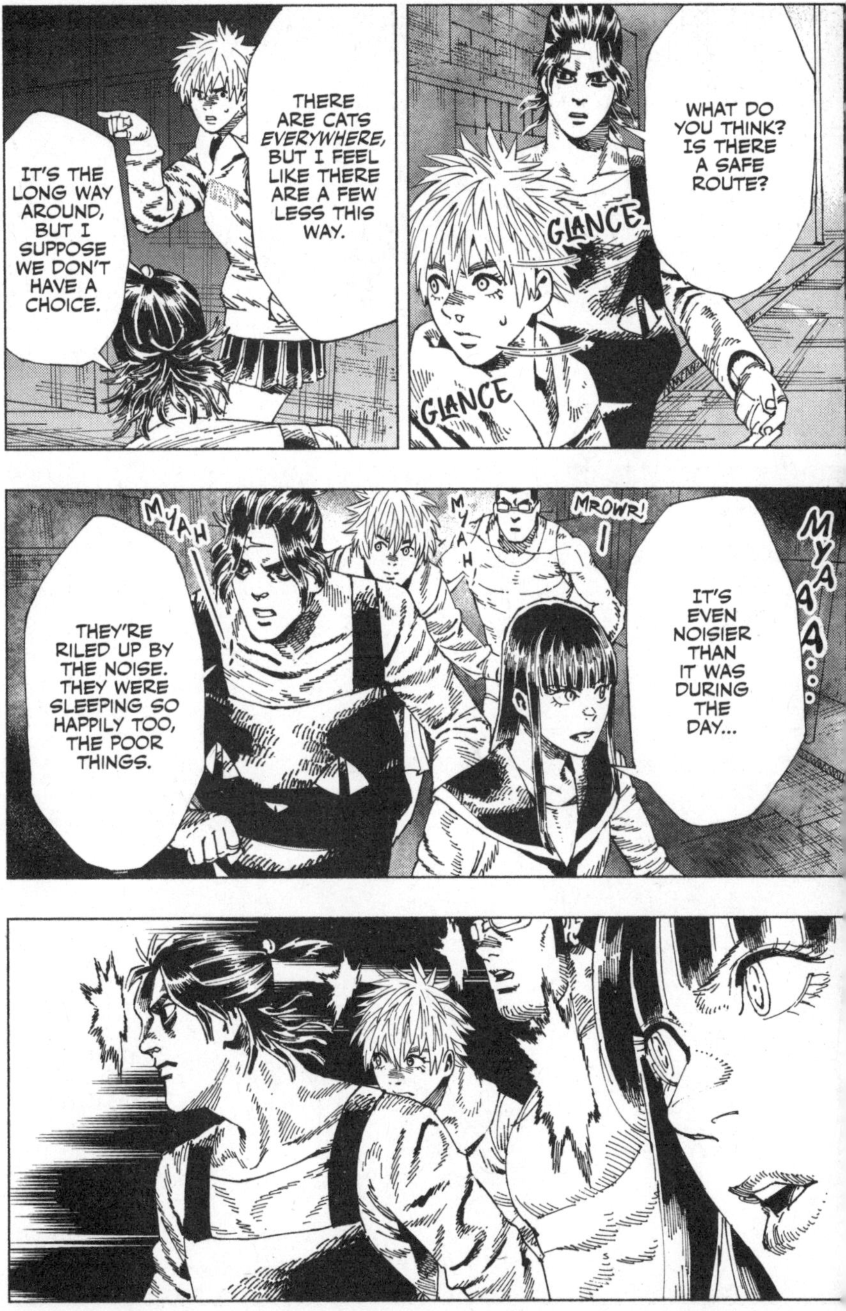
WHAT DO YOU THINK? IS THERE A SAFE ROUTE?
GLANCE
GLANCE
THERE ARE CATS *EVERYWHERE,* BUT I FEEL LIKE THERE ARE A FEW LESS THIS WAY.
IT'S THE LONG WAY AROUND, BUT I SUPPOSE WE DON'T HAVE A CHOICE.
MYAAA...
IT'S EVEN NOISIER THAN IT WAS DURING THE DAY...
MROWR!
MYAH
MYAH
THEY'RE RILED UP BY THE NOISE. THEY WERE SLEEPING SO HAPPILY TOO, THE POOR THINGS.

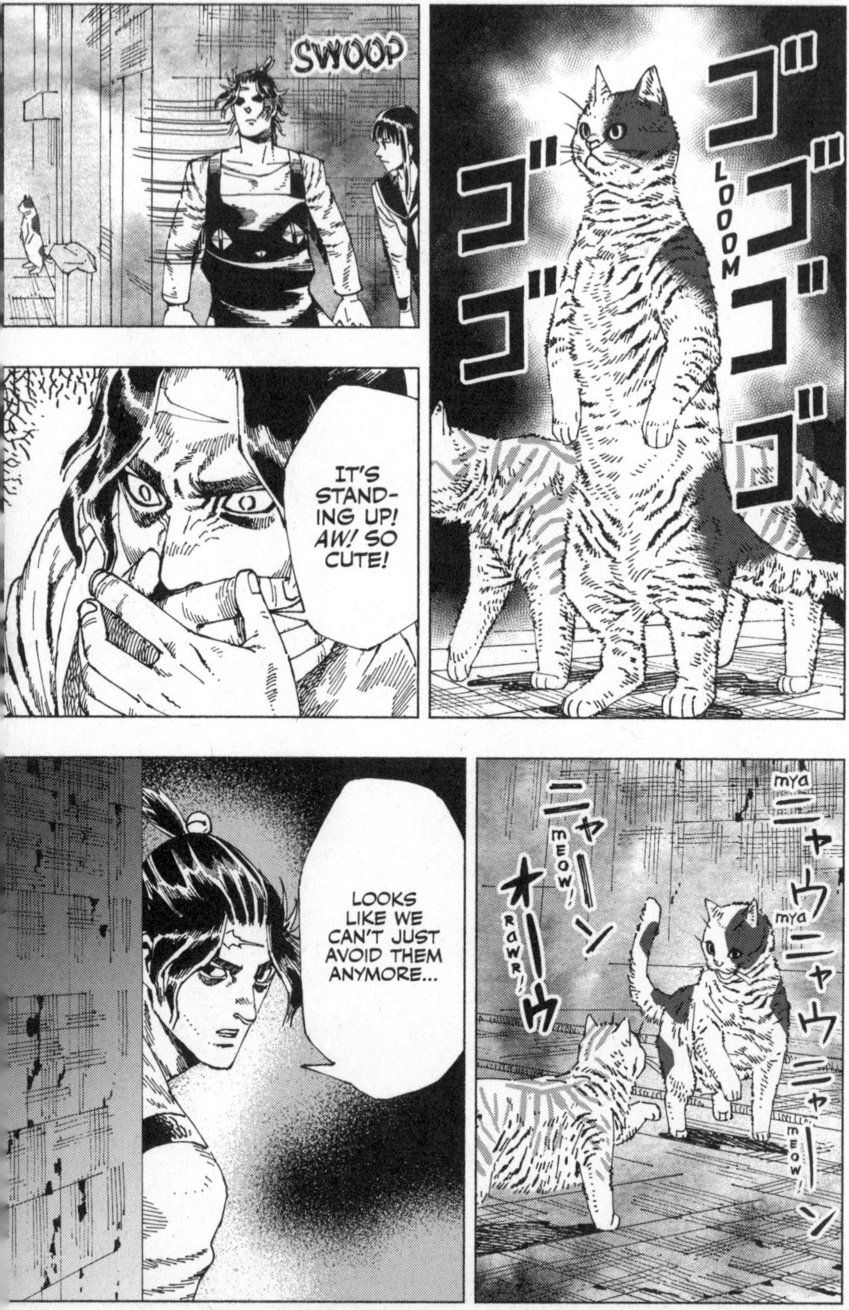

ゴゴゴゴ
LOOOM
SWOOP
IT'S STANDING UP! AW! SO CUTE!
mya
ニャウ
mya
ニャウニャーン
MEOW!
ニャーン
MEOW!
オーーウ
RAWR!
LOOKS LIKE WE CAN'T JUST AVOID THEM ANYMORE...

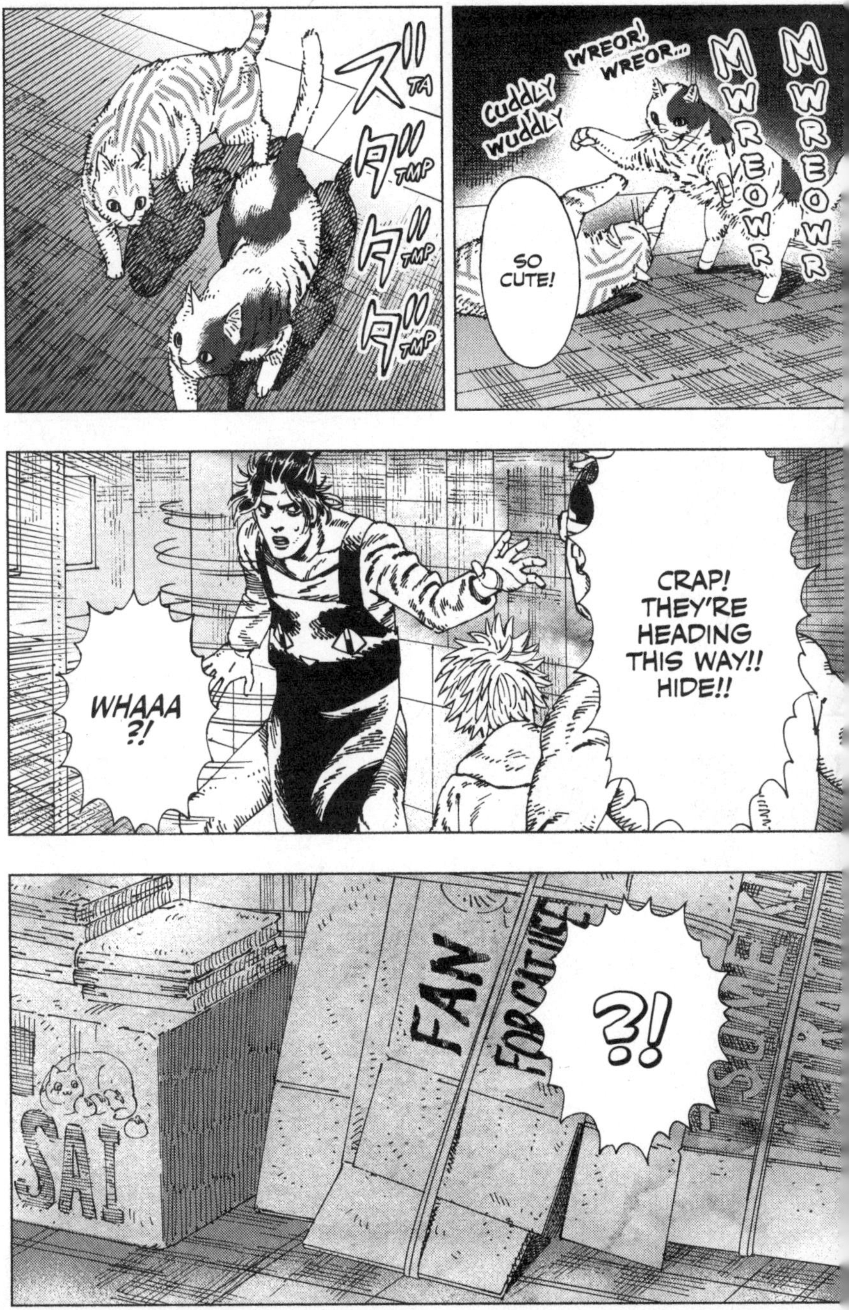
MWREOWR
MWREOWR
WREOR! WREOR...
cuddly wuddly
SO CUTE!
TA
TMP
TMP
TMP
CRAP! THEY'RE HEADING THIS WAY!! HIDE!!
WHAAA ?!
?!
FAN
SAI

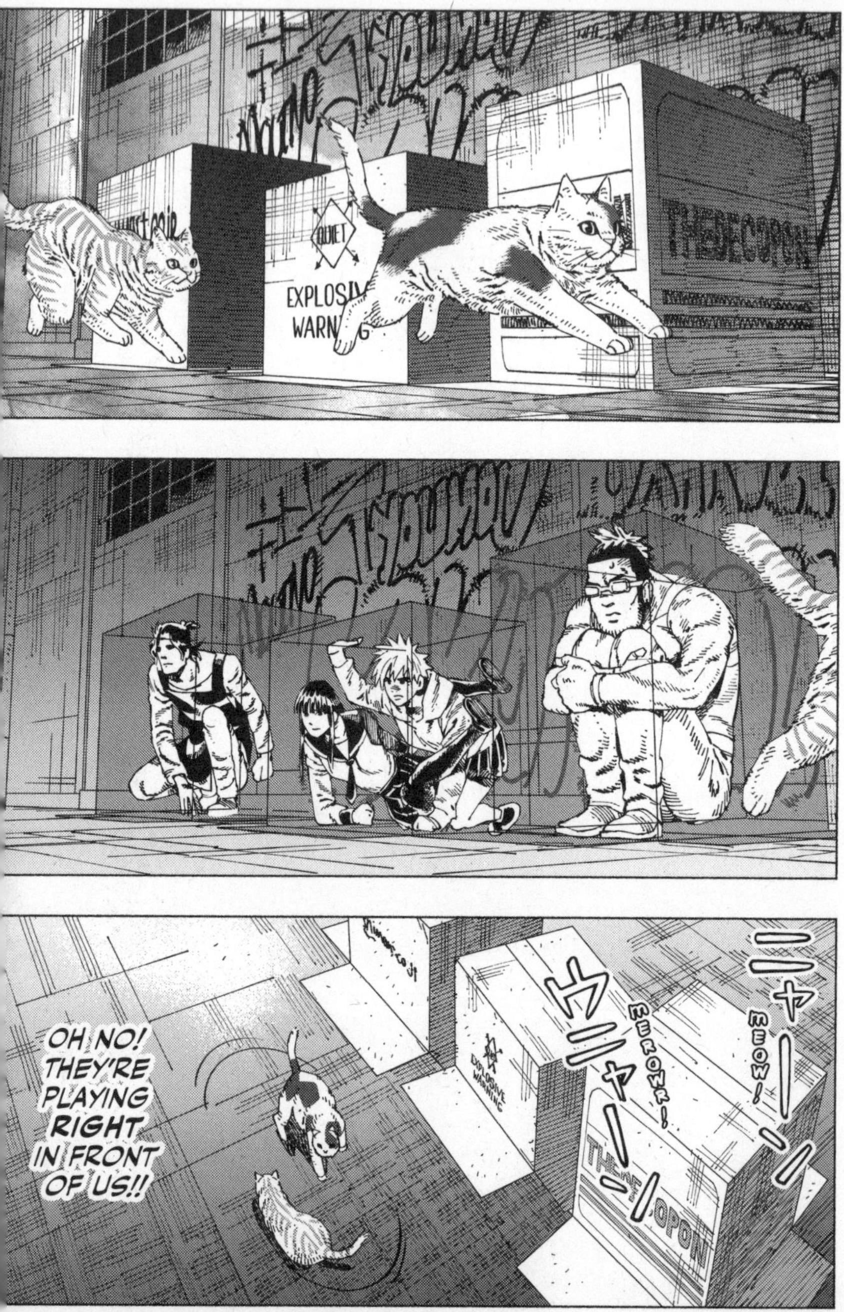

QUIET
EXPLOSIVE WARNING
ニャーーー
MEOW!
ウニャーー
MEROWR!
OH NO! THEY'RE PLAYING RIGHT IN FRONT OF US!!

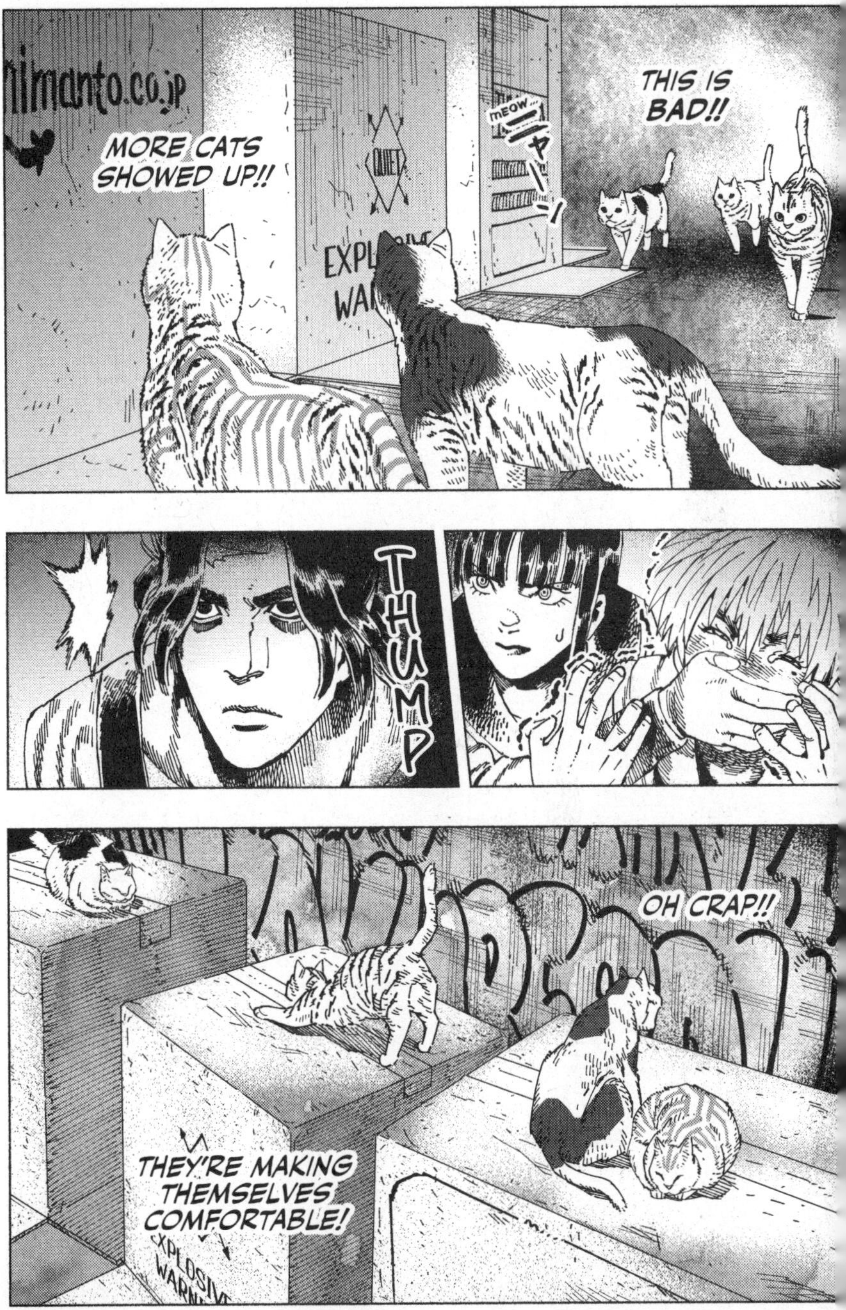
THIS IS BAD!!
MEOW...
MORE CATS SHOWED UP!!
QUIET
THUMP
OH CRAP!!
THEY'RE MAKING THEMSELVES COMFORTABLE!

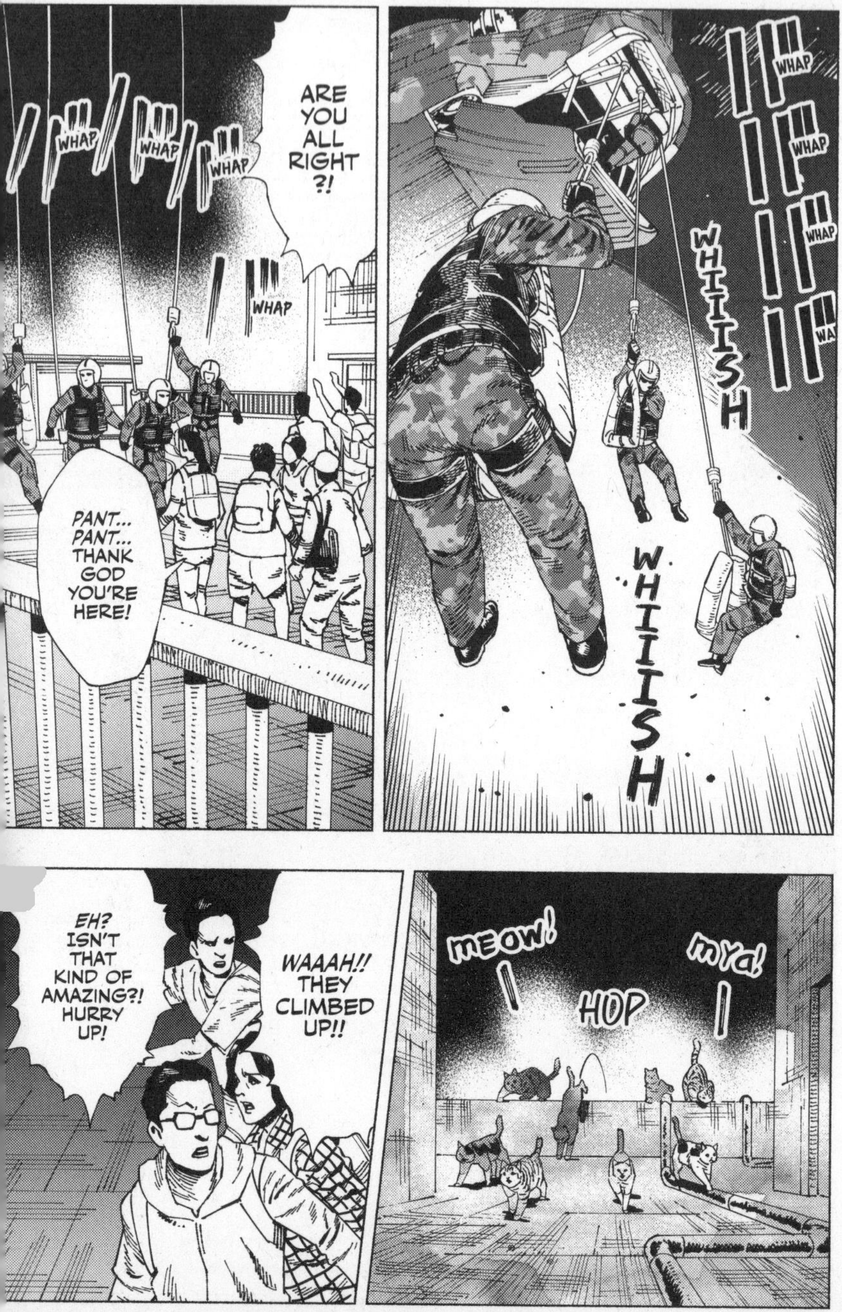
WHAP
WHAP
WHAP
WA
WHIIISH
WHIIISH
ARE YOU ALL RIGHT?!
WHAP
WHAP
WHAP
WHAP
PANT... PANT... THANK GOD YOU'RE HERE!
mya!
HOP
meow!
WAAAH!! THEY CLIMBED UP!!
EH? ISN'T THAT KIND OF AMAZING?! HURRY UP!

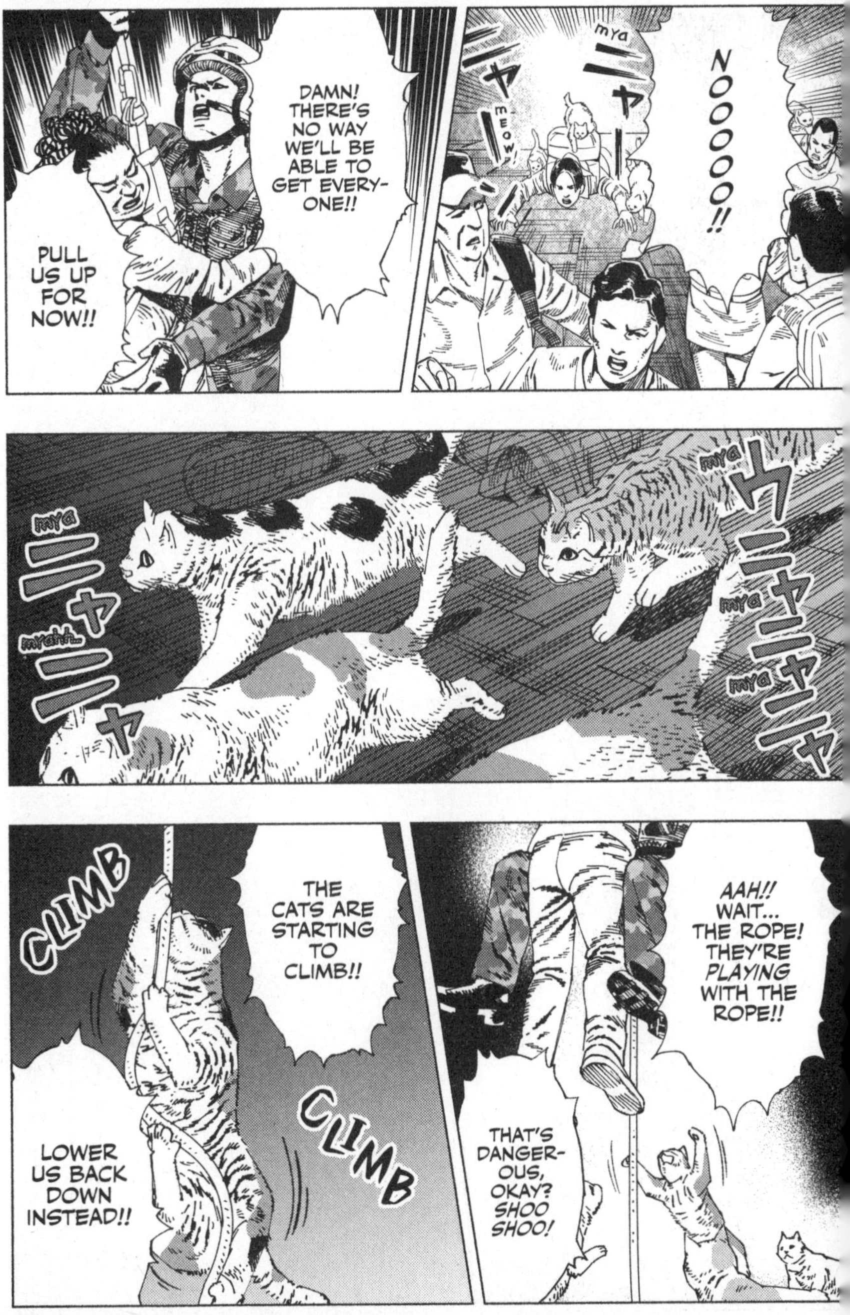

mya
ニャー
MEOW!
ニャー
NOOOOOO!!
DAMN! THERE'S NO WAY WE'LL BE ABLE TO GET EVERY-ONE!!
PULL US UP FOR NOW!!
mya
ウニャンニャンニャ
mya
mya
mya
ニャニャ
myahh...
AAH!! WAIT... THE ROPE! THEY'RE *PLAYING* WITH THE ROPE!!
THAT'S DANGER-OUS, OKAY? *SHOO SHOO!*
CLIMB
THE CATS ARE STARTING TO CLIMB!!
CLIMB
LOWER US BACK DOWN INSTEAD!!

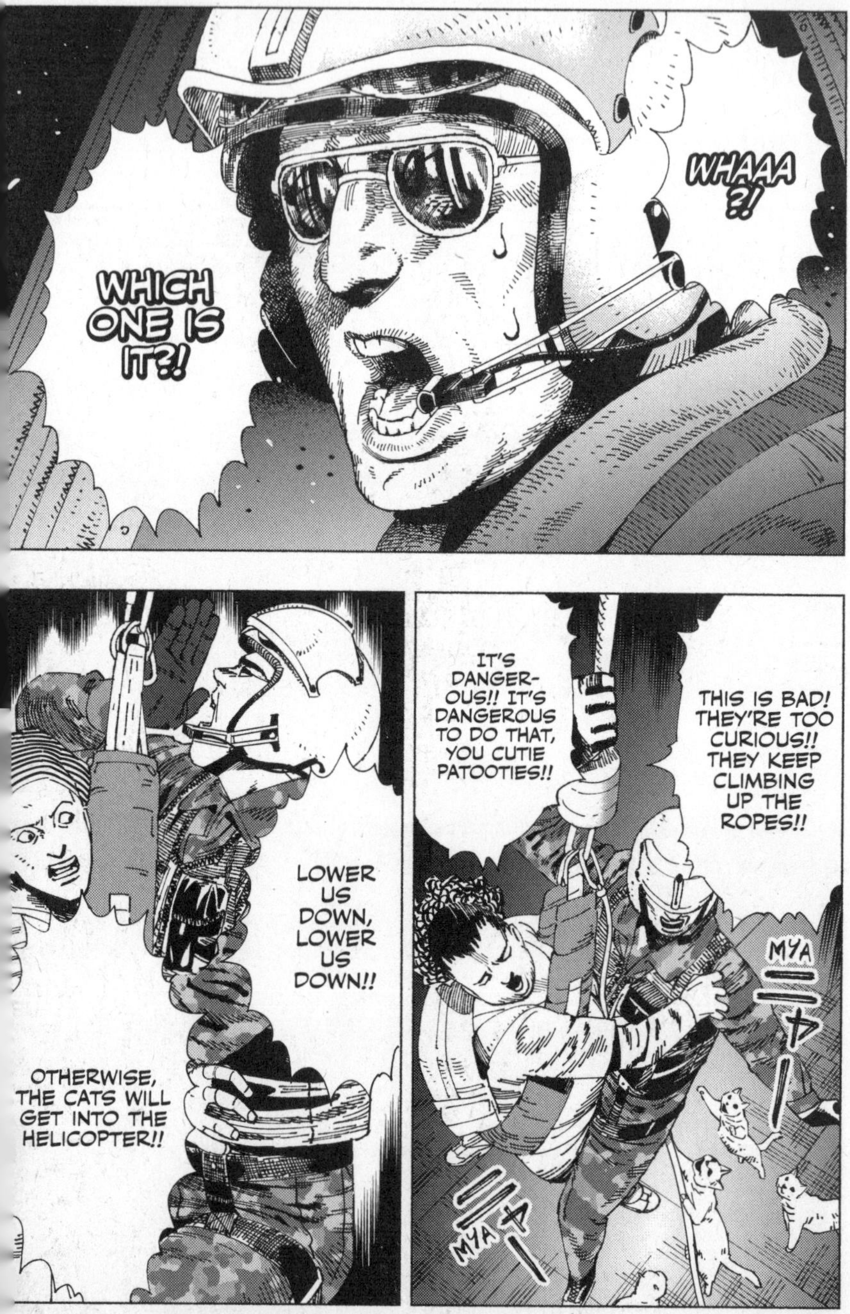
WHAAA ?!
WHICH ONE IS IT?!
THIS IS BAD! THEY'RE TOO CURIOUS!! THEY KEEP CLIMBING UP THE ROPES!!
IT'S DANGER-OUS!! IT'S DANGEROUS TO DO THAT, YOU CUTIE PATOOTIES!!
MYA
MYA
LOWER US DOWN, LOWER US DOWN!!
OTHERWISE, THE CATS WILL GET INTO THE HELICOPTER!!

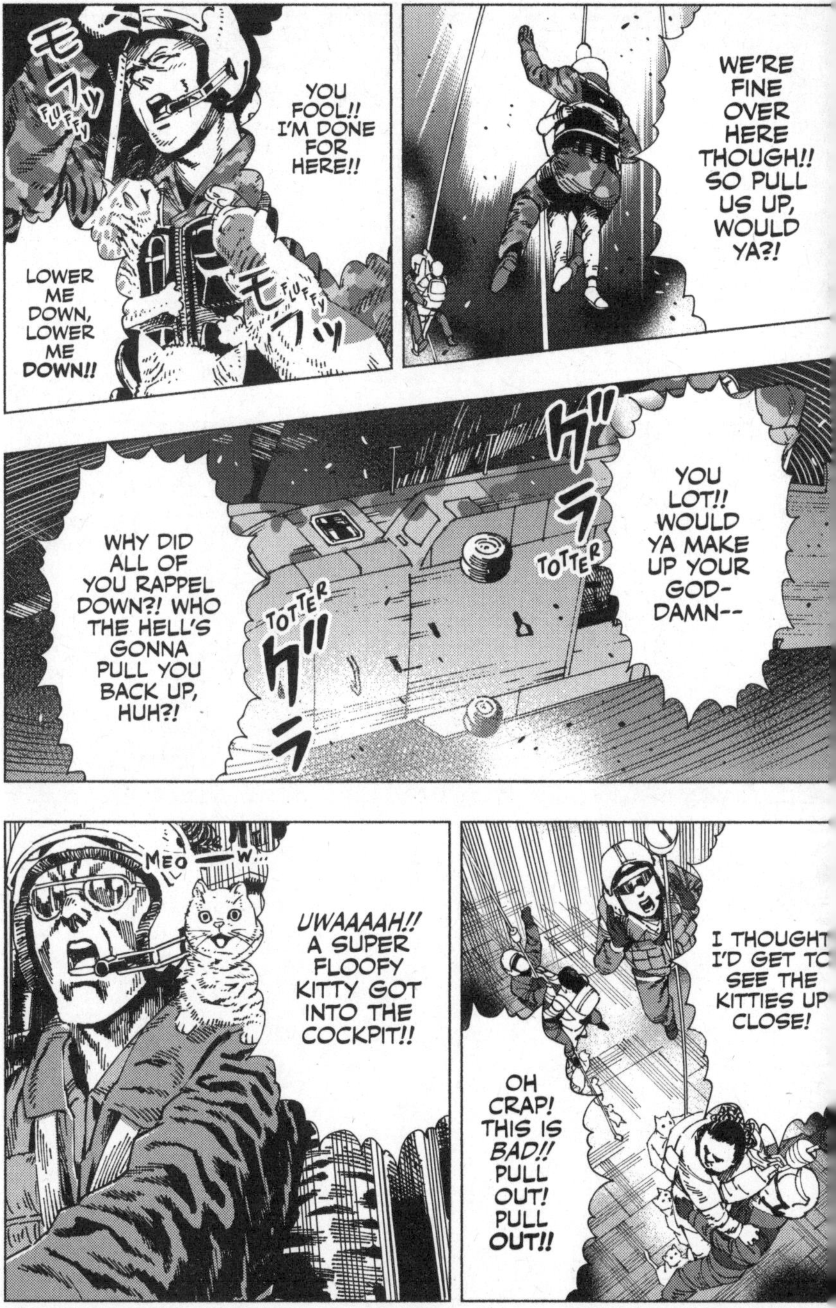
WE'RE FINE OVER HERE THOUGH!! SO PULL US UP, WOULD YA?!
YOU FOOL!! I'M DONE FOR HERE!!
モフッ FLUFFY
LOWER ME DOWN, LOWER ME DOWN!!
モフッ FLUFFY
YOU LOT!! WOULD YA MAKE UP YOUR GOD-DAMN--
グラ TOTTER
WHY DID ALL OF YOU RAPPEL DOWN?! WHO THE HELL'S GONNA PULL YOU BACK UP, HUH?!
グラ TOTTER
I THOUGHT I'D GET TO SEE THE KITTIES UP CLOSE!
OH CRAP! THIS IS BAD!! PULL OUT! PULL OUT!!
MEO——W...
UWAAAAH!! A SUPER FLOOFY KITTY GOT INTO THE COCKPIT!!

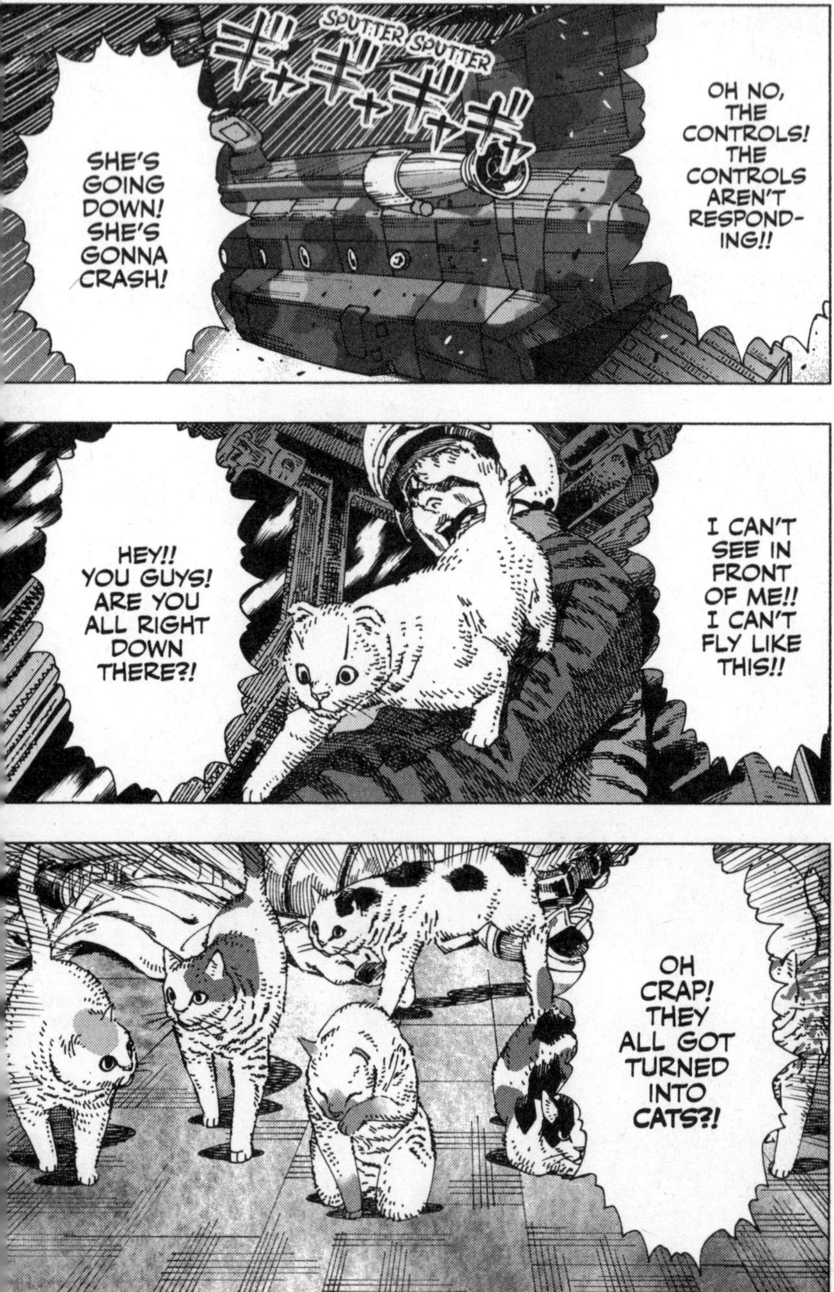
OH NO, THE CONTROLS! THE CONTROLS AREN'T RESPOND-ING!!
SPUTTER SPUTTER
SHE'S GOING DOWN! SHE'S GONNA CRASH!
I CAN'T SEE IN FRONT OF ME!! I CAN'T FLY LIKE THIS!!
HEY!! YOU GUYS! ARE YOU ALL RIGHT DOWN THERE?!
OH CRAP! THEY ALL GOT TURNED INTO CATS?!

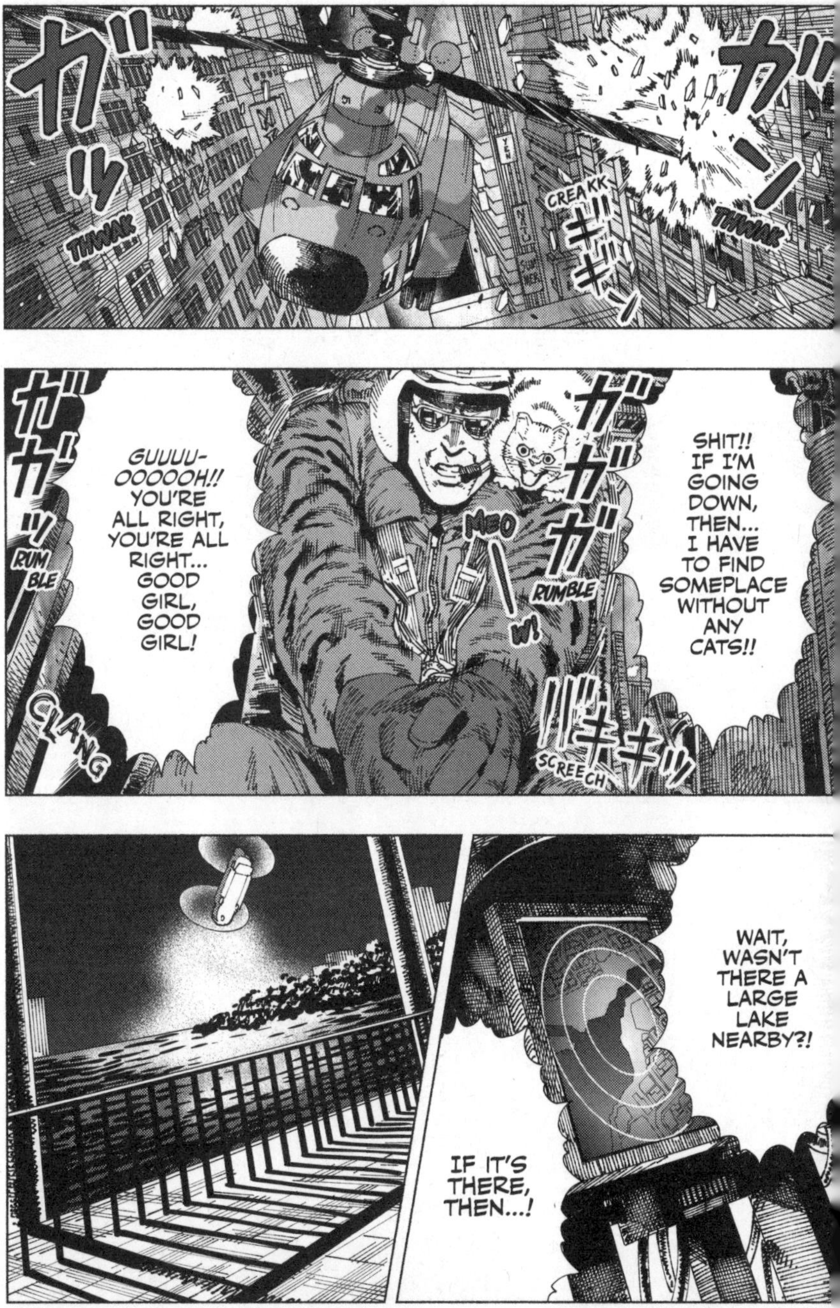
THWAK
CREAKK
THWAK
SHIT!! IF I'M GOING DOWN, THEN... I HAVE TO FIND SOMEPLACE WITHOUT ANY CATS!!
RUMBLE
MEO W!
SCREECH
GUUUU-OOOOOH!! YOU'RE ALL RIGHT, YOU'RE ALL RIGHT... GOOD GIRL, GOOD GIRL!
RUMBLE
CLANG
WAIT, WASN'T THERE A LARGE LAKE NEARBY?!
IF IT'S THERE, THEN...!

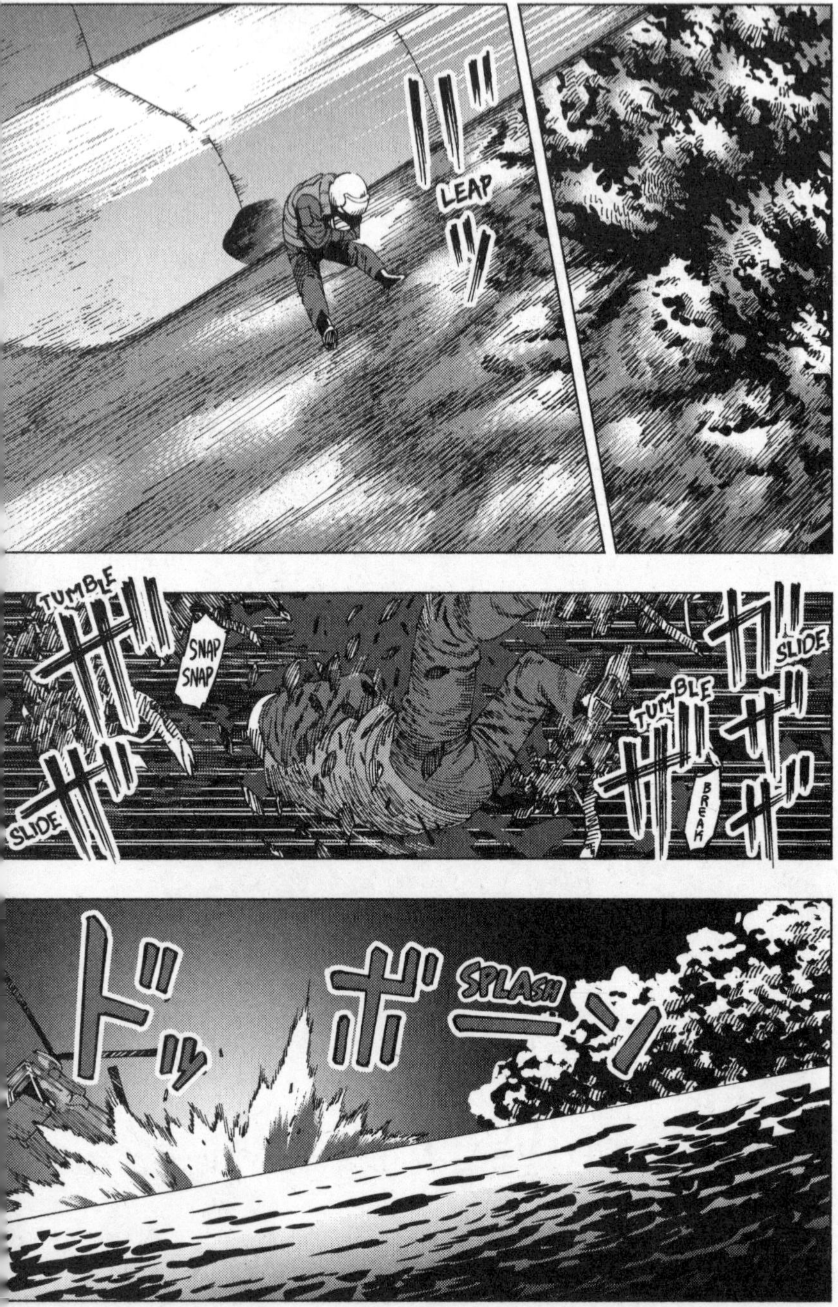

LEAP
SLIDE
TUMBLE
BREAK
SNAP SNAP
TUMBLE
SLIDE
SPLASH

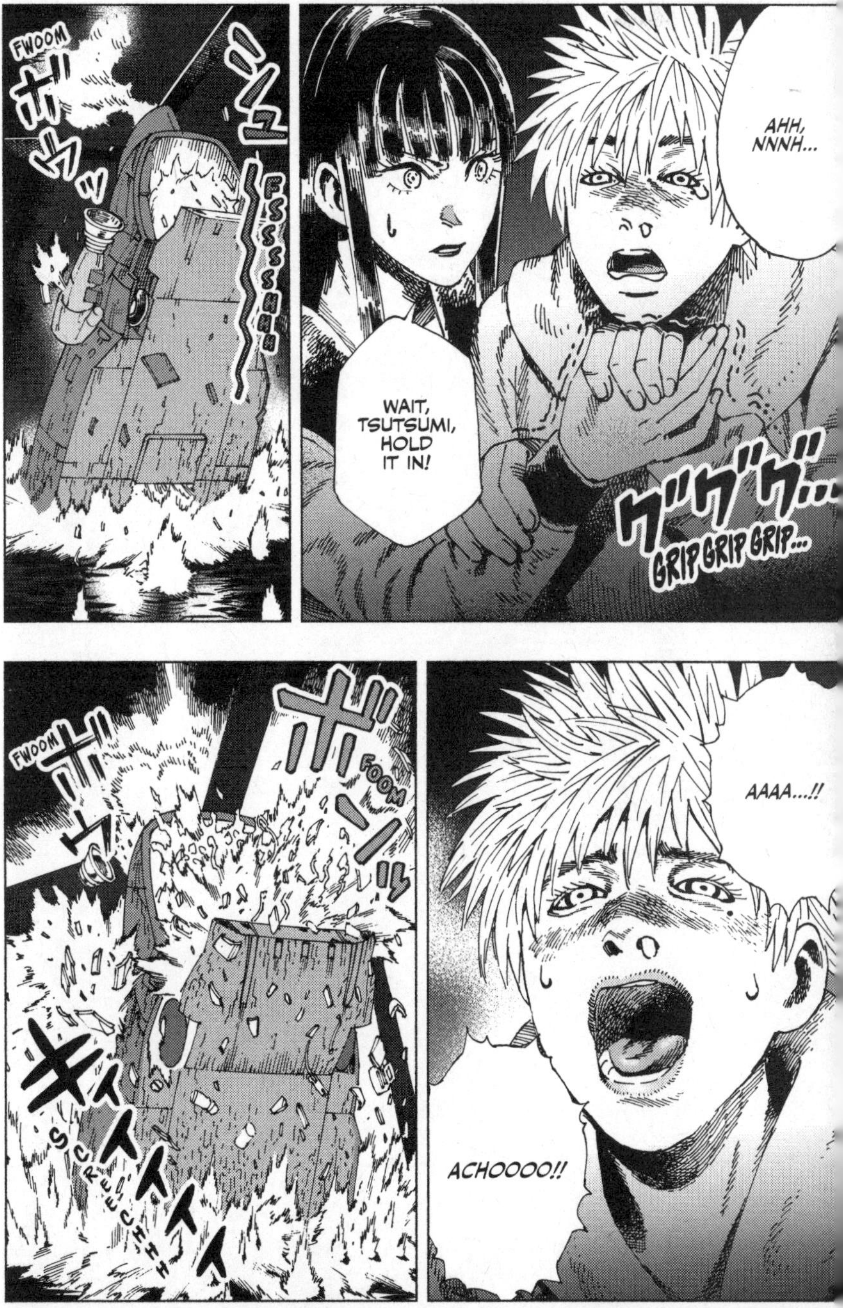
AHH, NNNH...
WAIT, TSUTSUMI, HOLD IT IN!
GRIP GRIP GRIP...
FWOOM
FSSSSHHH
AAAA...!!
ACHOOOO!!
FWOOM
FOOM
SCREECHHH

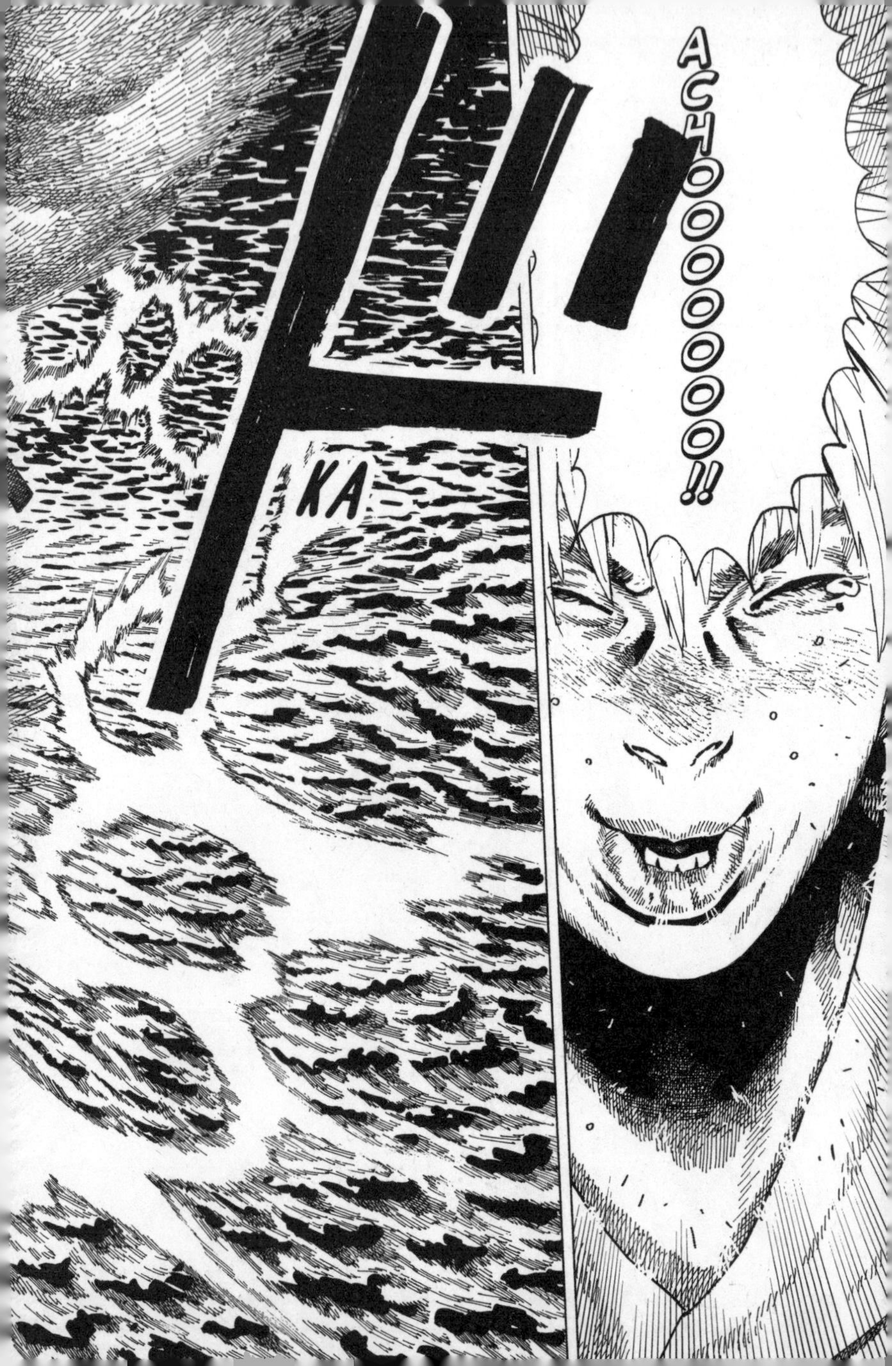
ACHOOOOOOO!!
KA

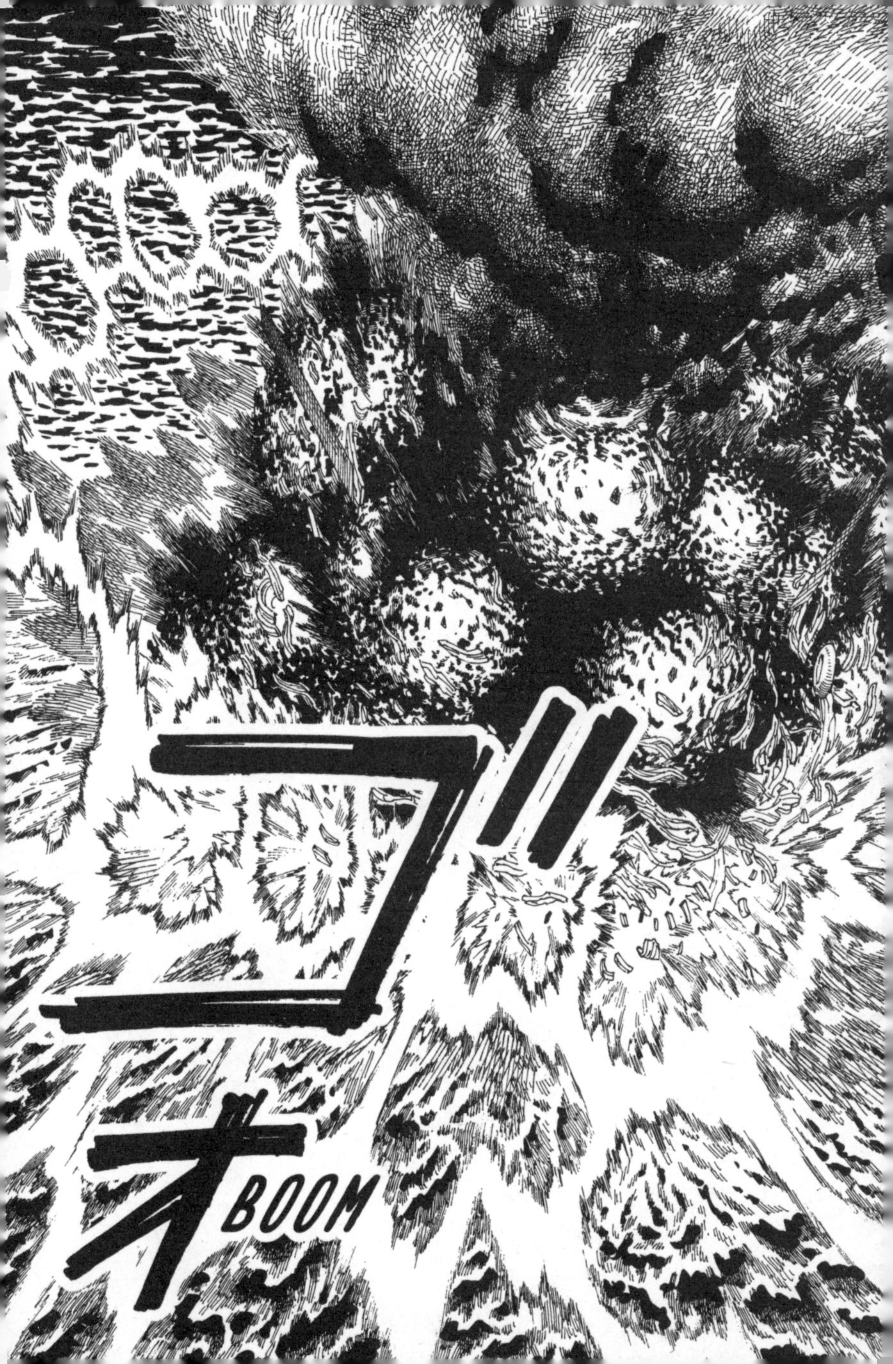
ゴオ
BOOM

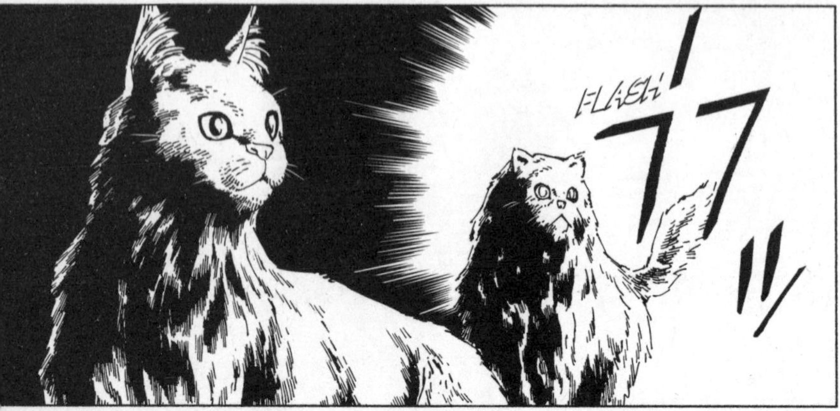
FLASH

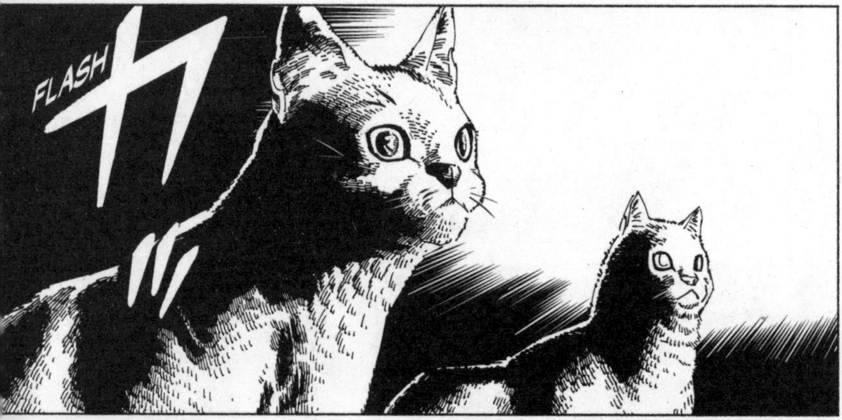
FLASH

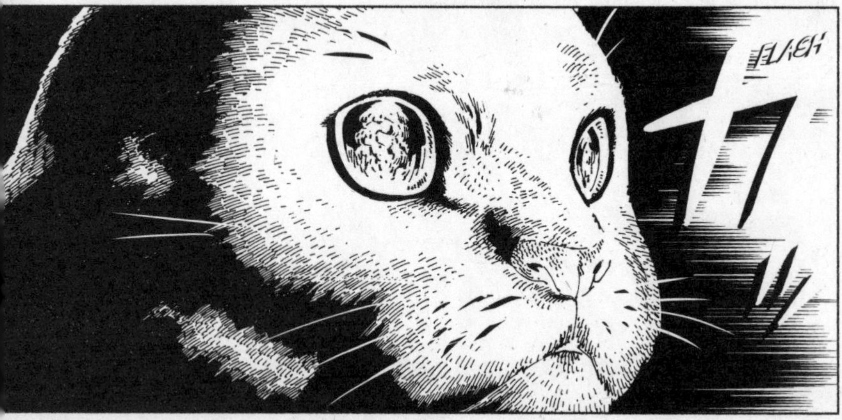
FLASH

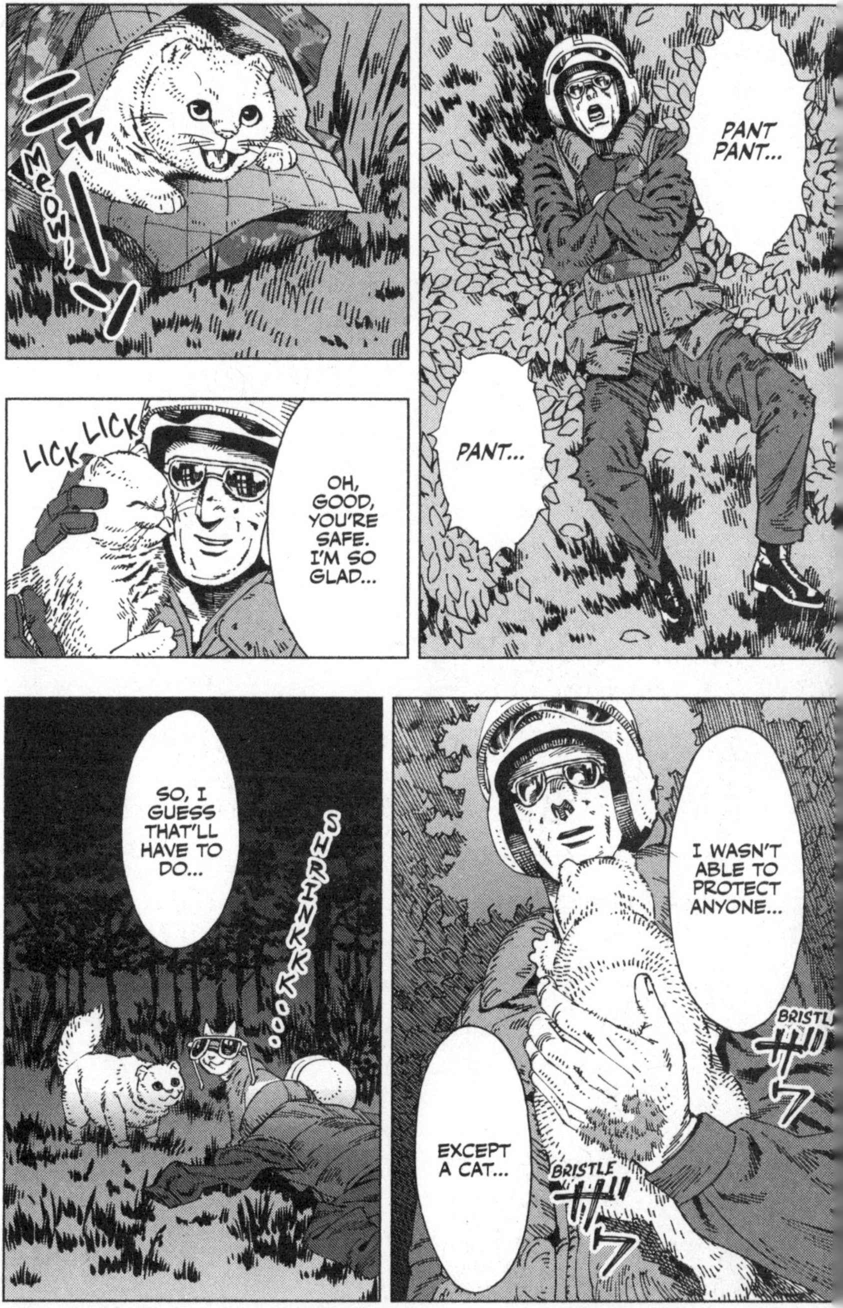
PANT PANT...
PANT...
MEOW!
LICK LICK
OH, GOOD, YOU'RE SAFE. I'M SO GLAD...
I WASN'T ABLE TO PROTECT ANYONE...
BRISTL
EXCEPT A CAT...
BRISTLE
SO, I GUESS THAT'LL HAVE TO DO...
SHRINKKKooo

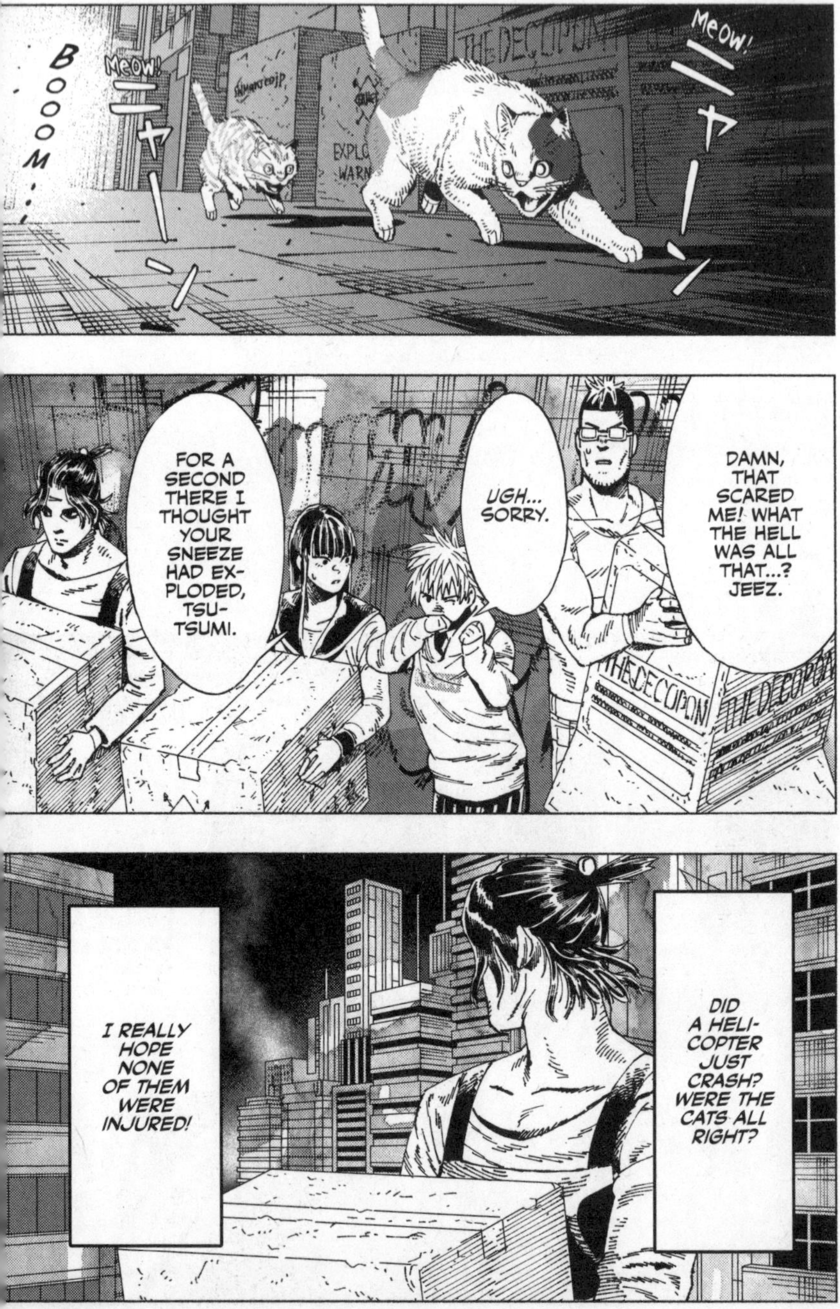
MEOW!
THE DECOPON
MEOW!
BOOOOM...
DAMN, THAT SCARED ME! WHAT THE HELL WAS ALL THAT...? JEEZ.
THE DECOPON
THE DECOPON
UGH... SORRY.
FOR A SECOND THERE I THOUGHT YOUR SNEEZE HAD EXPLODED, TSUTSUMI.
DID A HELICOPTER JUST CRASH? WERE THE CATS ALL RIGHT?
I REALLY HOPE NONE OF THEM WERE INJURED!

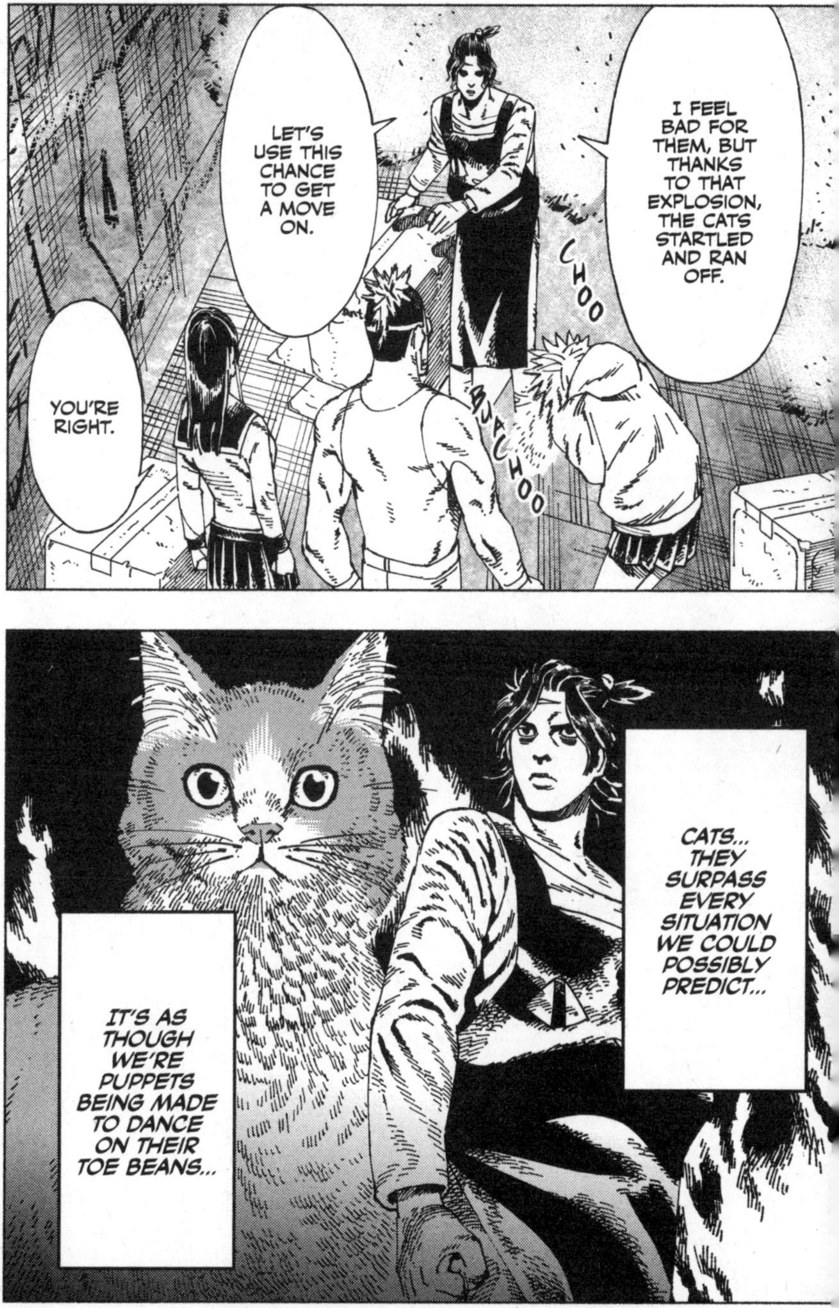
I FEEL BAD FOR THEM, BUT THANKS TO THAT EXPLOSION, THE CATS STARTLED AND RAN OFF.
CHOO
LET'S USE THIS CHANCE TO GET A MOVE ON.
BUACHOO
YOU'RE RIGHT.
CATS... THEY SURPASS EVERY SITUATION WE COULD POSSIBLY PREDICT...
IT'S AS THOUGH WE'RE PUPPETS BEING MADE TO DANCE ON THEIR TOE BEANS...

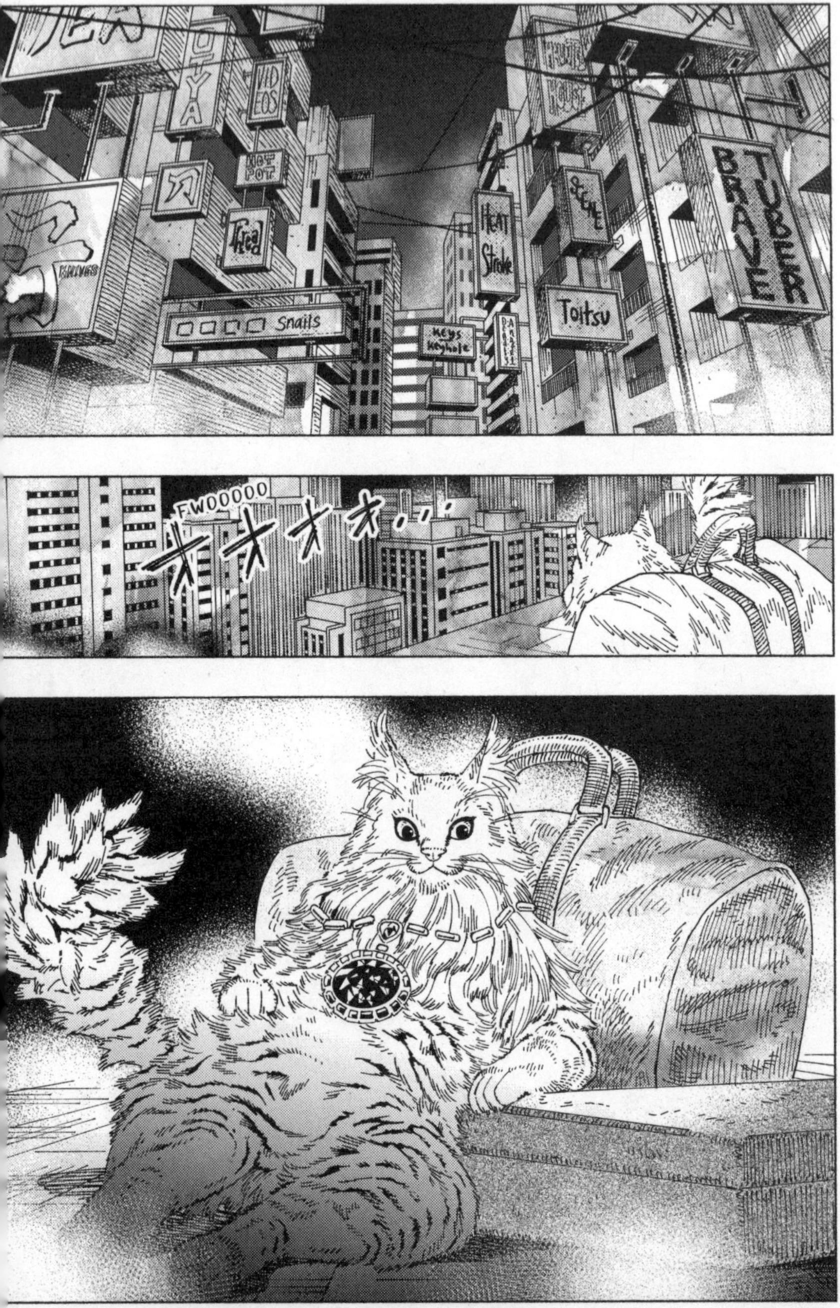
BRAVE
TUBER
Toitsu
SCENE
Heat Stroke
Keys Keyhole
Snails
Thread
HOT POT
VIDEOS
FWOOOOO

Babel

Perhaps it's because he just became a cat, but he walks on two legs beautifully. If a cat should ever appear that's capable of walking like that, it would no doubt be an existence closest to a god.

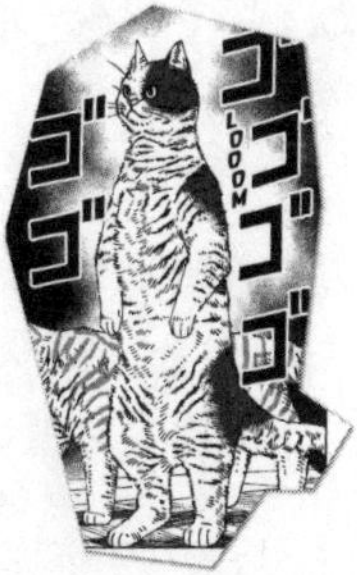
LOOOM

NYAIGHT
OF THE
LIVING
CAT 2

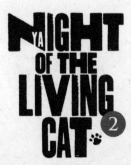

Chapter 6
The Cat is a Harsh Mistress

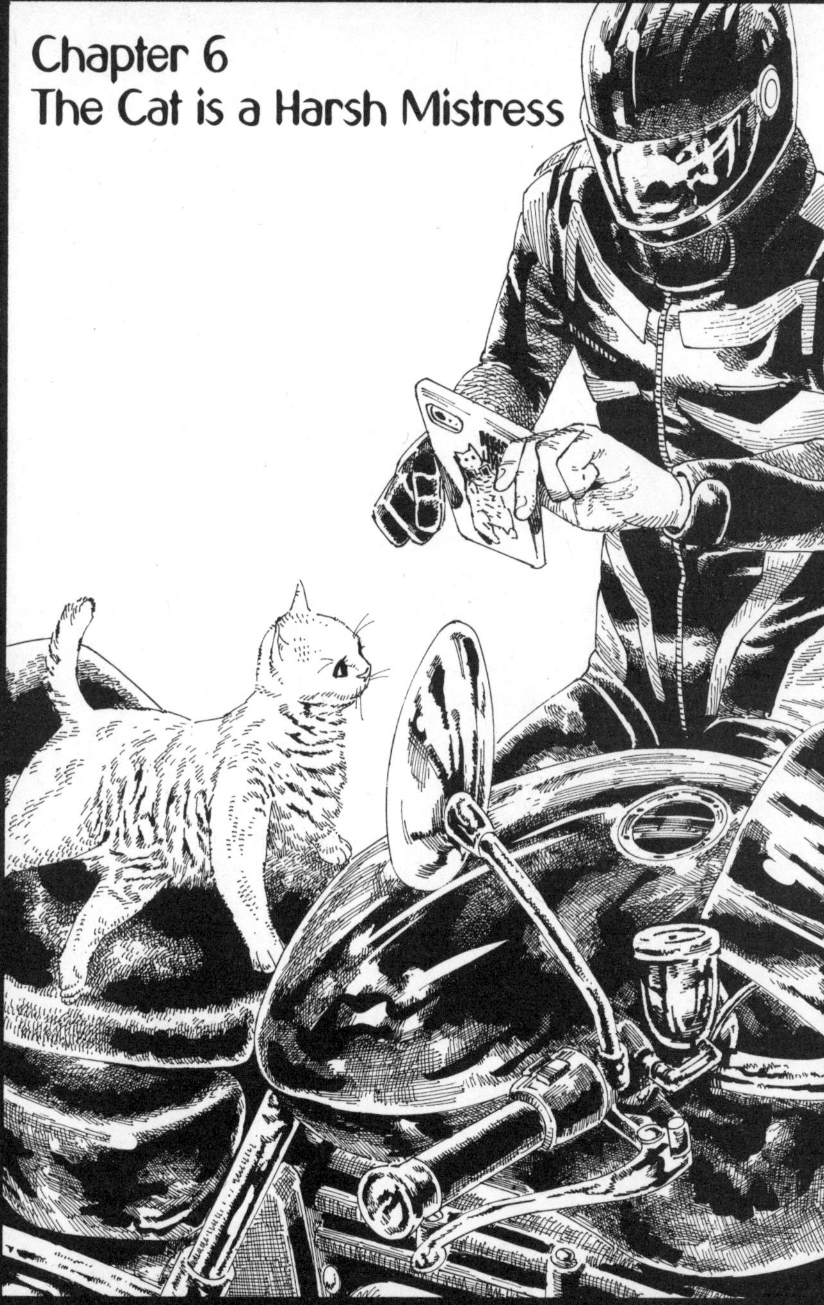

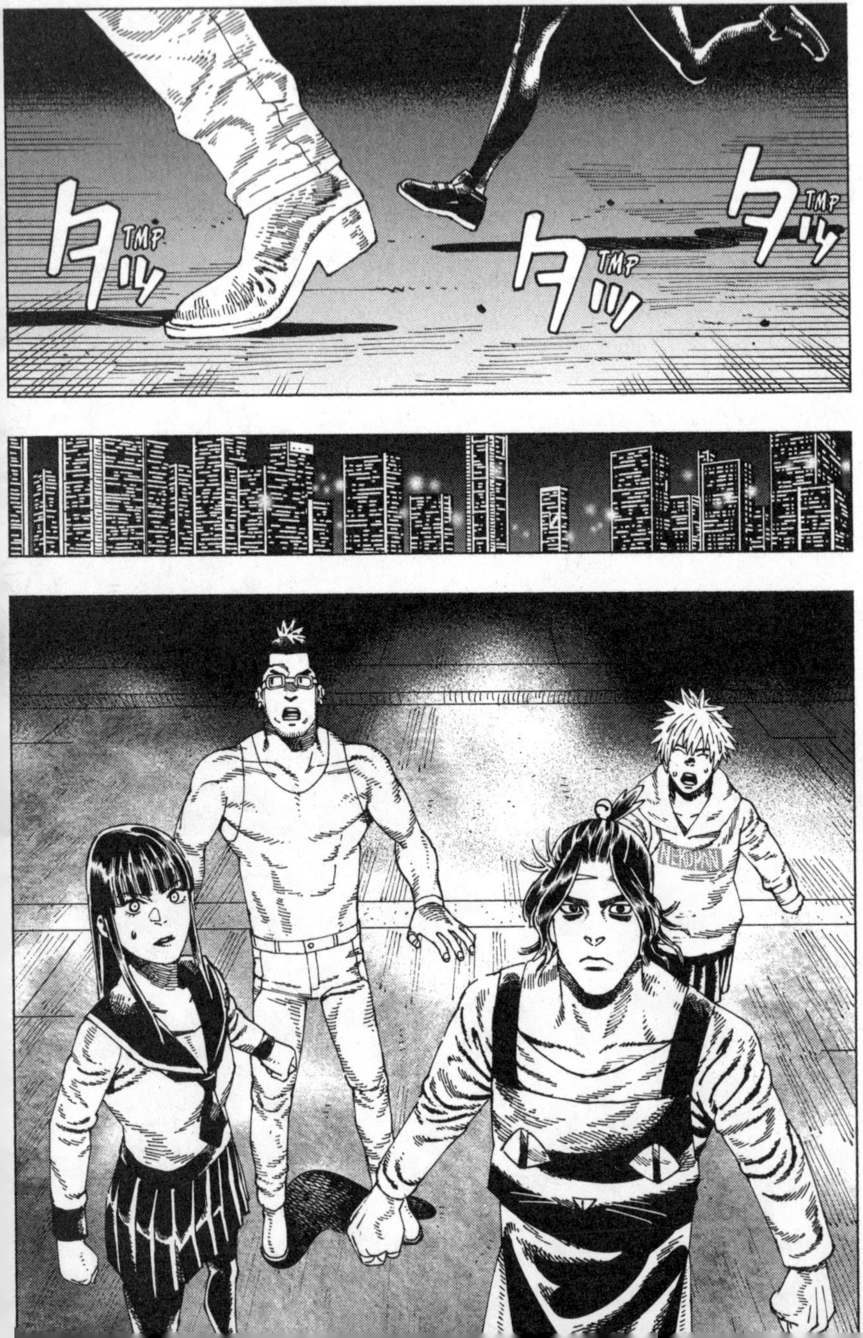
タッ
TMP
タッ
TMP
タッ
TMP

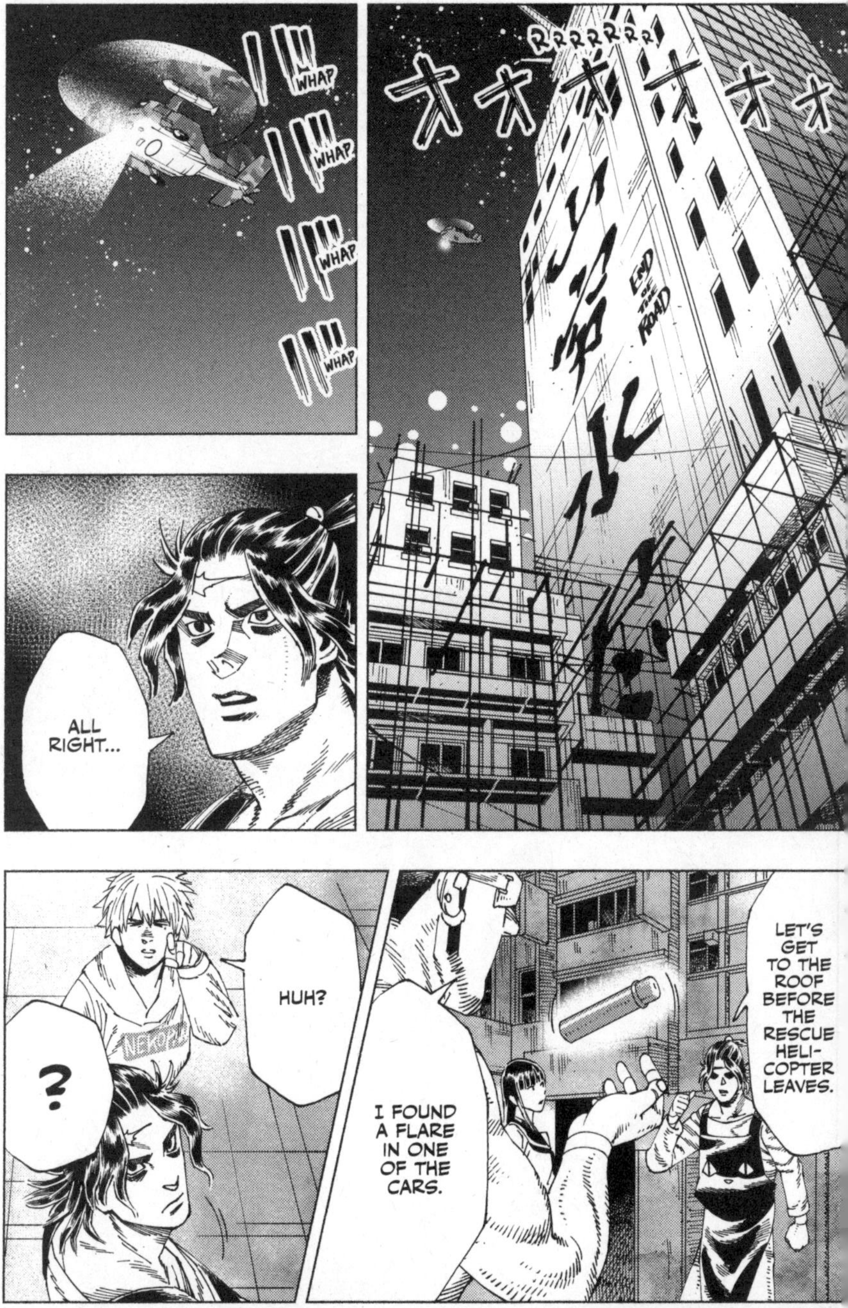
RRRRRRRR
END OF THE ROAD
WHAP
WHAP
WHAP
WHAP
ALL RIGHT...
LET'S GET TO THE ROOF BEFORE THE RESCUE HELI-COPTER LEAVES.
I FOUND A FLARE IN ONE OF THE CARS.
HUH?
?

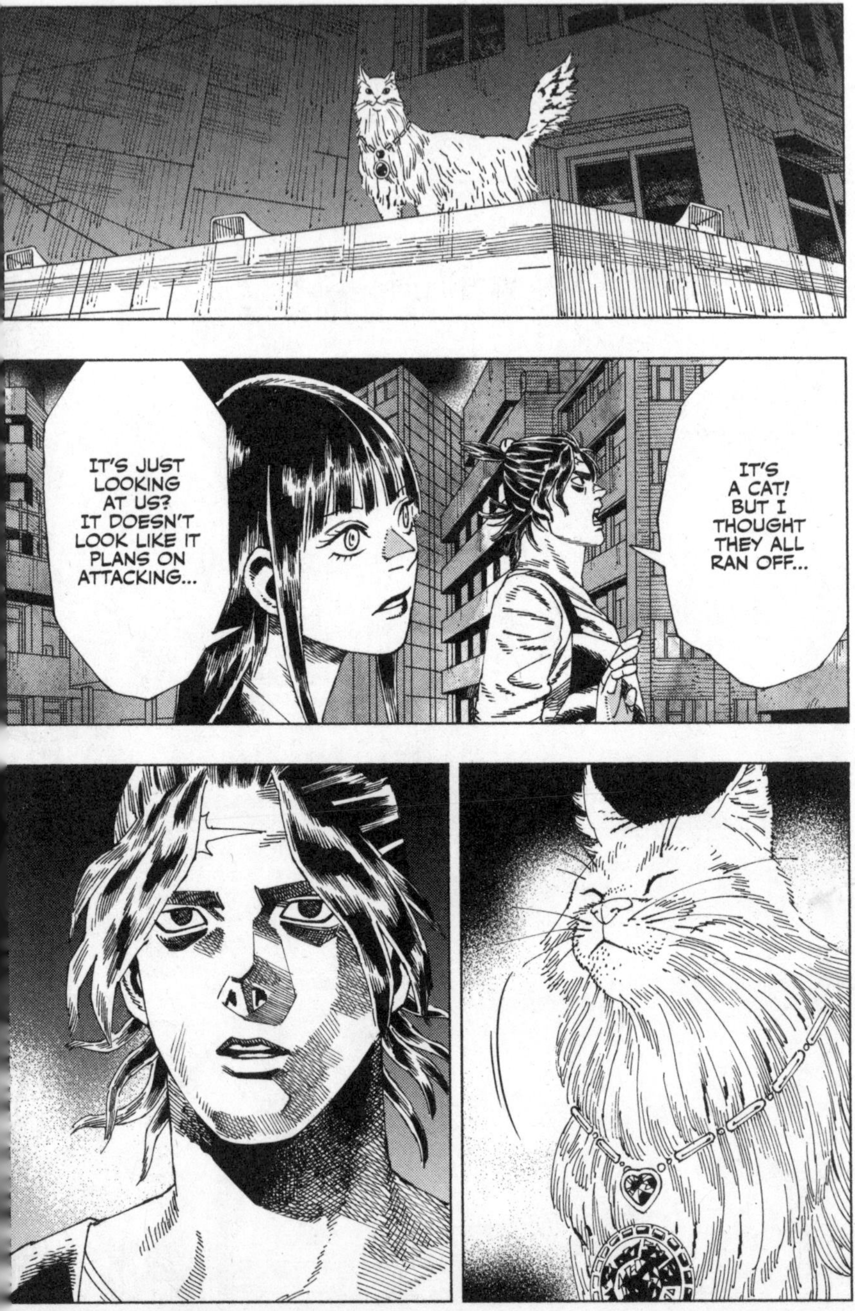
IT'S A CAT! BUT I THOUGHT THEY ALL RAN OFF...
IT'S JUST LOOKING AT US? IT DOESN'T LOOK LIKE IT PLANS ON ATTACKING...

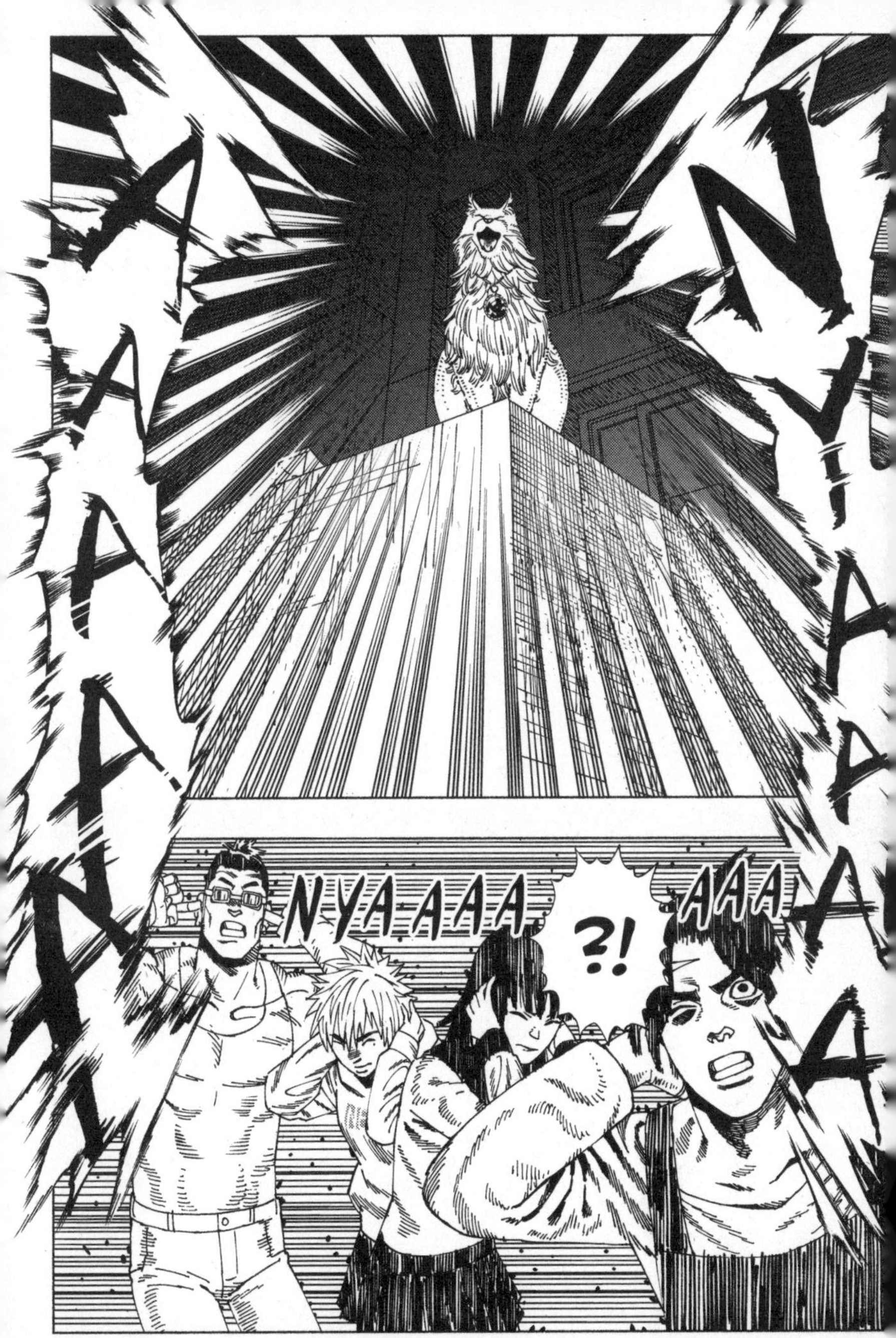
NYAAAAAAAAAAA
NYAAAAA
NYAAA
?!
AAA

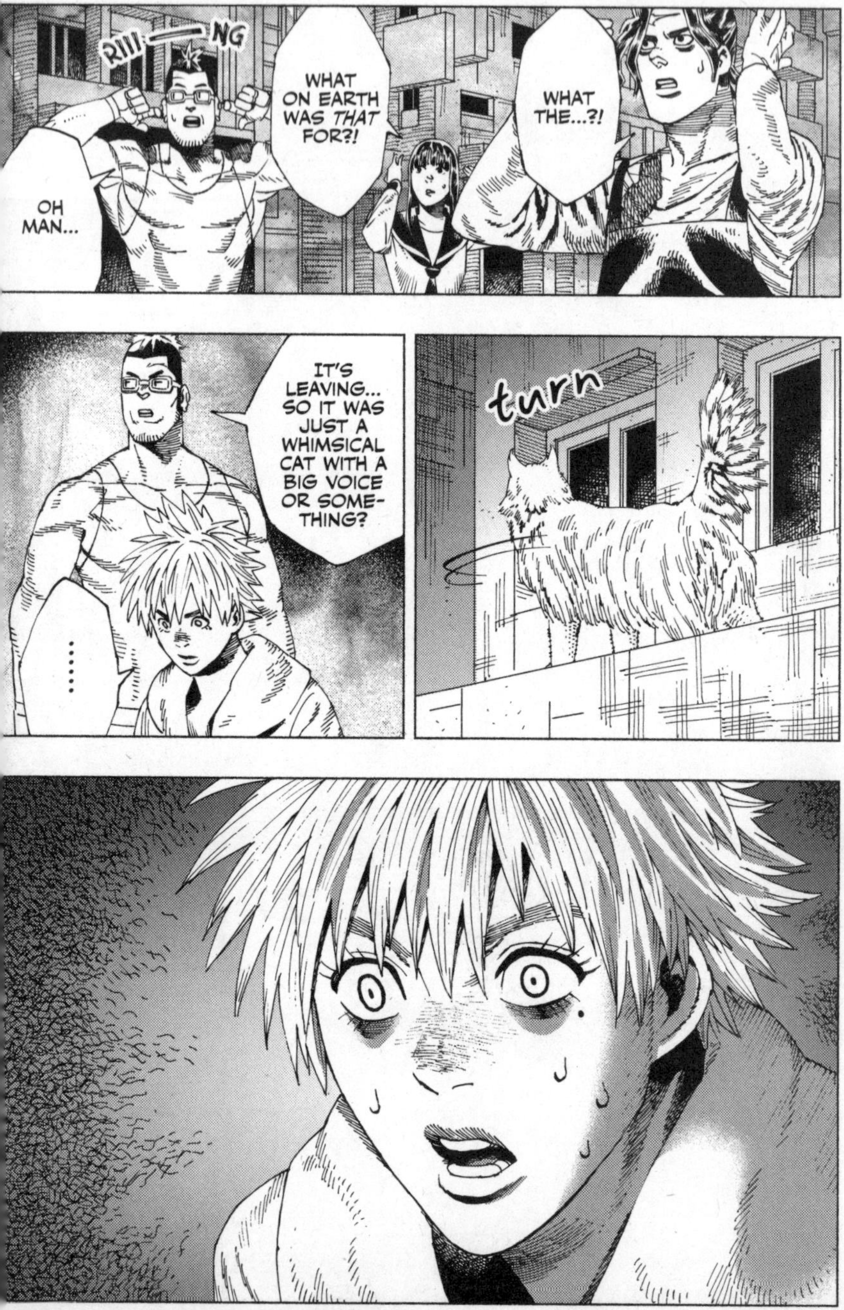
WHAT THE...?!
WHAT ON EARTH WAS *THAT* FOR?!
RIII——NG
OH MAN...
turn
IT'S LEAVING... SO IT WAS JUST A WHIMSICAL CAT WITH A BIG VOICE OR SOMETHING?
......

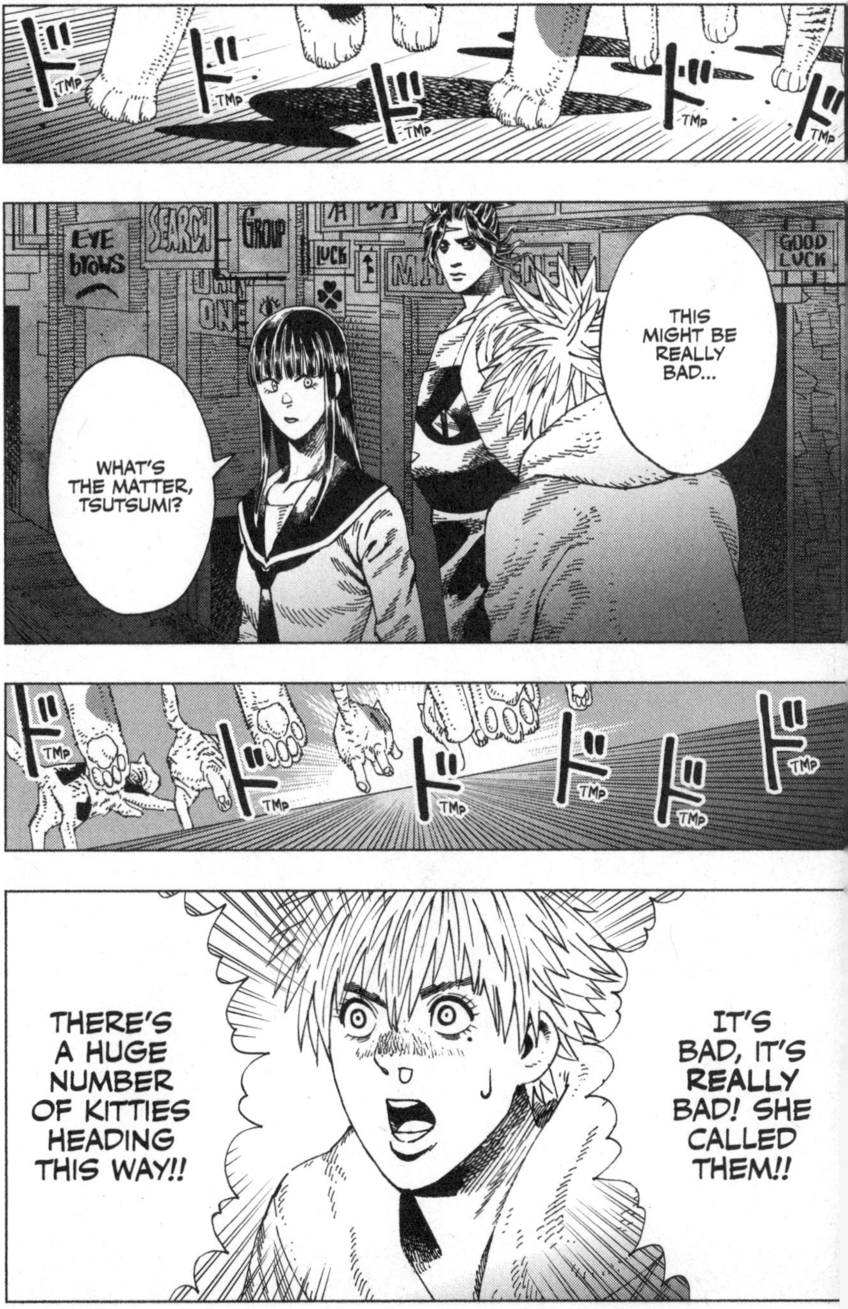
ド TMP
ド TMP
ド TMP
ド TMP
ド TMP
GOOD LUCK
THIS MIGHT BE REALLY BAD...
LUCK
GROUP
SEARCH
EYE brows
WHAT'S THE MATTER, TSUTSUMI?
ド TMP
ド TMP
ド TMP
ド TMP
ド TMP
ド TMP
IT'S BAD, IT'S REALLY BAD! SHE CALLED THEM!!
THERE'S A HUGE NUMBER OF KITTIES HEADING THIS WAY!!

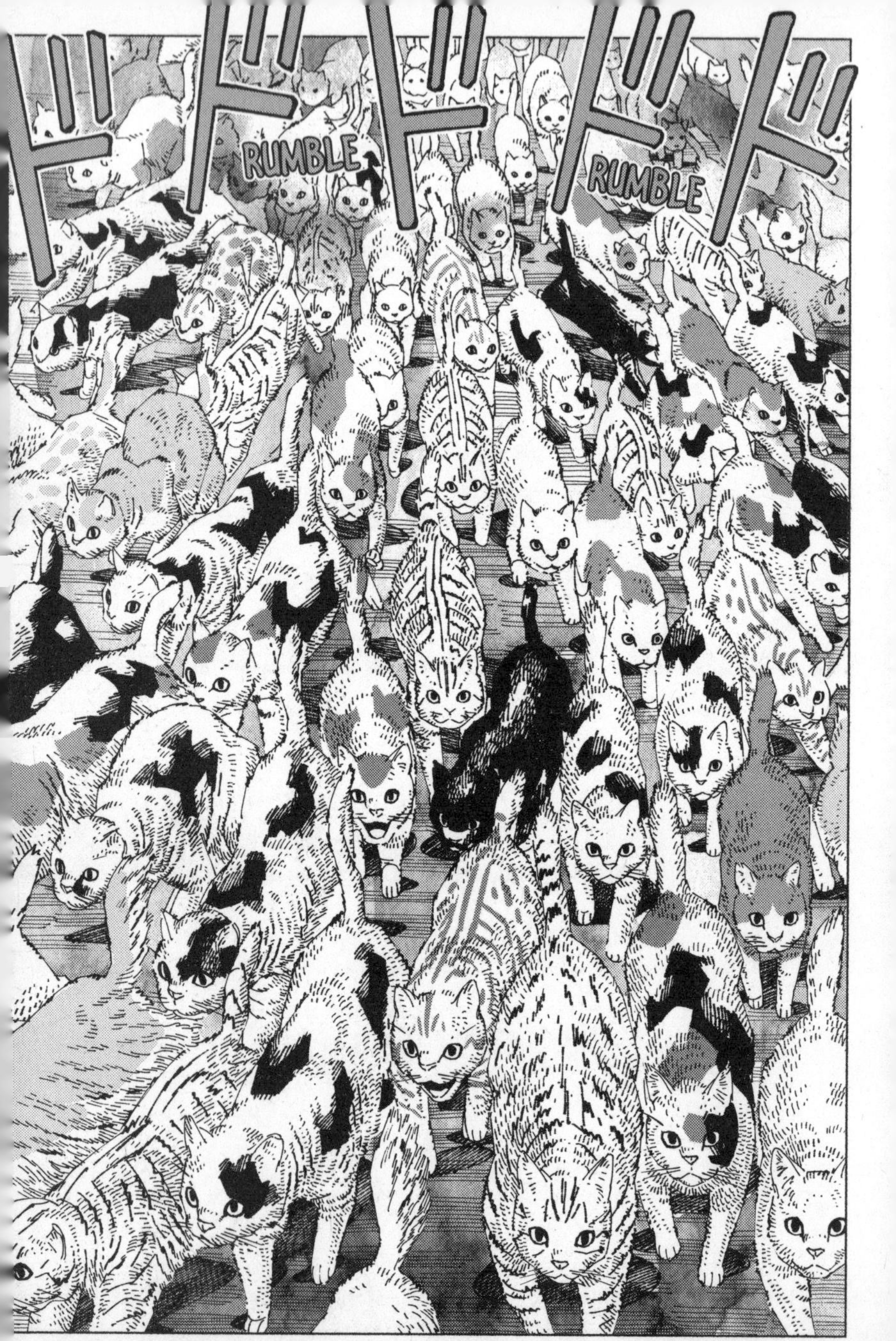
ドドドドドド
RUMBLE
RUMBLE

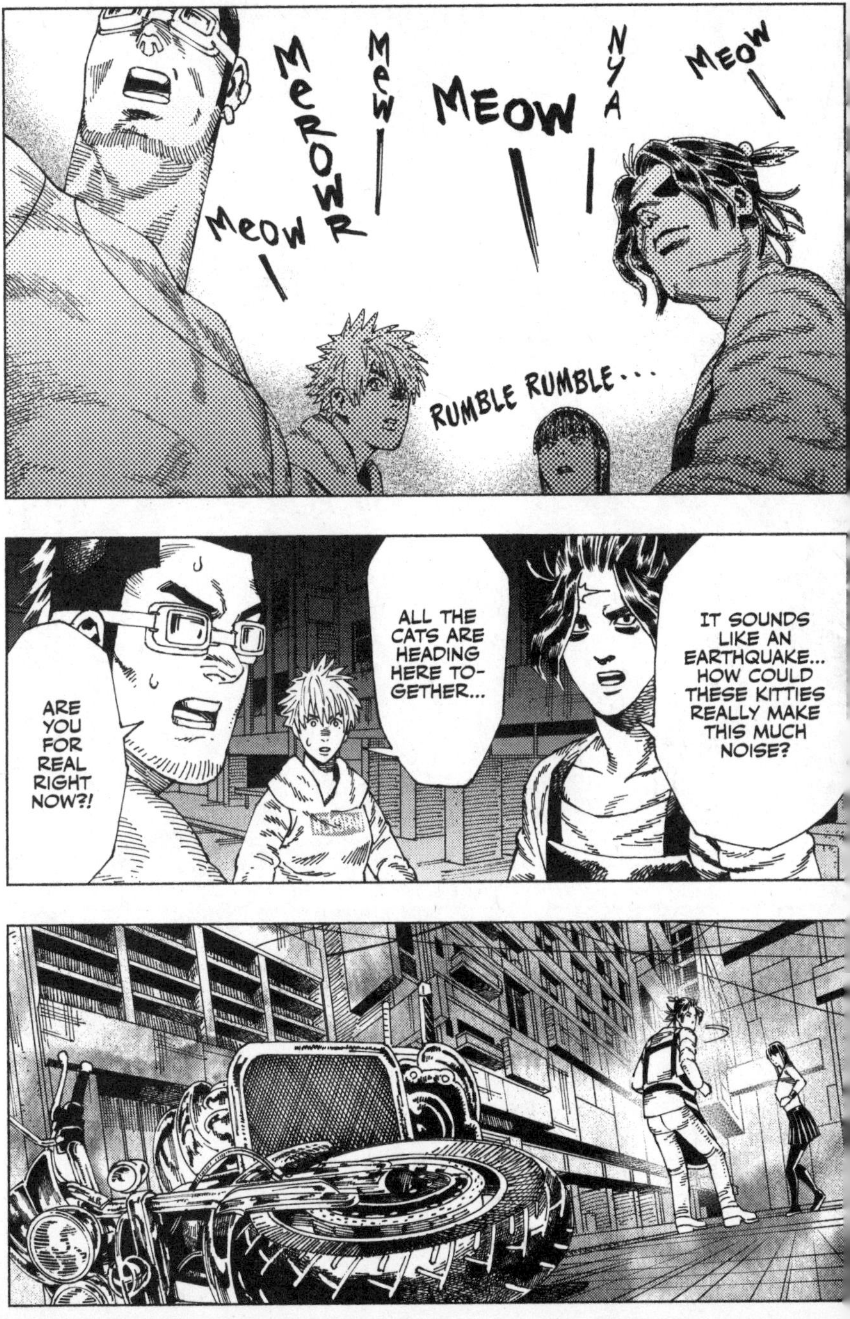
MEOW
NYA
MEOW
Mew
MEROWR
Meow
RUMBLE RUMBLE...
IT SOUNDS LIKE AN EARTHQUAKE... HOW COULD THESE KITTIES REALLY MAKE THIS MUCH NOISE?
ALL THE CATS ARE HEADING HERE TO-GETHER...
ARE YOU FOR REAL RIGHT NOW?!

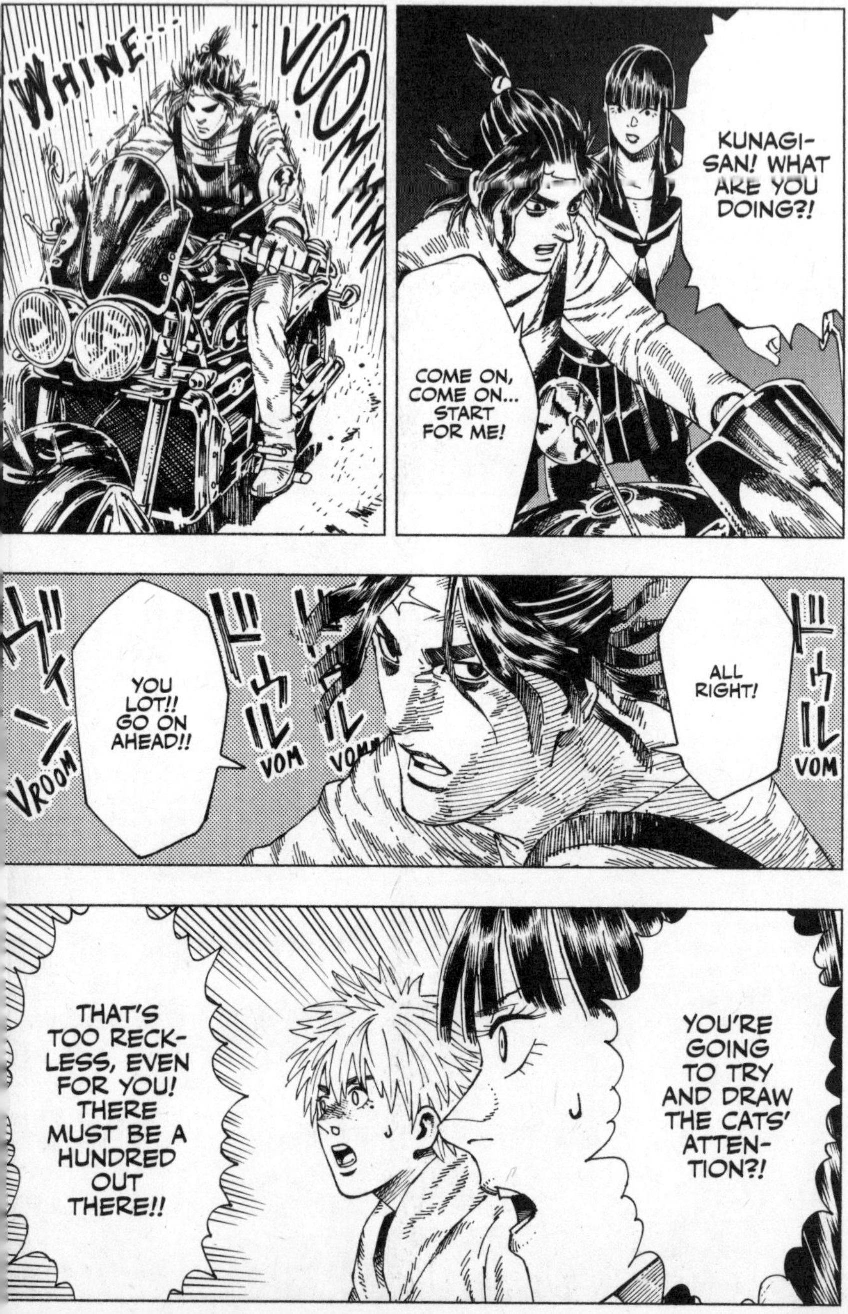
KUNAGI-SAN! WHAT ARE YOU DOING?!
COME ON, COME ON... START FOR ME!
VOOMMM
WHINE...
VOM
ALL RIGHT!
VOM
VOM
YOU LOT!! GO ON AHEAD!!
VROOM
YOU'RE GOING TO TRY AND DRAW THE CATS' ATTEN-TION?!
THAT'S TOO RECK-LESS, EVEN FOR YOU! THERE MUST BE A HUNDRED OUT THERE!!

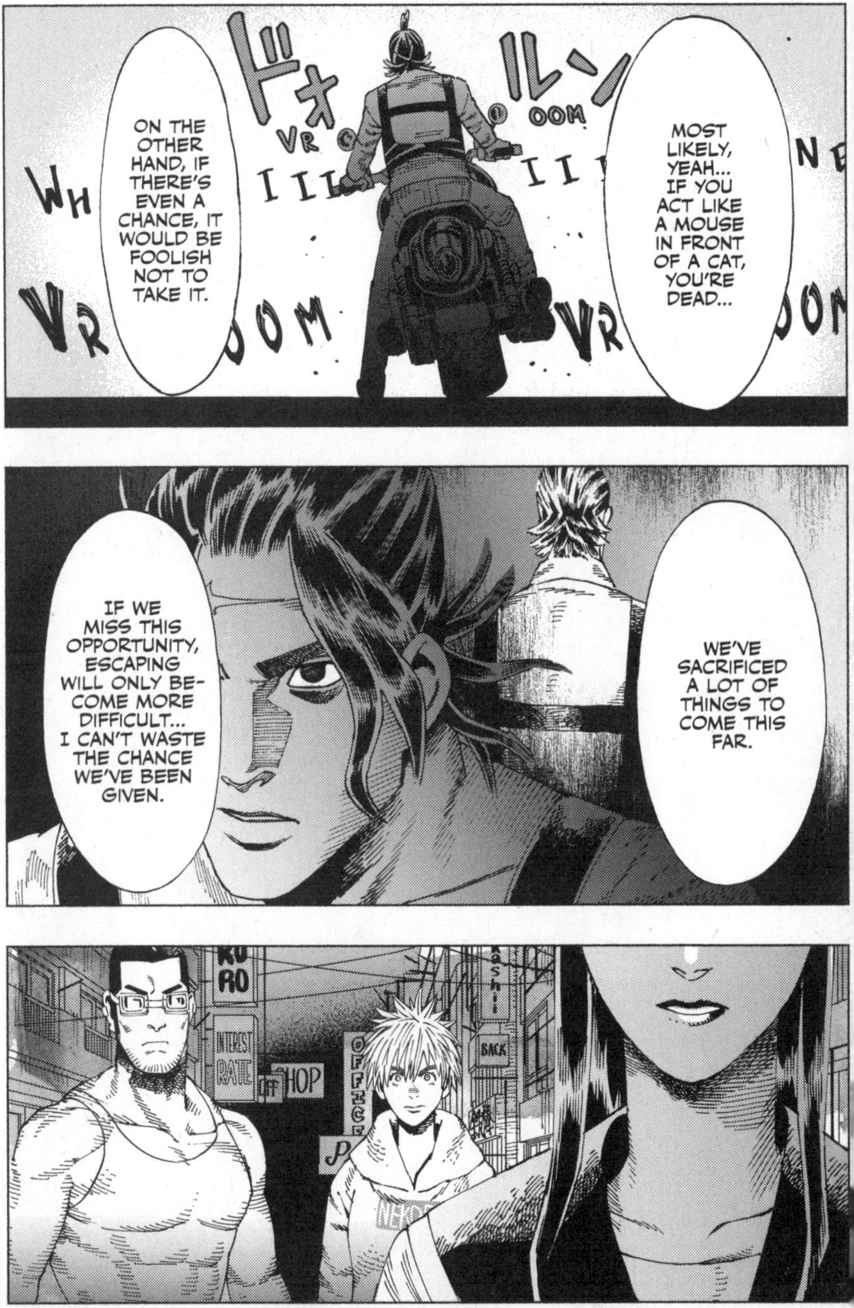
MOST LIKELY, YEAH... IF YOU ACT LIKE A MOUSE IN FRONT OF A CAT, YOU'RE DEAD...
ON THE OTHER HAND, IF THERE'S EVEN A CHANCE, IT WOULD BE FOOLISH NOT TO TAKE IT.
WE'VE SACRIFICED A LOT OF THINGS TO COME THIS FAR.
IF WE MISS THIS OPPORTUNITY, ESCAPING WILL ONLY BECOME MORE DIFFICULT... I CAN'T WASTE THE CHANCE WE'VE BEEN GIVEN.
BACK
SHOP
INTEREST RATE

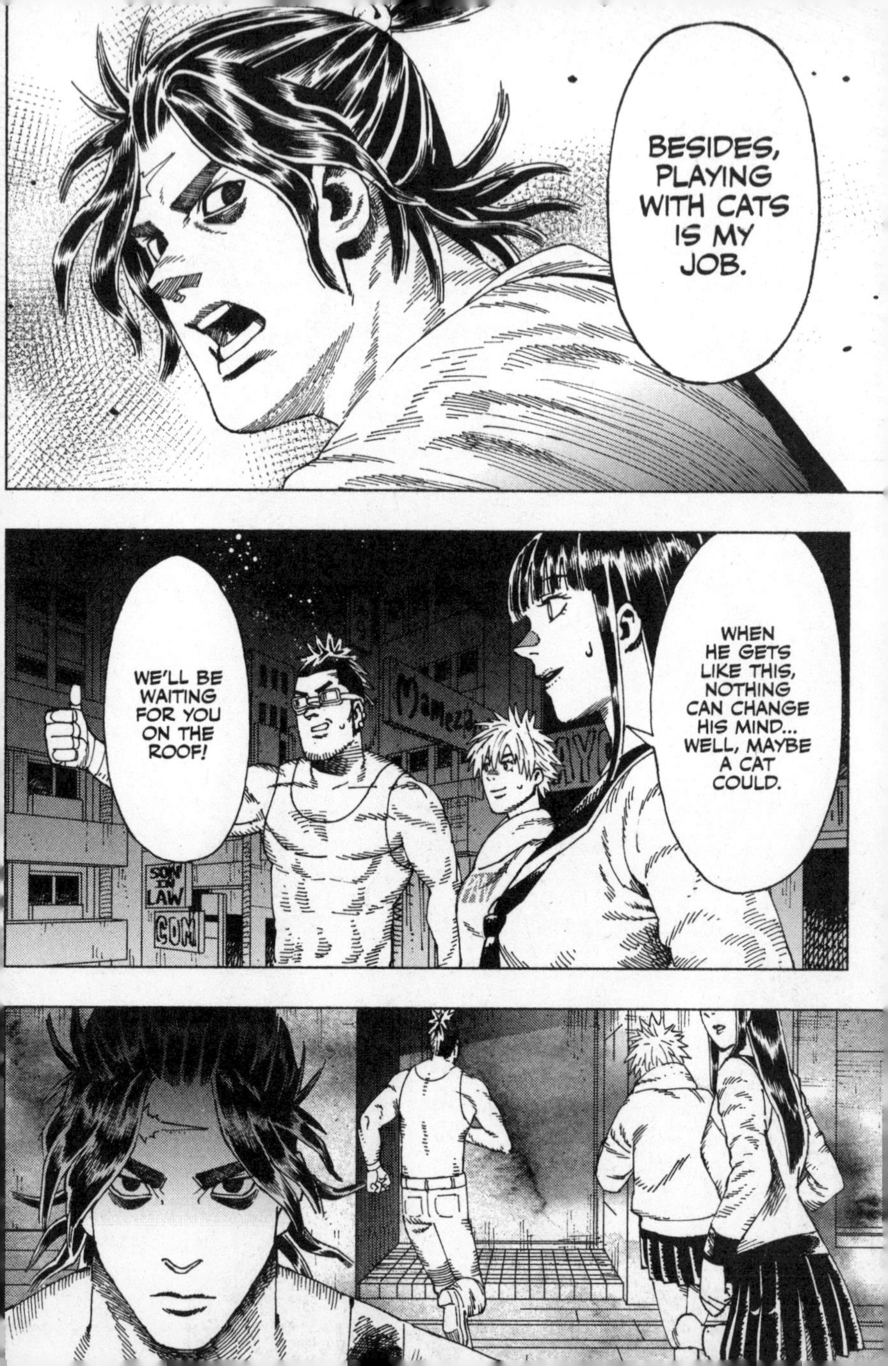
BESIDES, PLAYING WITH CATS IS MY JOB.
WHEN HE GETS LIKE THIS, NOTHING CAN CHANGE HIS MIND... WELL, MAYBE A CAT COULD.
WE'LL BE WAITING FOR YOU ON THE ROOF!
SON IN LAW
COM

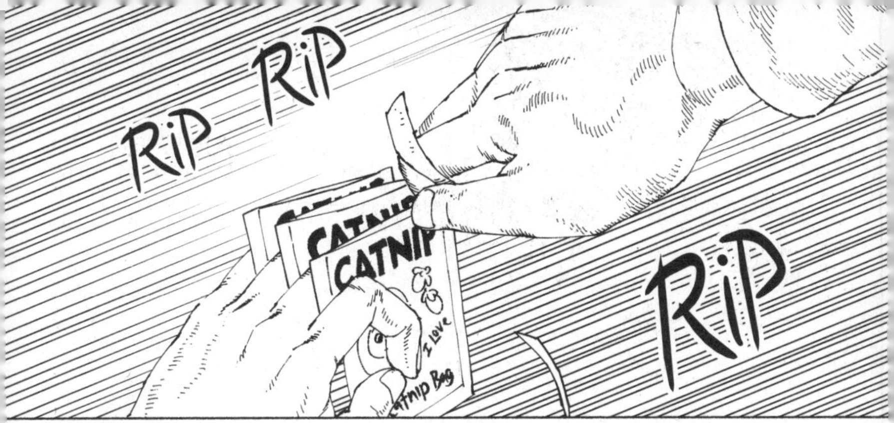
RIP RIP
RIP
CATNIP
CATNIP
I LOVE

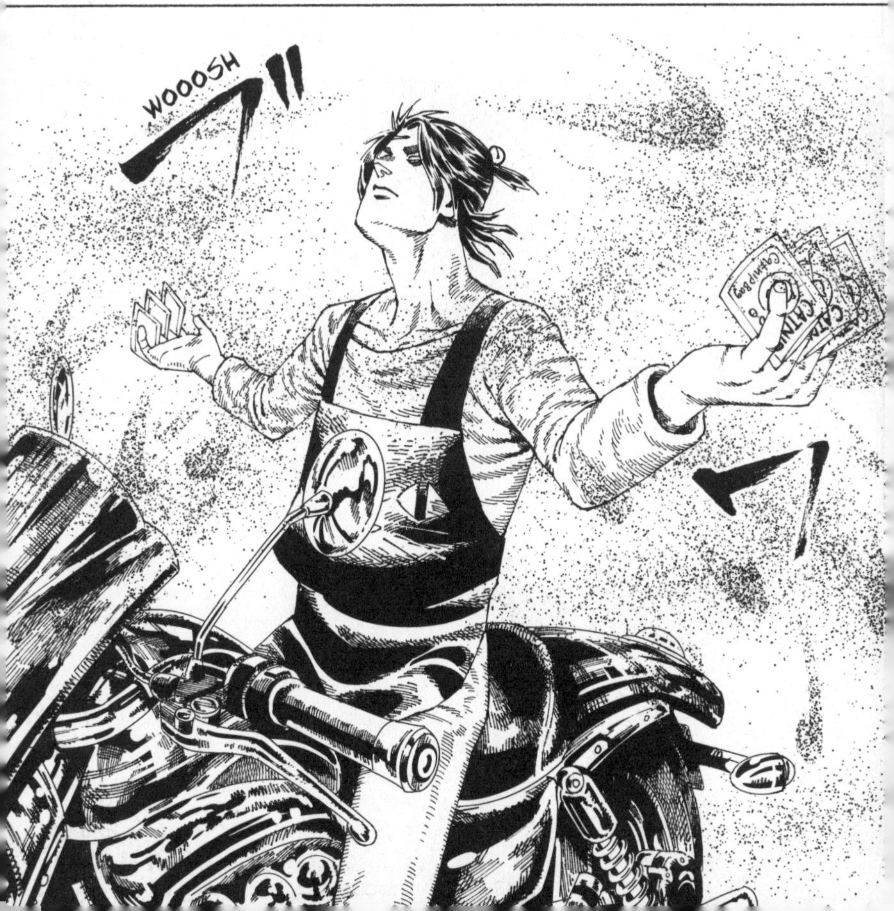
WOOOSH

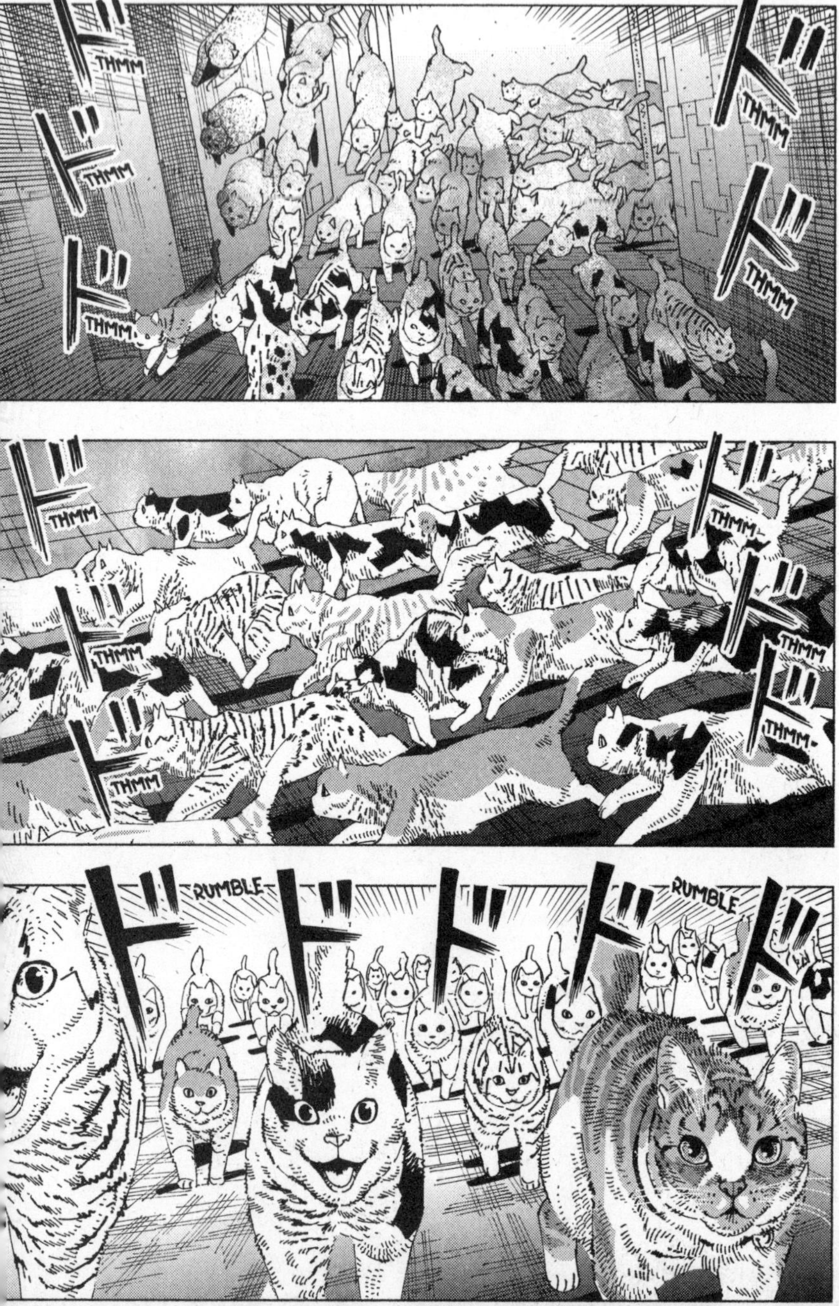
ド
THMM
ド
THMM
ド
THMM
ド
THMM
ド
THMM
ド
THMM-
ド
THMM
ド
THMM-
ド
THMM
ド
THMM
ド
THMM
ド
RUMBLE
ド
ド
ド
RUMBLE
ド

Satsuki-chan from Honda-san's household. ⇧

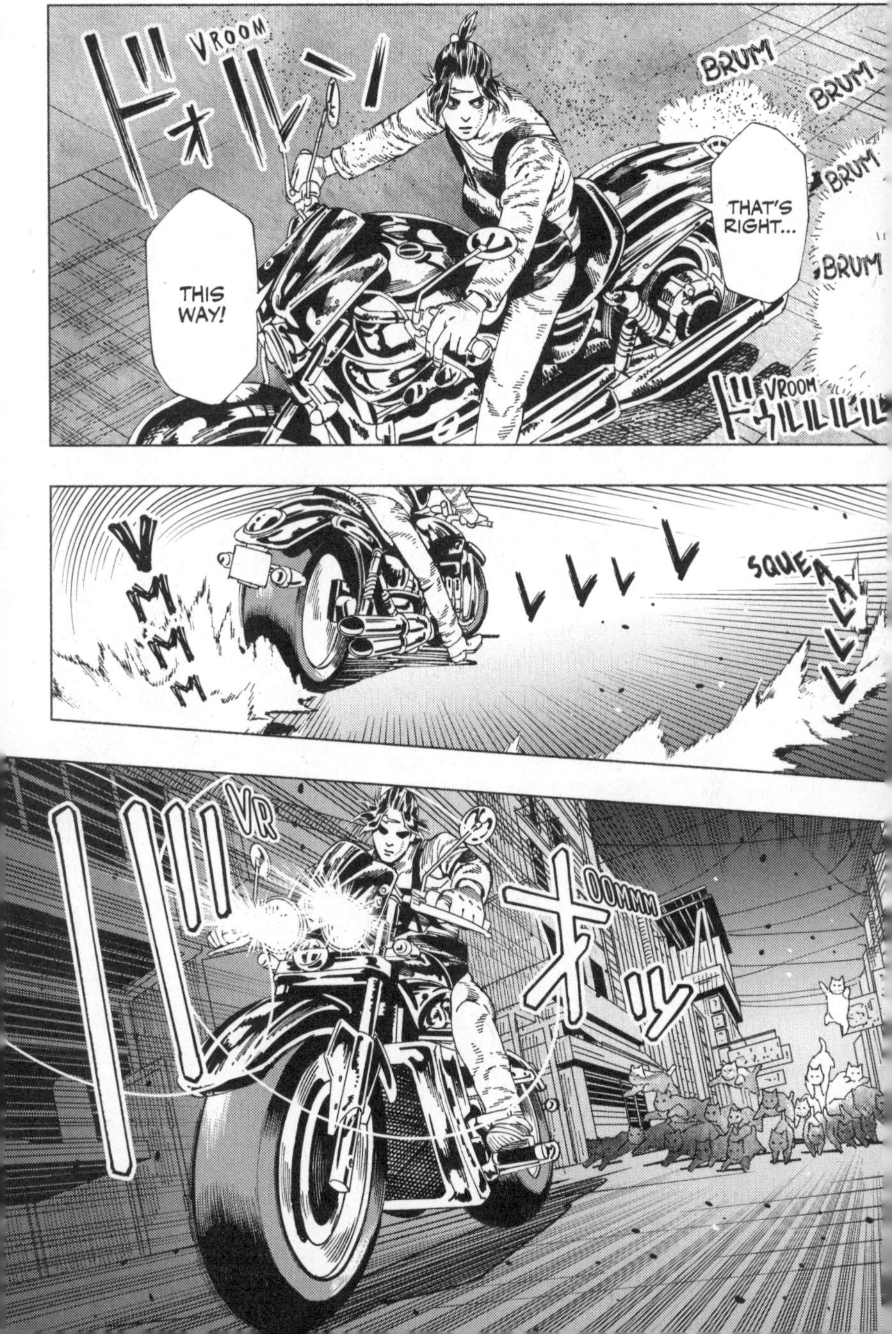
BRUM
BRUM
BRUM
BRUM
THAT'S RIGHT...
VROOM
THIS WAY!
VROOM
SQUEAAAAAA
VVVVV
VMMMMM
VR
OOMMM

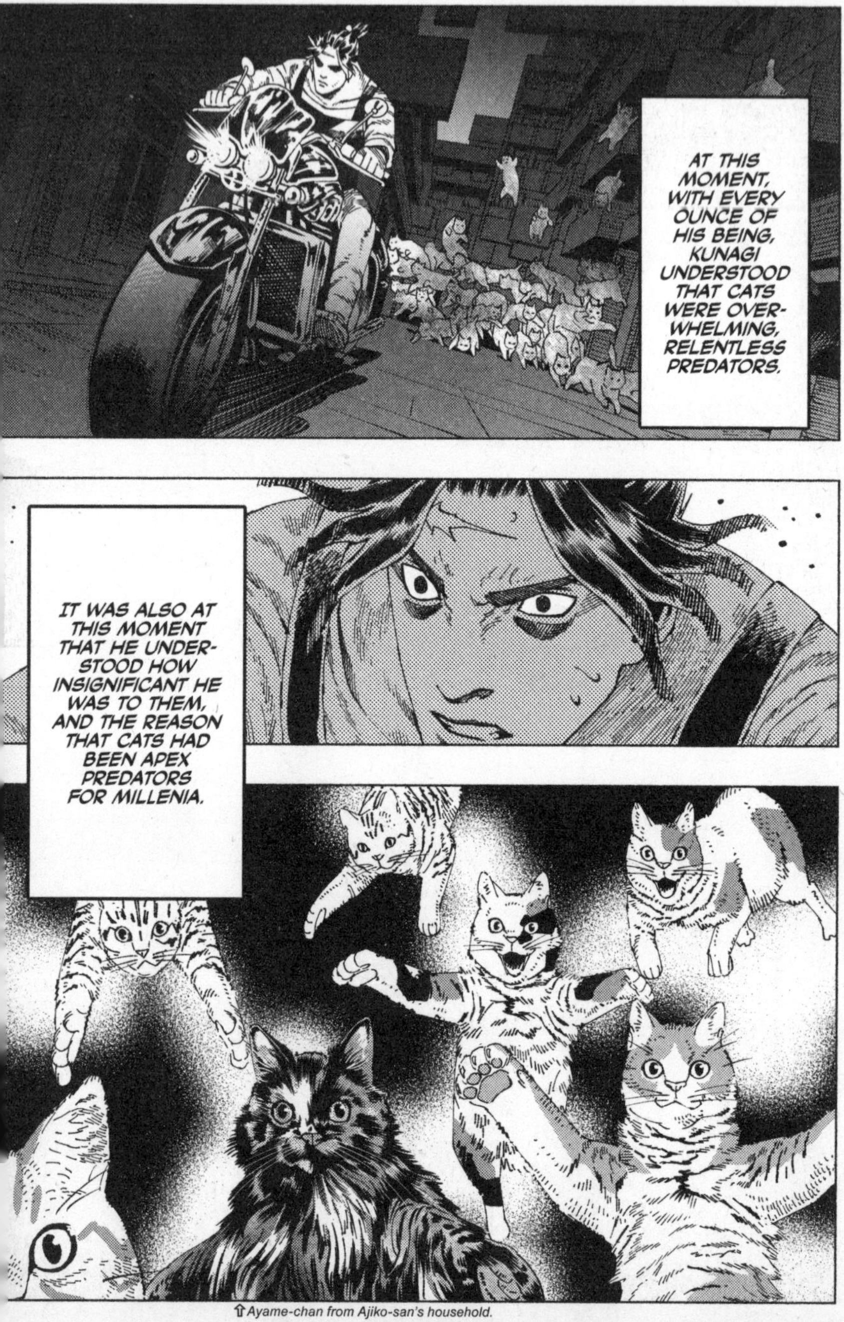
AT THIS MOMENT, WITH EVERY OUNCE OF HIS BEING, KUNAGI UNDERSTOOD THAT CATS WERE OVER-WHELMING, RELENTLESS PREDATORS.
IT WAS ALSO AT THIS MOMENT THAT HE UNDER-STOOD HOW INSIGNIFICANT HE WAS TO THEM, AND THE REASON THAT CATS HAD BEEN APEX PREDATORS FOR MILLENIA.

⇧Ayame-chan from Ajiko-san's household.

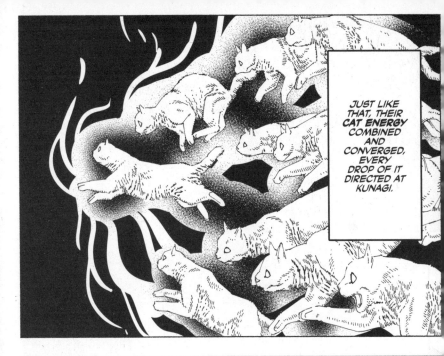

JUST LIKE THAT, THEIR **CAT ENERGY** COMBINED AND CONVERGED, EVERY DROP OF IT DIRECTED AT KUNAGI.

IT'S SAID WHEN A LIVING CREATURE CONFRONTS SOMETHING STRONGER THAN ITSELF, IT TENDS TO SEE ITS ADVERSARY AS FAR BIGGER THAN IT TRULY IS.

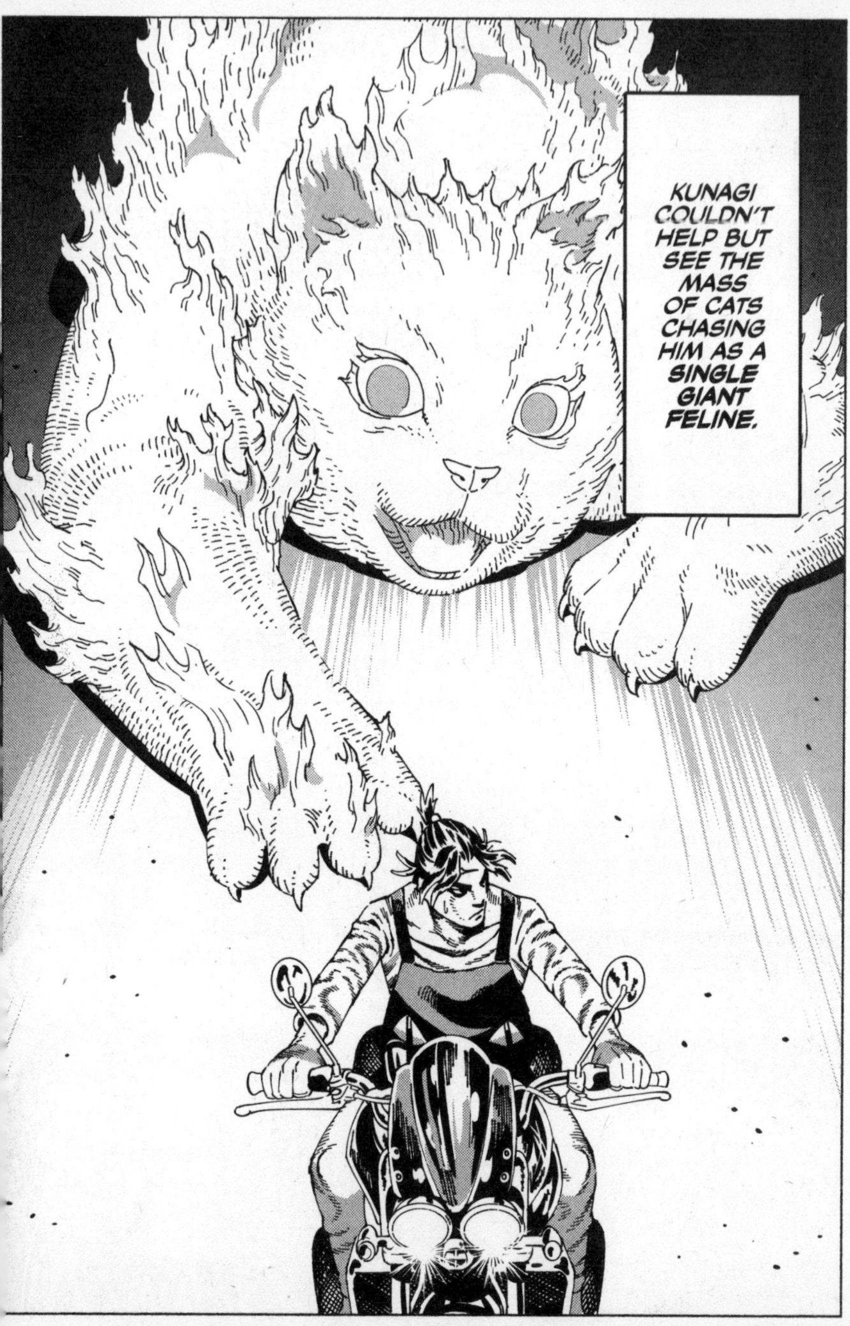
KUNAGI COULDN'T HELP BUT SEE THE MASS OF CATS CHASING HIM AS A SINGLE GIANT FELINE.

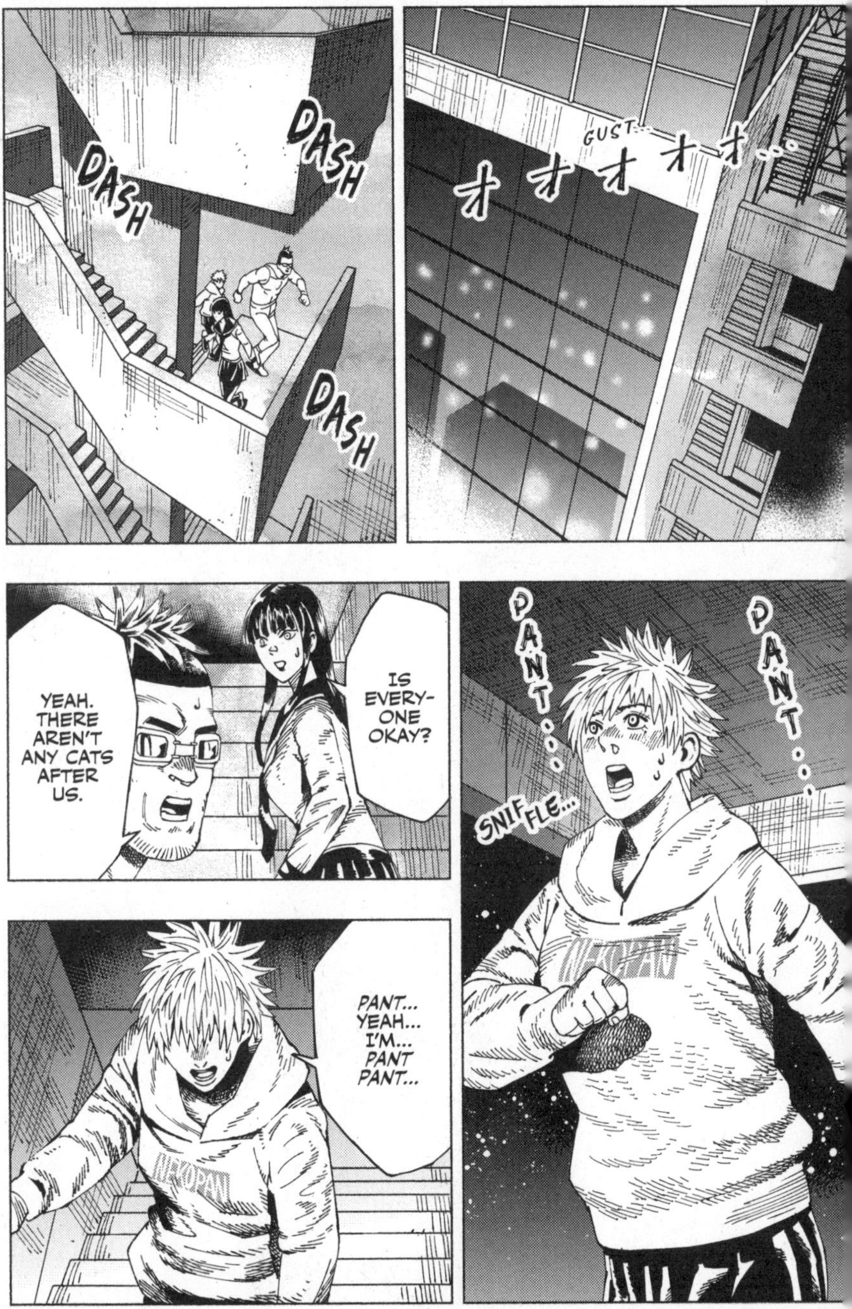
GUST
オオオオオ...
DASH
DASH
DASH
PANT...
PANT...
SNIFFLE...
IS EVERYONE OKAY?
YEAH. THERE AREN'T ANY CATS AFTER US.
PANT... YEAH... I'M... PANT PANT...
NEKOPAN
NEKOPAN

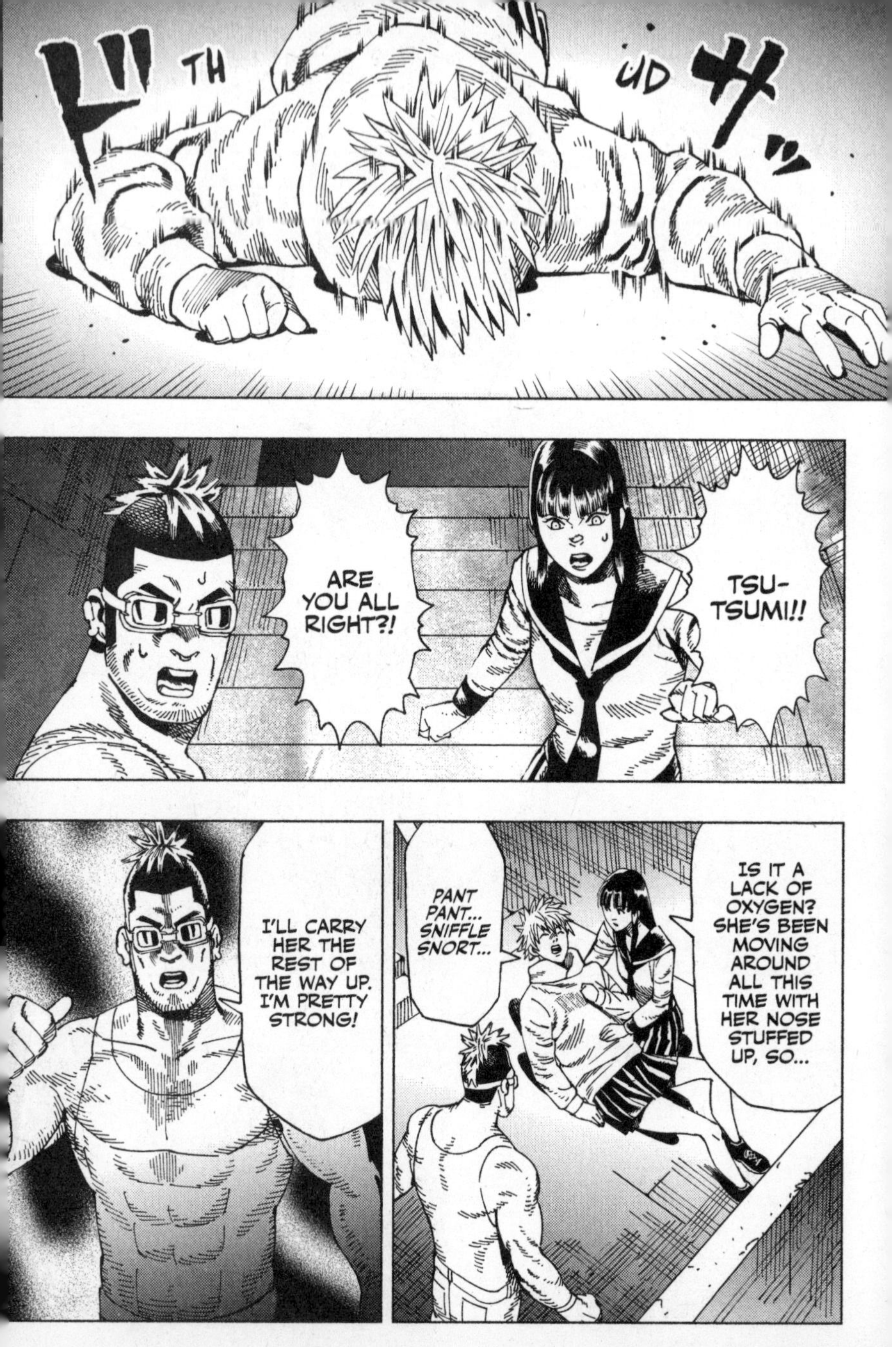
TH
UD
TSU-TSUMI!!
ARE YOU ALL RIGHT?!
IS IT A LACK OF OXYGEN? SHE'S BEEN MOVING AROUND ALL THIS TIME WITH HER NOSE STUFFED UP, SO...
PANT PANT... SNIFFLE SNORT...
I'LL CARRY HER THE REST OF THE WAY UP. I'M PRETTY STRONG!

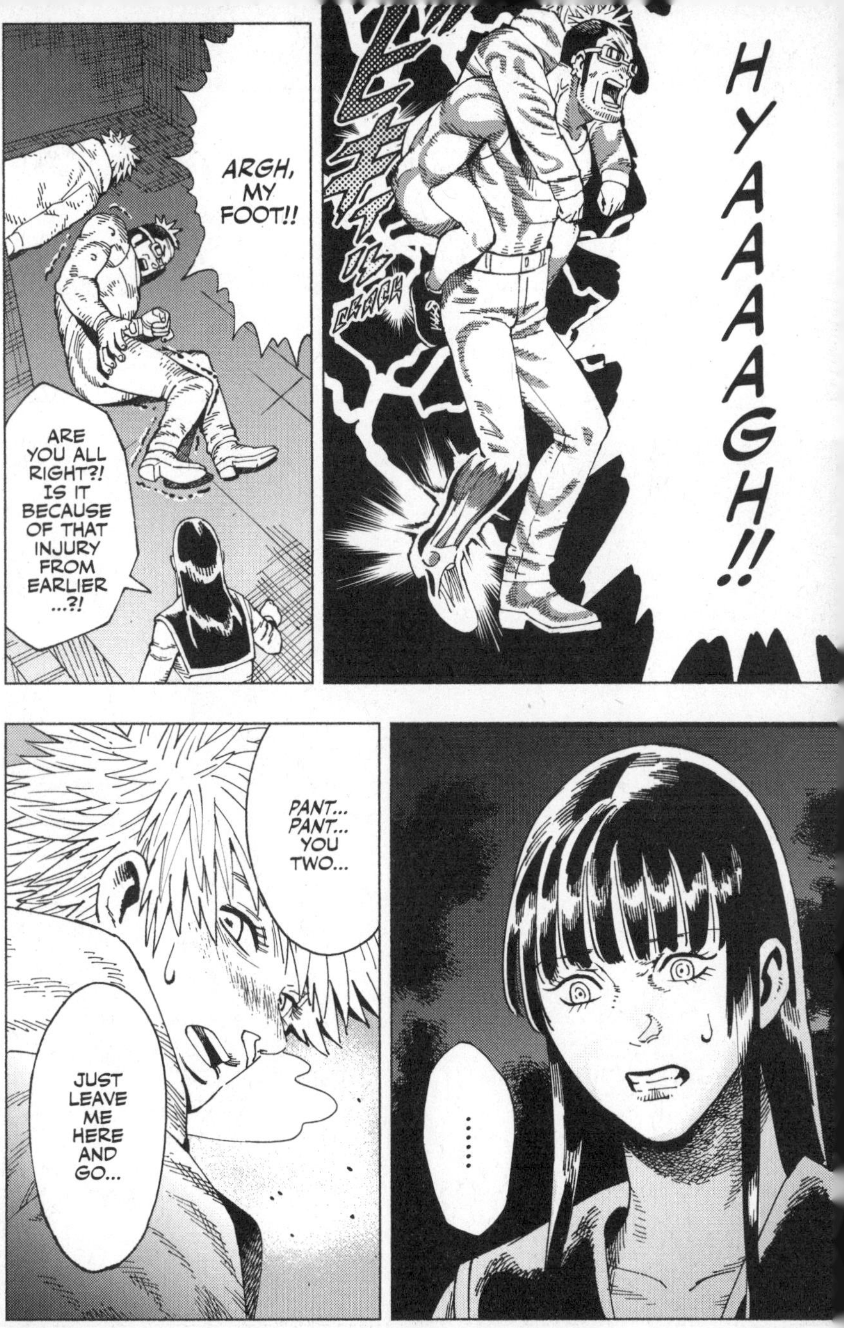
HYAAAAAGH!!
CRACK
ARGH, MY FOOT!!
ARE YOU ALL RIGHT?! IS IT BECAUSE OF THAT INJURY FROM EARLIER ...?!
......
PANT... PANT... YOU TWO...
JUST LEAVE ME HERE AND GO...

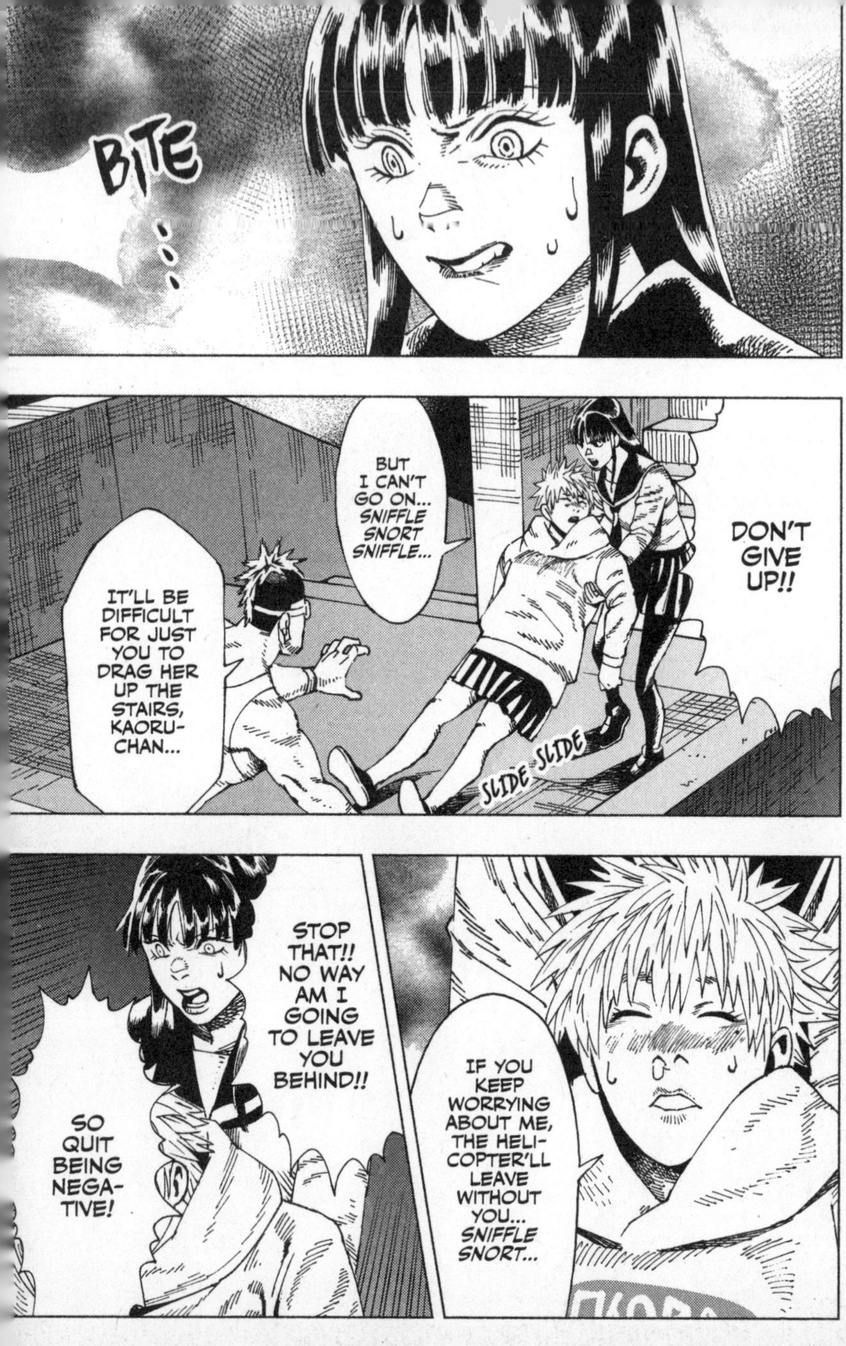
BITE
...
DON'T GIVE UP!!
BUT I CAN'T GO ON... SNIFFLE SNORT SNIFFLE...
IT'LL BE DIFFICULT FOR JUST YOU TO DRAG HER UP THE STAIRS, KAORU-CHAN...
SLIDE SLIDE
IF YOU KEEP WORRYING ABOUT ME, THE HELI-COPTER'LL LEAVE WITHOUT YOU... SNIFFLE SNORT...
STOP THAT!! NO WAY AM I GOING TO LEAVE YOU BEHIND!!
SO QUIT BEING NEGA-TIVE!

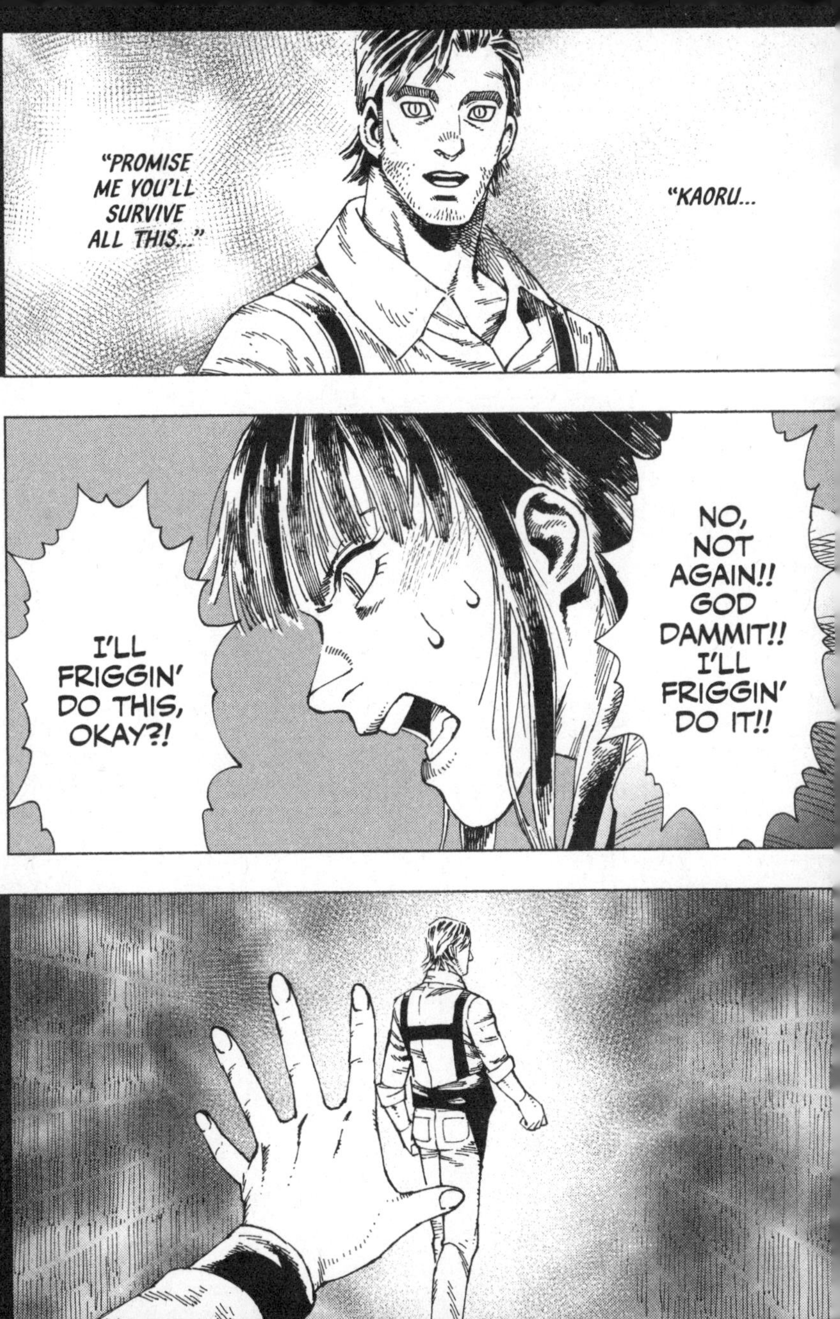
"KAORU...
"PROMISE ME YOU'LL SURVIVE ALL THIS..."
NO, NOT AGAIN!! GOD DAMMIT!! I'LL FRIGGIN' DO IT!!
I'LL FRIGGIN' DO THIS, OKAY?!

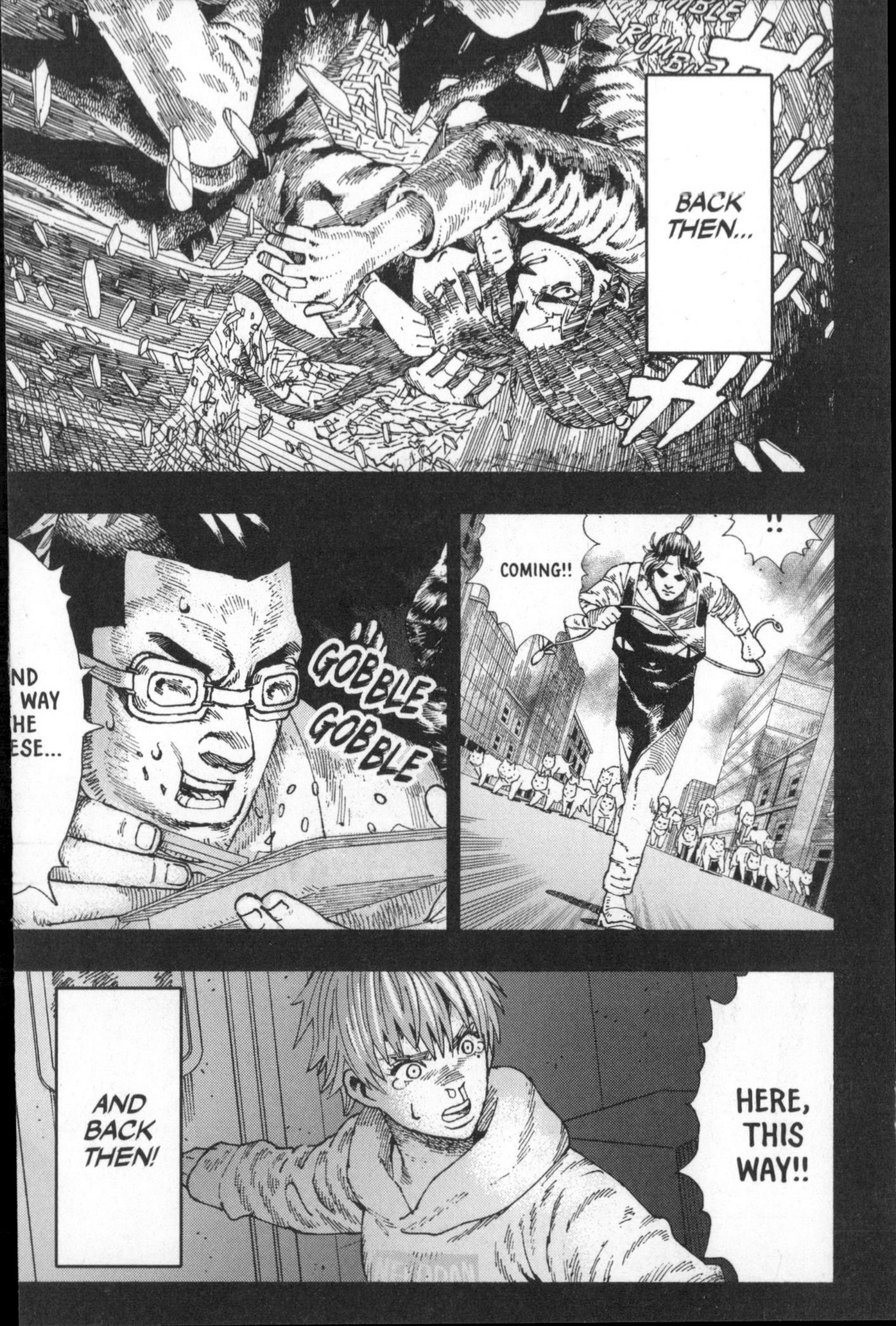
BACK THEN...
!!
COMING!!
GOBBLE GOBBLE
HERE, THIS WAY!!
AND BACK THEN!

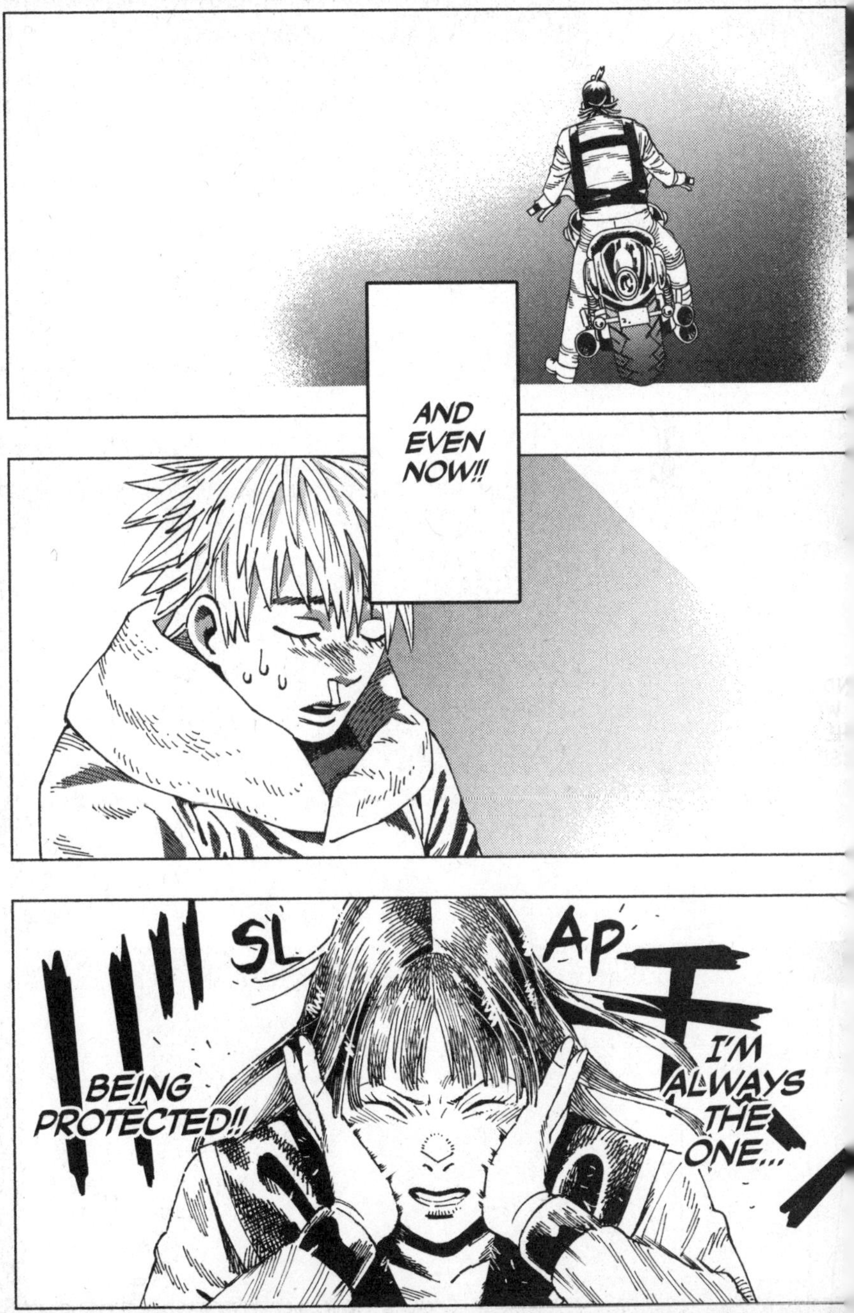
AND EVEN NOW!!
SL AP
I'M ALWAYS THE ONE...
BEING PROTECTED!!

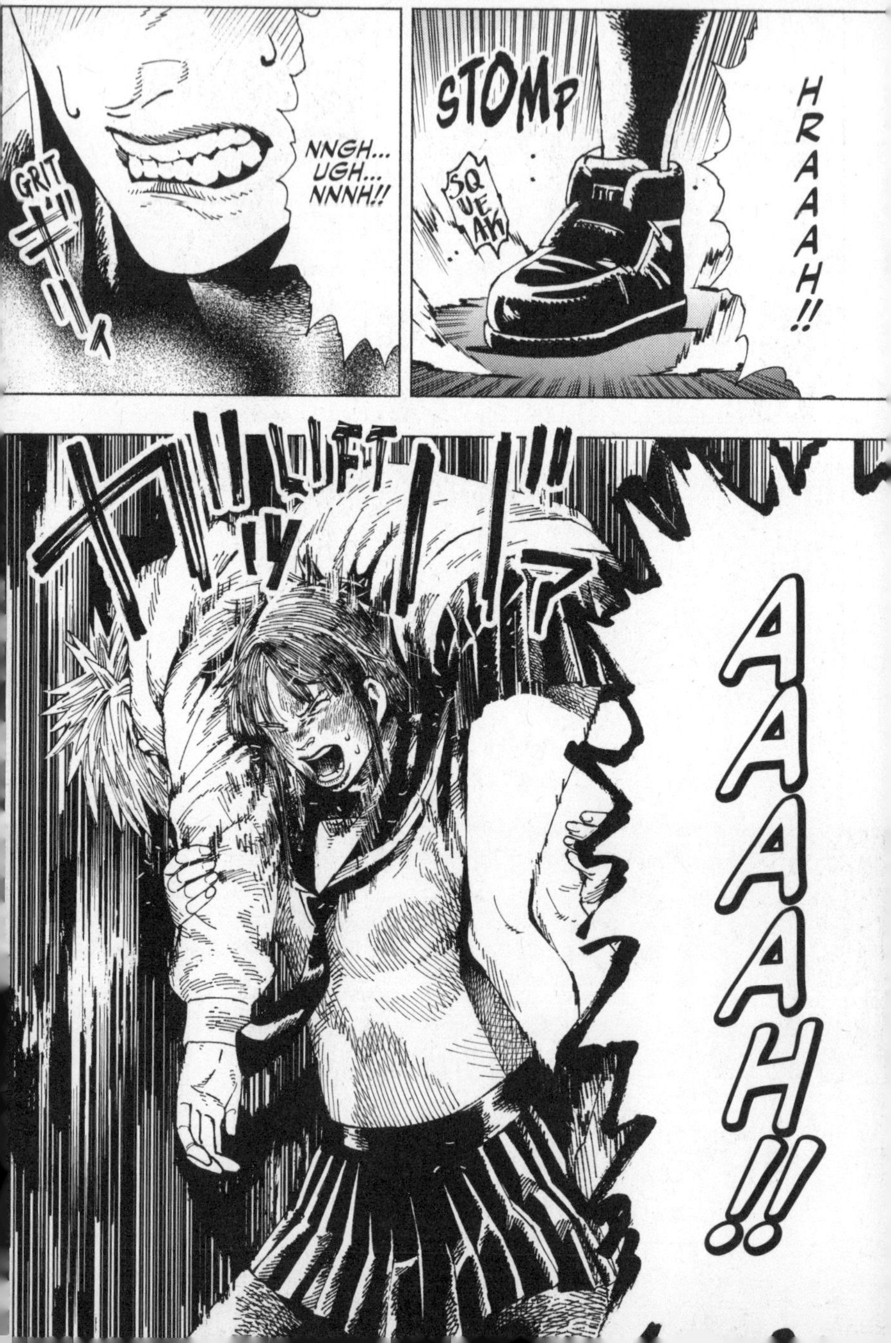
HRAAAAH!!
STOMP
SQUEAK
NNGH... UGH... NNNH!!
GRIT
LIFT
AAAAAH!!

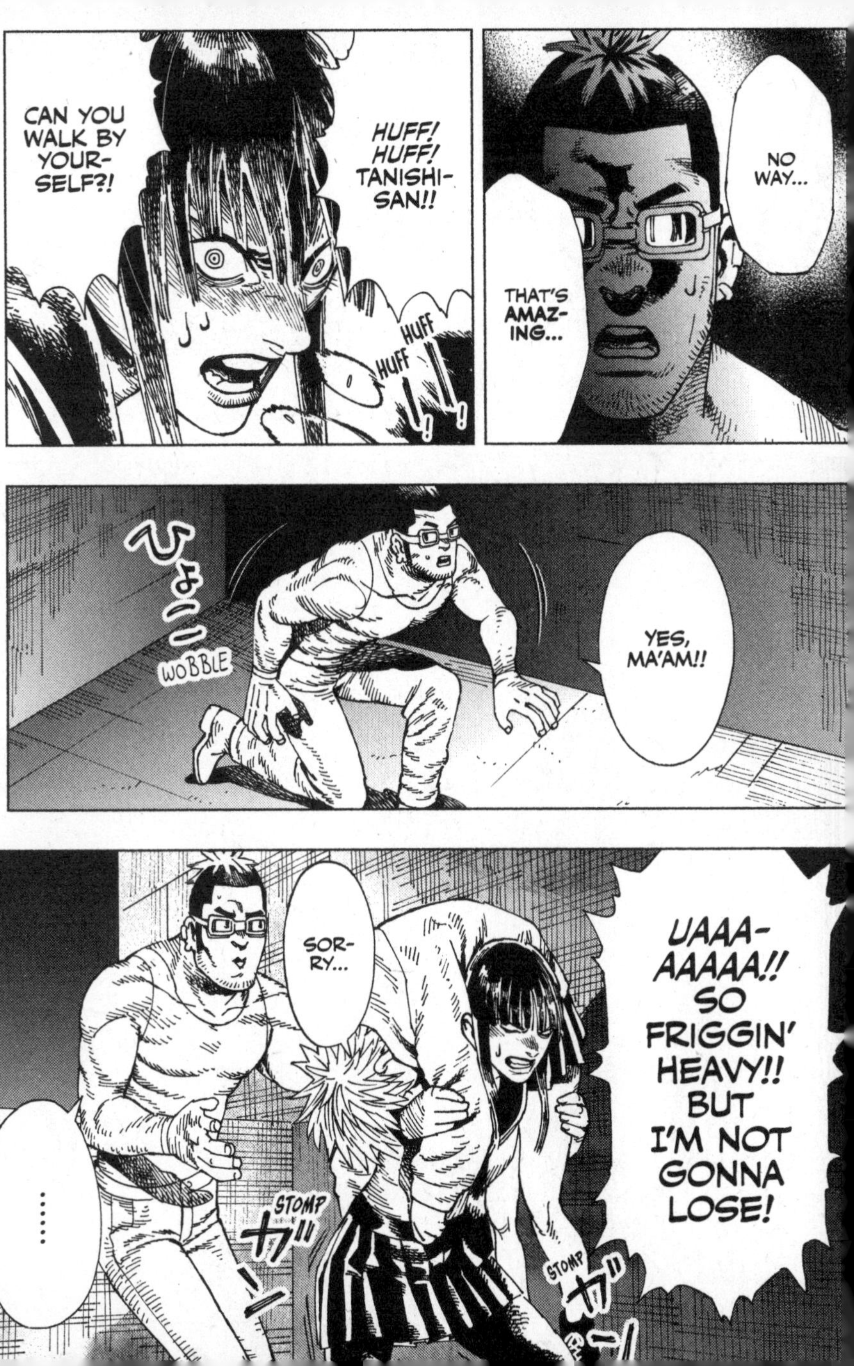
NO WAY...
THAT'S AMAZING...
HUFF! HUFF! TANISHI-SAN!!
CAN YOU WALK BY YOURSELF?!
HUFF HUFF
YES, MA'AM!!
WOBBLE
UAAA-AAAAA!! SO FRIGGIN' HEAVY!! BUT I'M NOT GONNA LOSE!
STOMP
SORRY...
STOMP
......

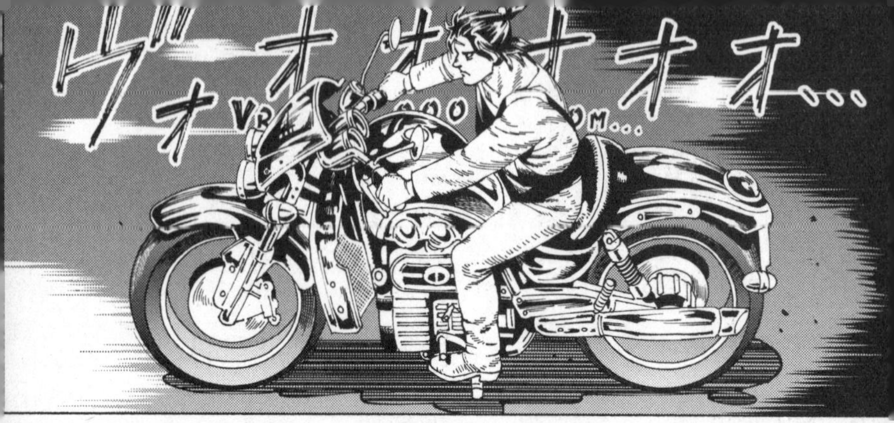
ヴォオオオオオ…
VR OOO OM...
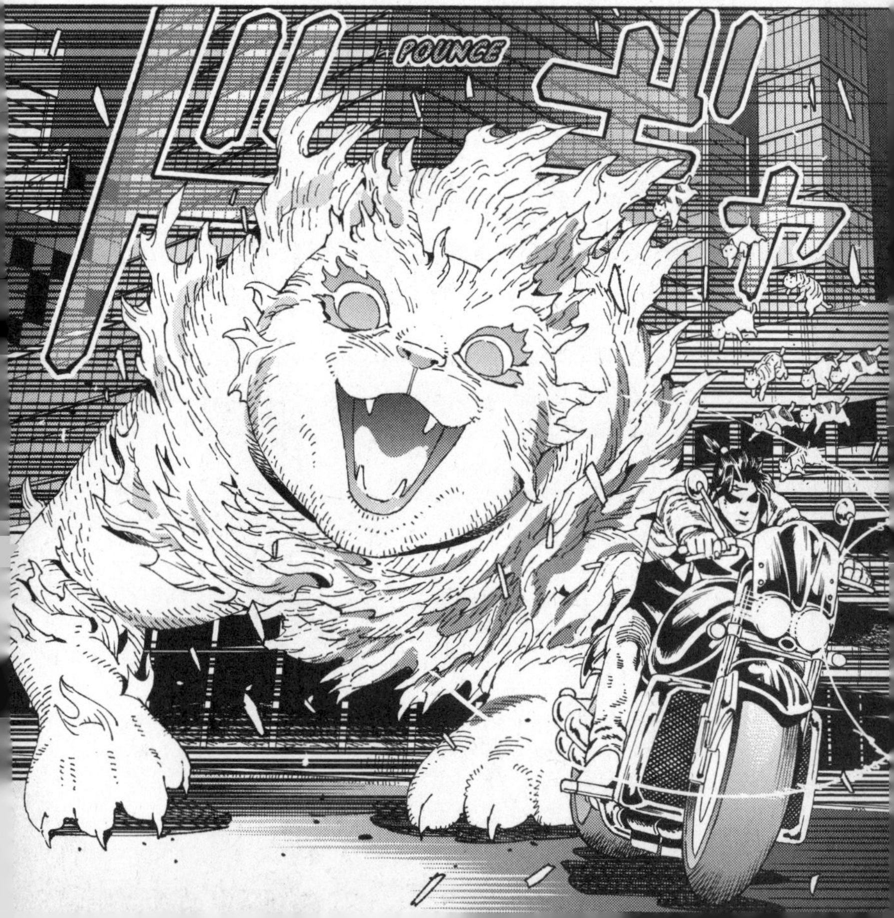
POUNCE
ギャ

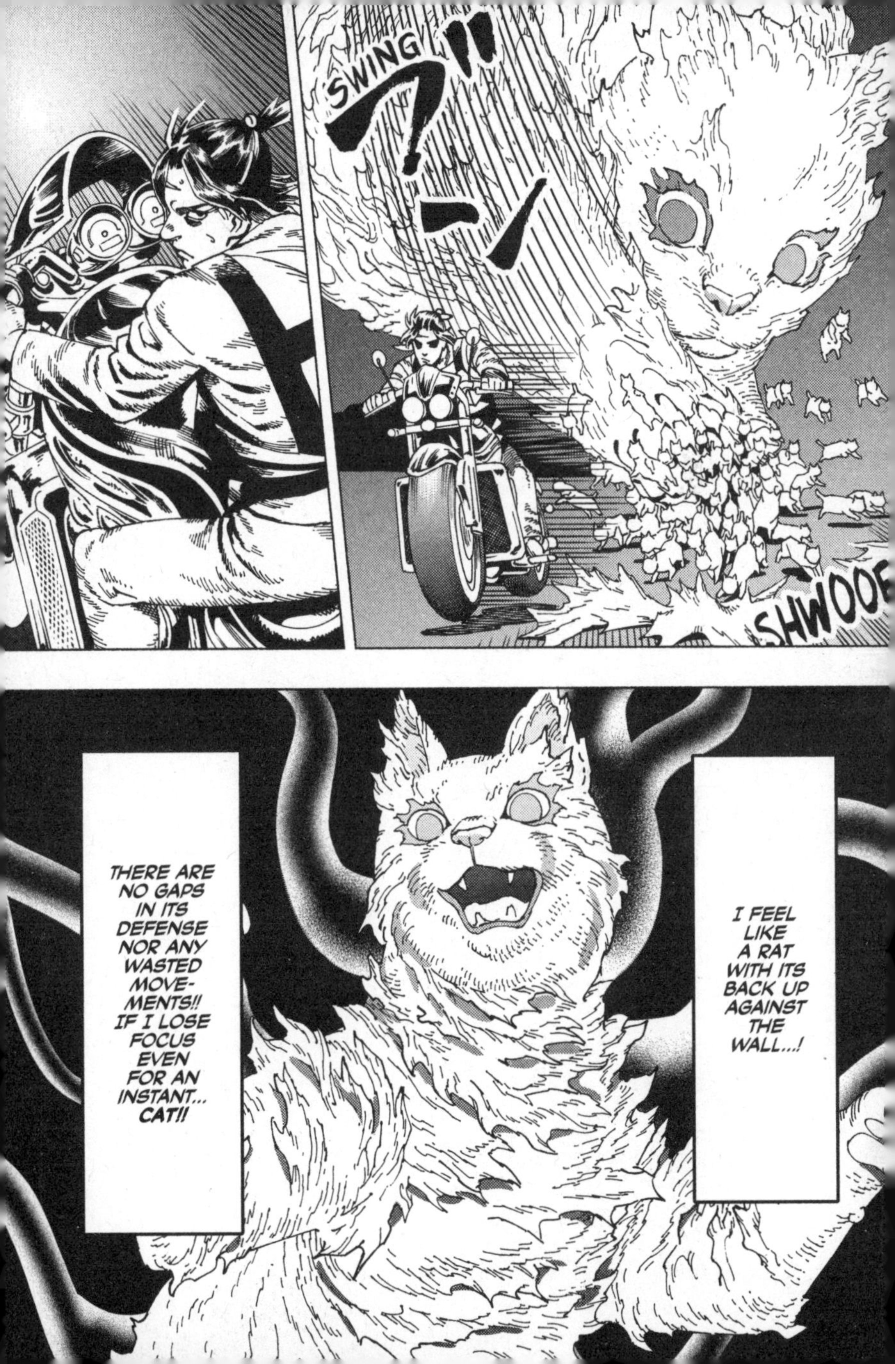
SWING
SHWOOF
I FEEL LIKE A RAT WITH ITS BACK UP AGAINST THE WALL...!
THERE ARE NO GAPS IN ITS DEFENSE NOR ANY WASTED MOVEMENTS!! IF I LOSE FOCUS EVEN FOR AN INSTANT... CAT!!

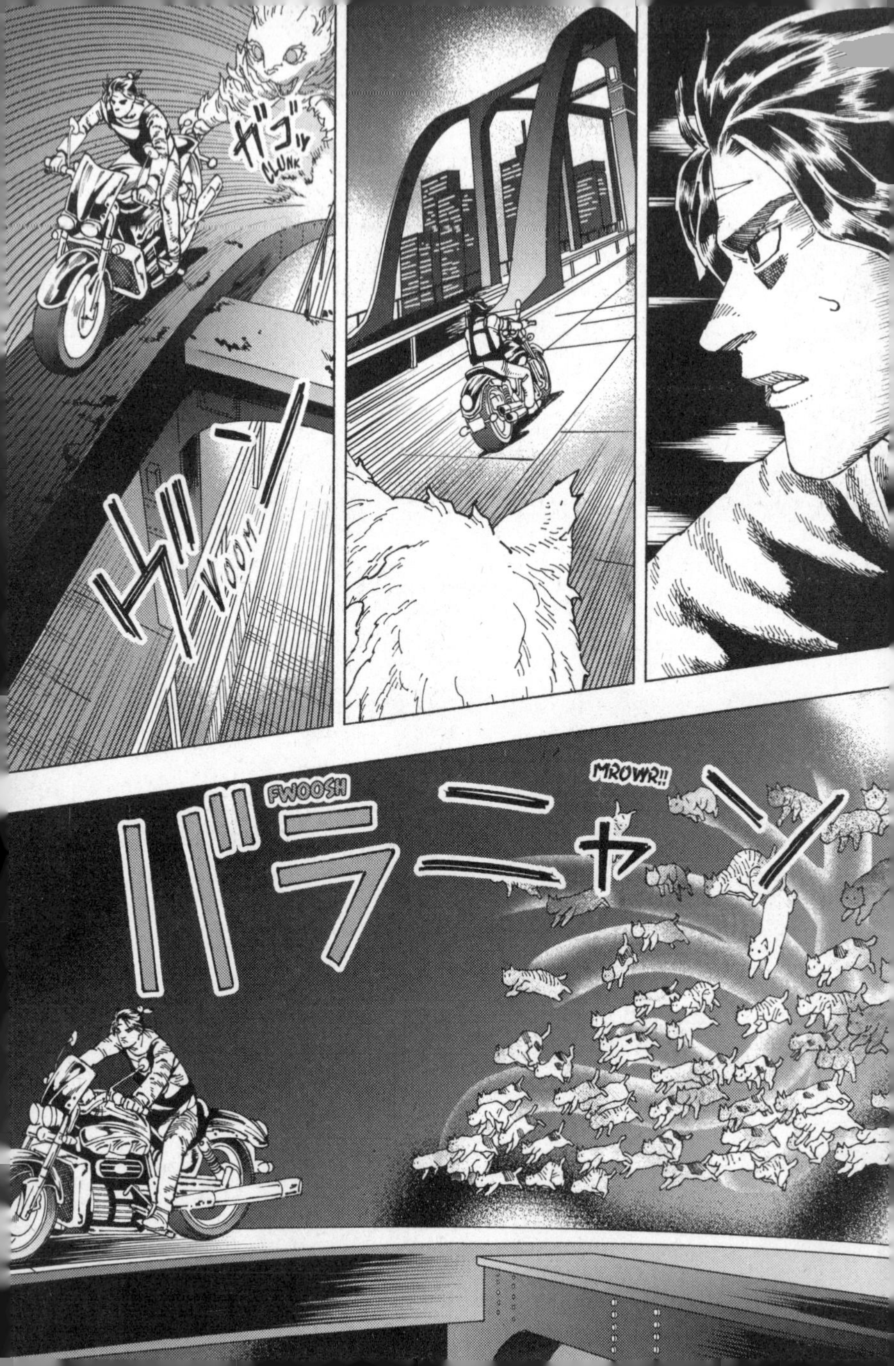
ガゴッ
CLUNK
VOOM
MROWR!!
FWOOSH

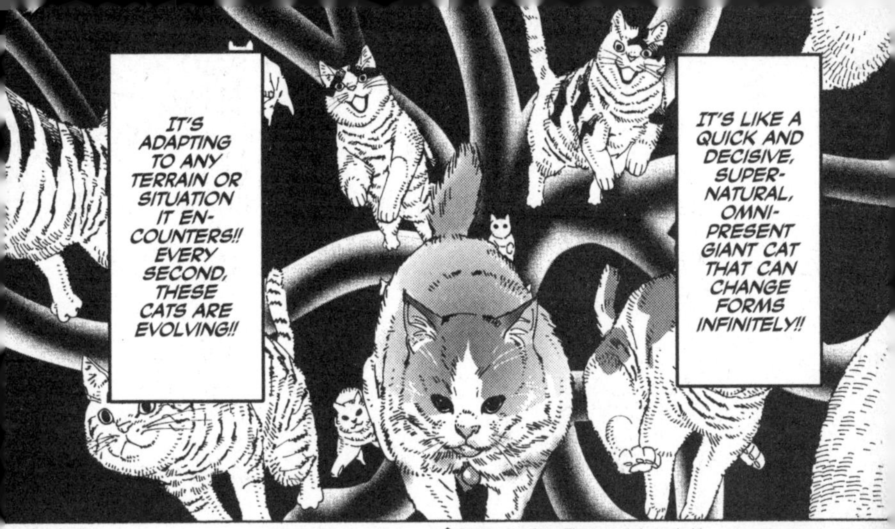
IT'S LIKE A QUICK AND DECISIVE, SUPER-NATURAL, OMNI-PRESENT GIANT CAT THAT CAN CHANGE FORMS INFINITELY!!
IT'S ADAPTING TO ANY TERRAIN OR SITUATION IT EN-COUNTERS!! EVERY SECOND, THESE CATS ARE EVOLVING!!

⇧ Chappy-kun from Ehara-san's household.

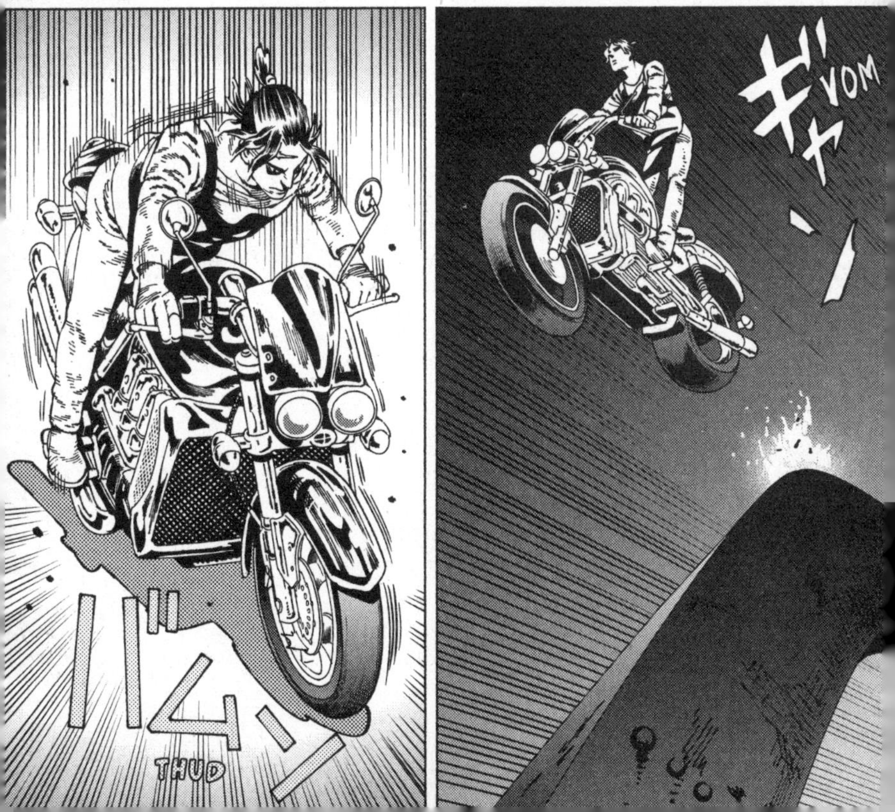
VOM
THUD

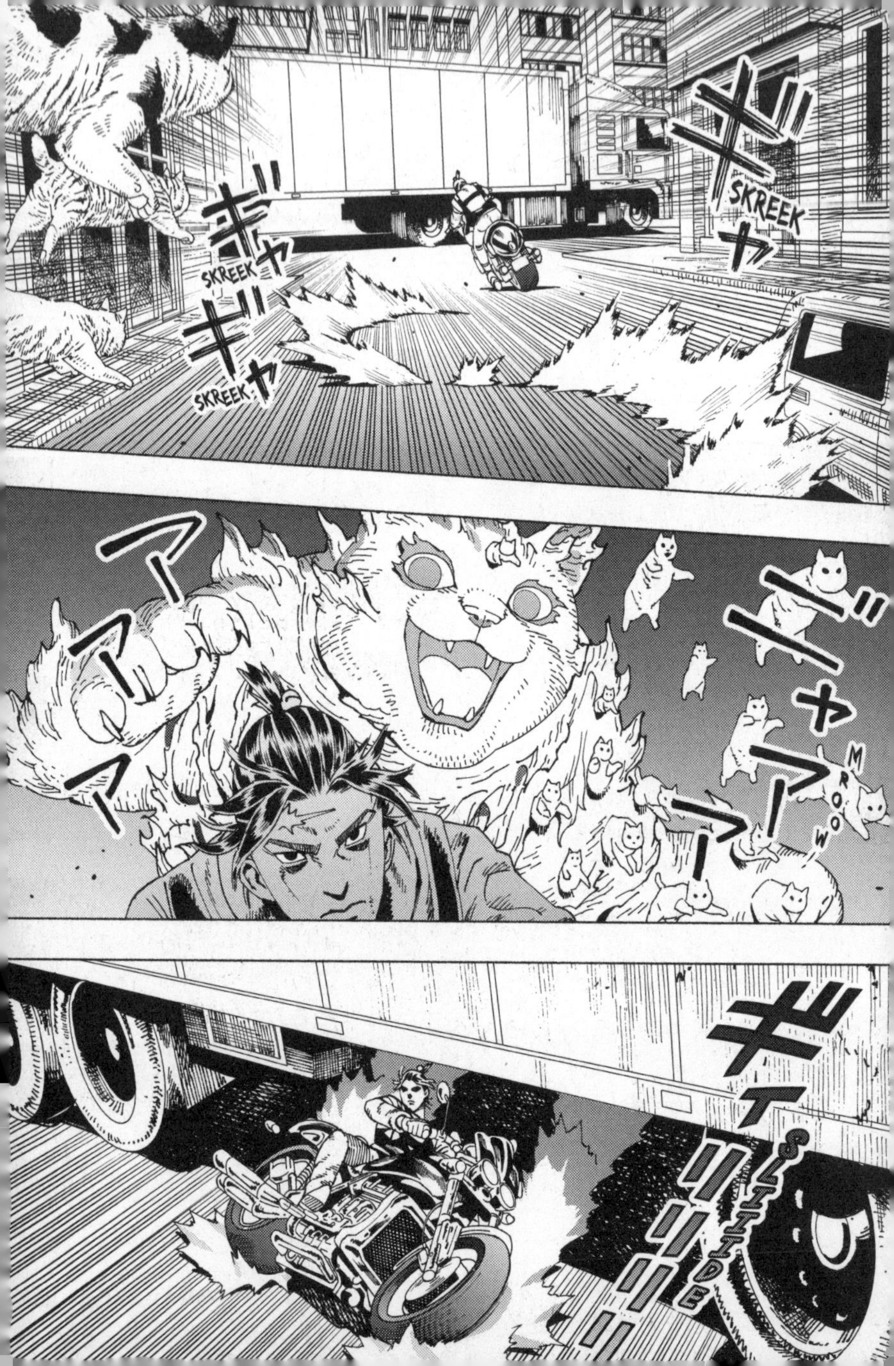
SKREEK
SKREEK
SKREEK
MROOW
SLIIIDE

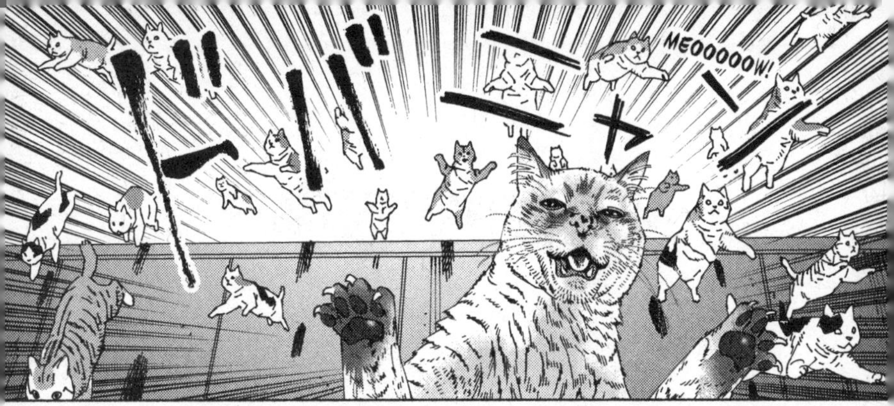
MEOOOOOW!

⇧Kinjiro-kun from the Shigii-san household.

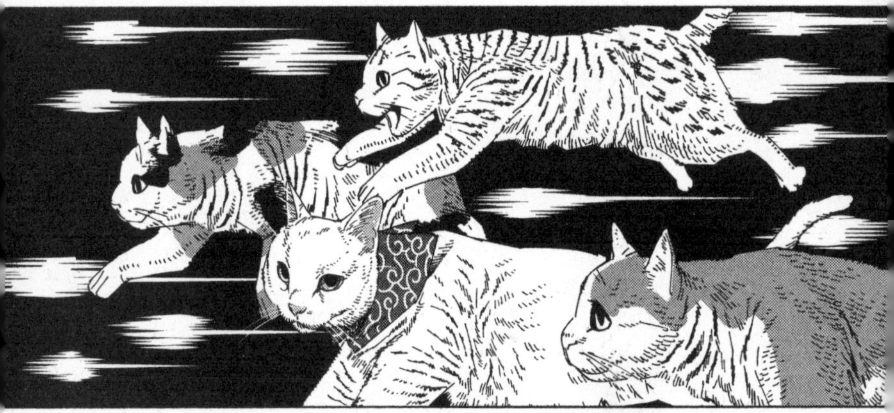

⇧Ren-kun from Seraku Miyachi-san's household.

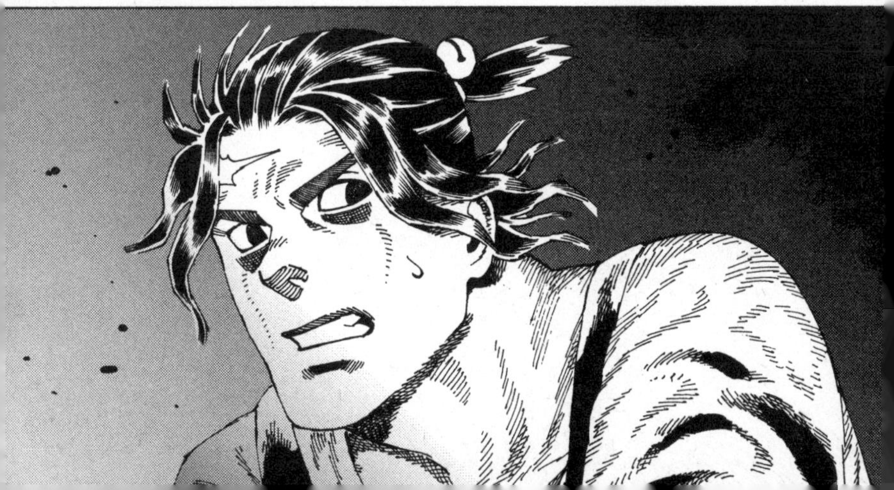

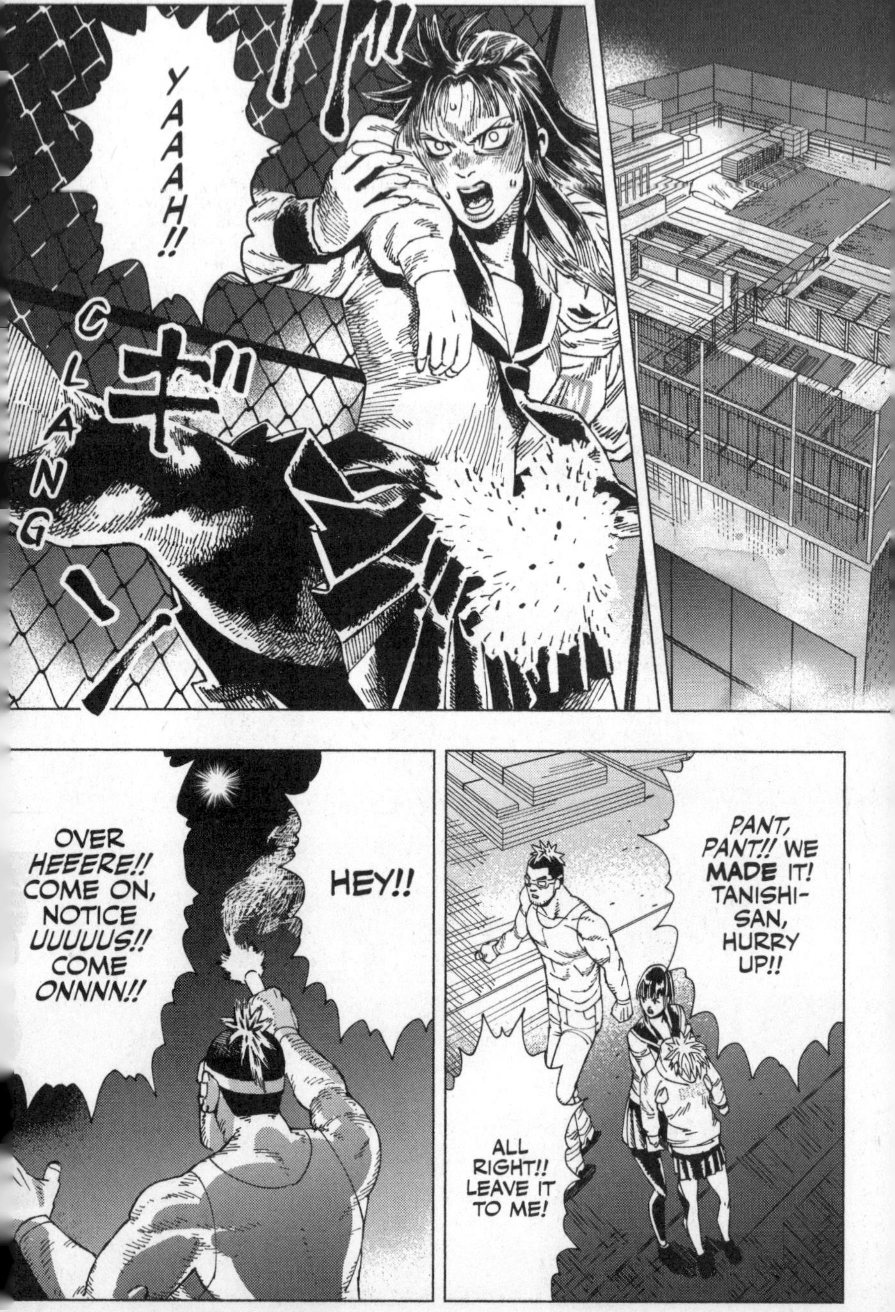

YAAAAH!!
CLANG!
PANT, PANT!! WE MADE IT! TANISHI-SAN, HURRY UP!!
ALL RIGHT!! LEAVE IT TO ME!
HEY!!
OVER HEEERE!! COME ON, NOTICE UUUUUS!! COME ONNNN!!

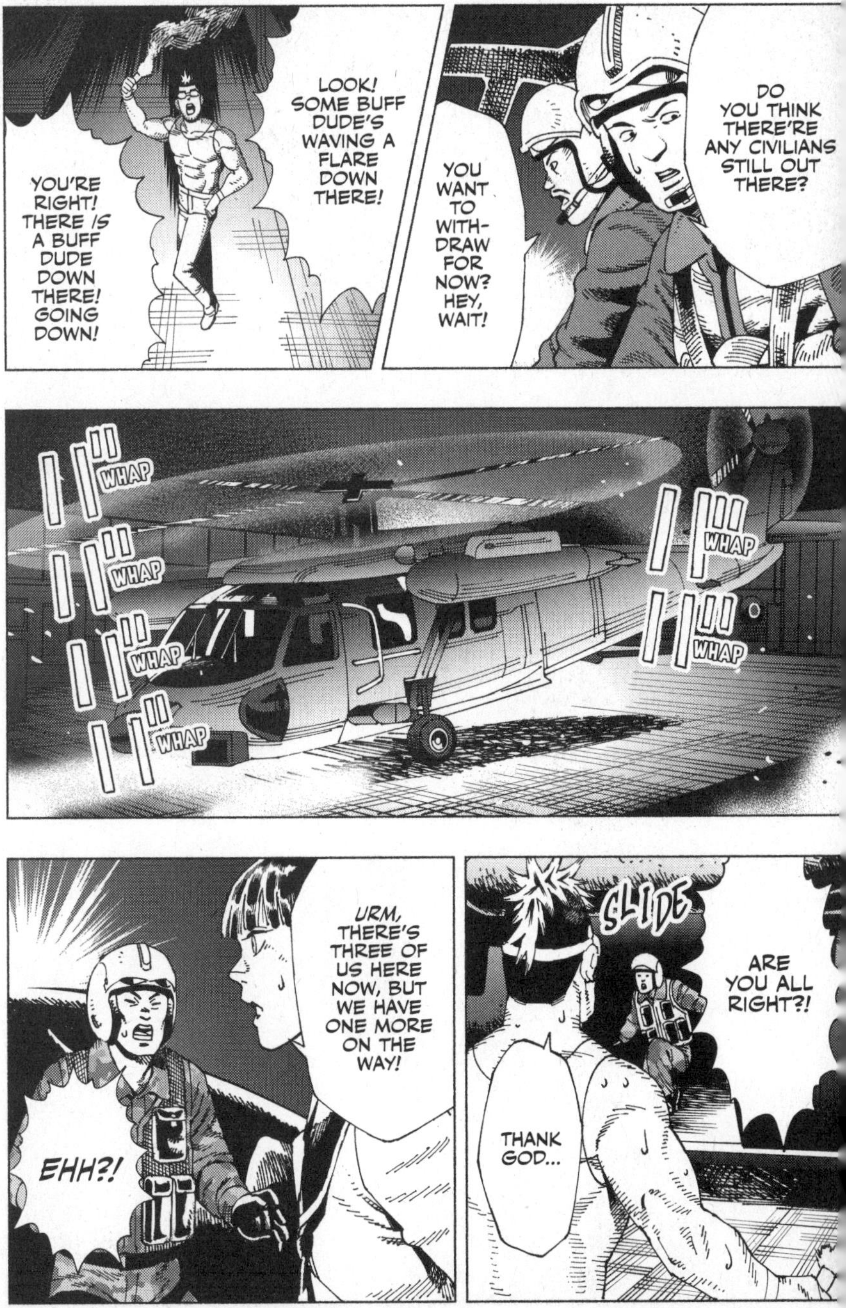
DO YOU THINK THERE'RE ANY CIVILIANS STILL OUT THERE?
YOU WANT TO WITH-DRAW FOR NOW? HEY, WAIT!
LOOK! SOME BUFF DUDE'S WAVING A FLARE DOWN THERE!
YOU'RE RIGHT! THERE *IS* A BUFF DUDE DOWN THERE! GOING DOWN!
WHAP
WHAP
WHAP
WHAP
WHAP
WHAP
SLIDE
ARE YOU ALL RIGHT?!
THANK GOD...
URM, THERE'S THREE OF US HERE NOW, BUT WE HAVE ONE MORE ON THE WAY!
EHH?!

FOR REAL?!

I'M SO SORRY, BUT UNFORTUNATELY, THE MOST THIS HELICOPTER CAN TAKE IS ONE EXTRA PERSON.

WE'LL BE FINE SO, PLEASE, TAKE HER!

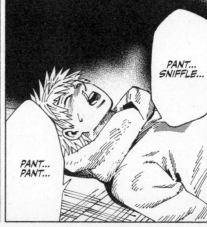

PANT... SNIFFLE...

PANT... PANT...

LIFT...

BLOW

BUT IF YOU DO THAT, YOU'LL ALL... SNIFFLE SNORT...

I DON'T WANT THAT...

WE'LL MANAGE!

DON'T YOU WORRY ABOUT US. WE WOULDN'T HAVE MADE IT THIS FAR WITHOUT YOU, TSUTSUMI.

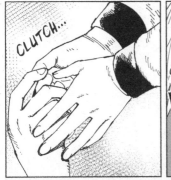

CLUTCH...

SOB

SOB

UEEEEEE...

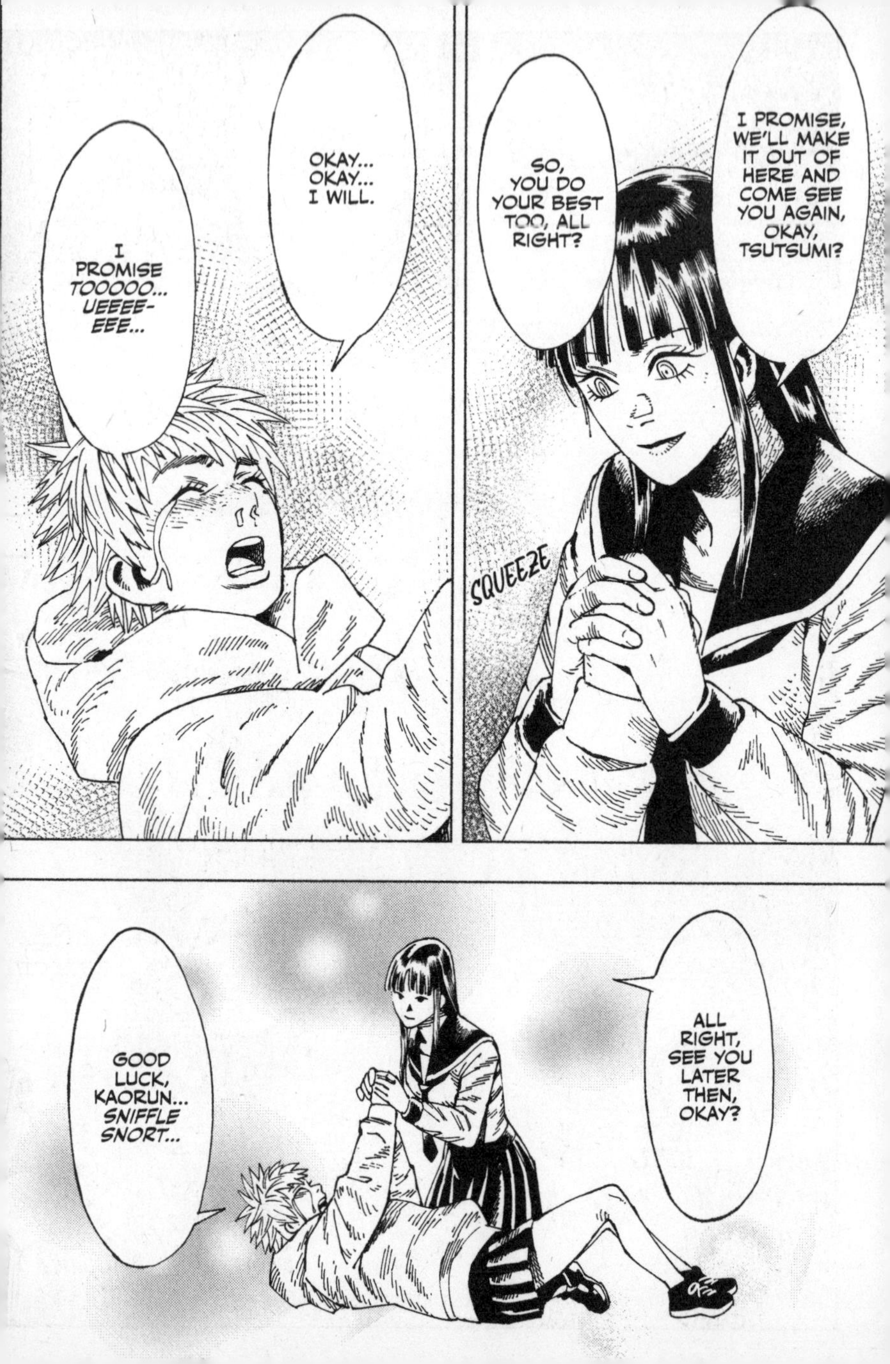
I PROMISE, WE'LL MAKE IT OUT OF HERE AND COME SEE YOU AGAIN, OKAY, TSUTSUMI?
SO, YOU DO YOUR BEST TOO, ALL RIGHT?
SQUEEZE
OKAY... OKAY... I WILL.
I PROMISE TOOOOO... UEEEE-EEE...
ALL RIGHT, SEE YOU LATER THEN, OKAY?
GOOD LUCK, KAORUN... SNIFFLE SNORT...

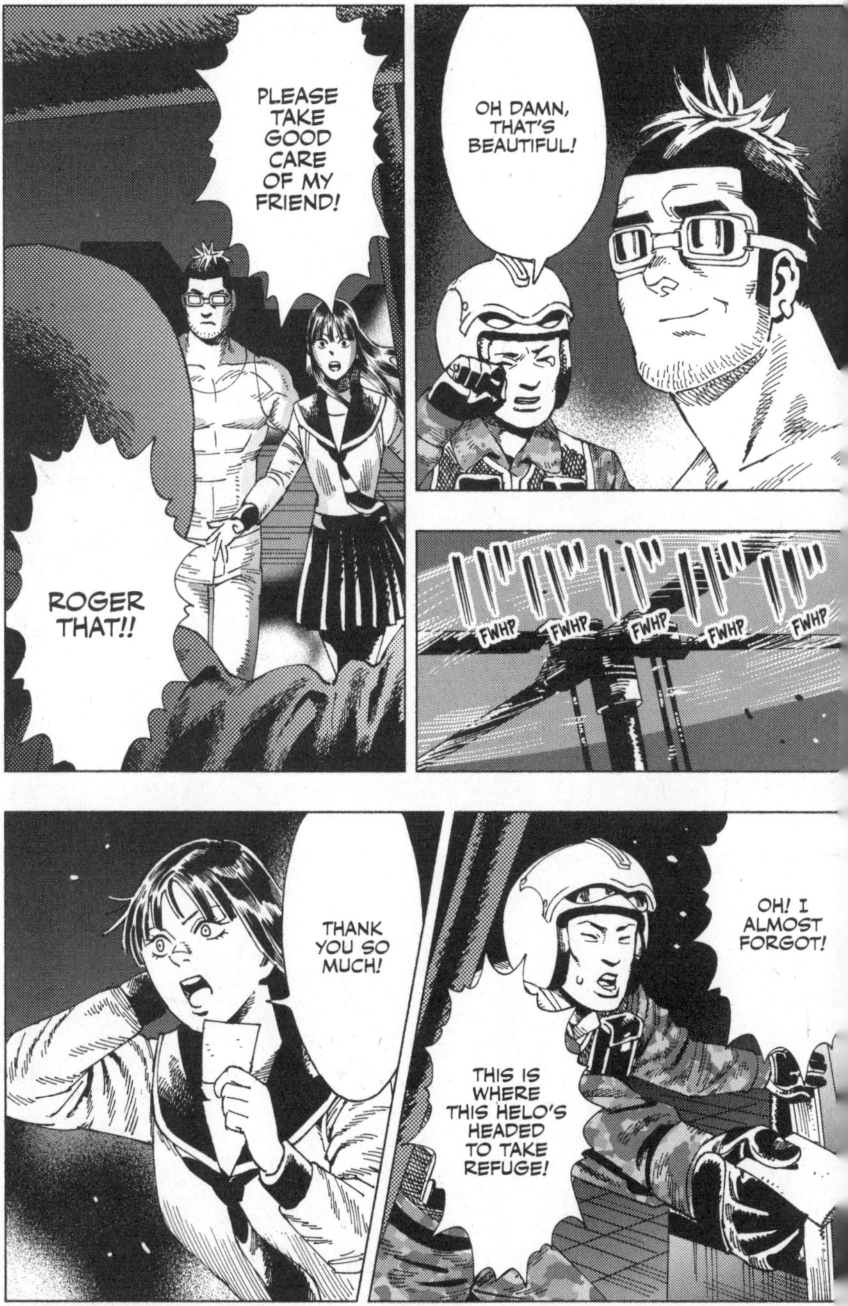
OH DAMN, THAT'S BEAUTIFUL!
FWHP
FWHP
FWHP
FWHP
FWHP
PLEASE TAKE GOOD CARE OF MY FRIEND!
ROGER THAT!!
OH! I ALMOST FORGOT!
THIS IS WHERE THIS HELO'S HEADED TO TAKE REFUGE!
THANK YOU SO MUCH!

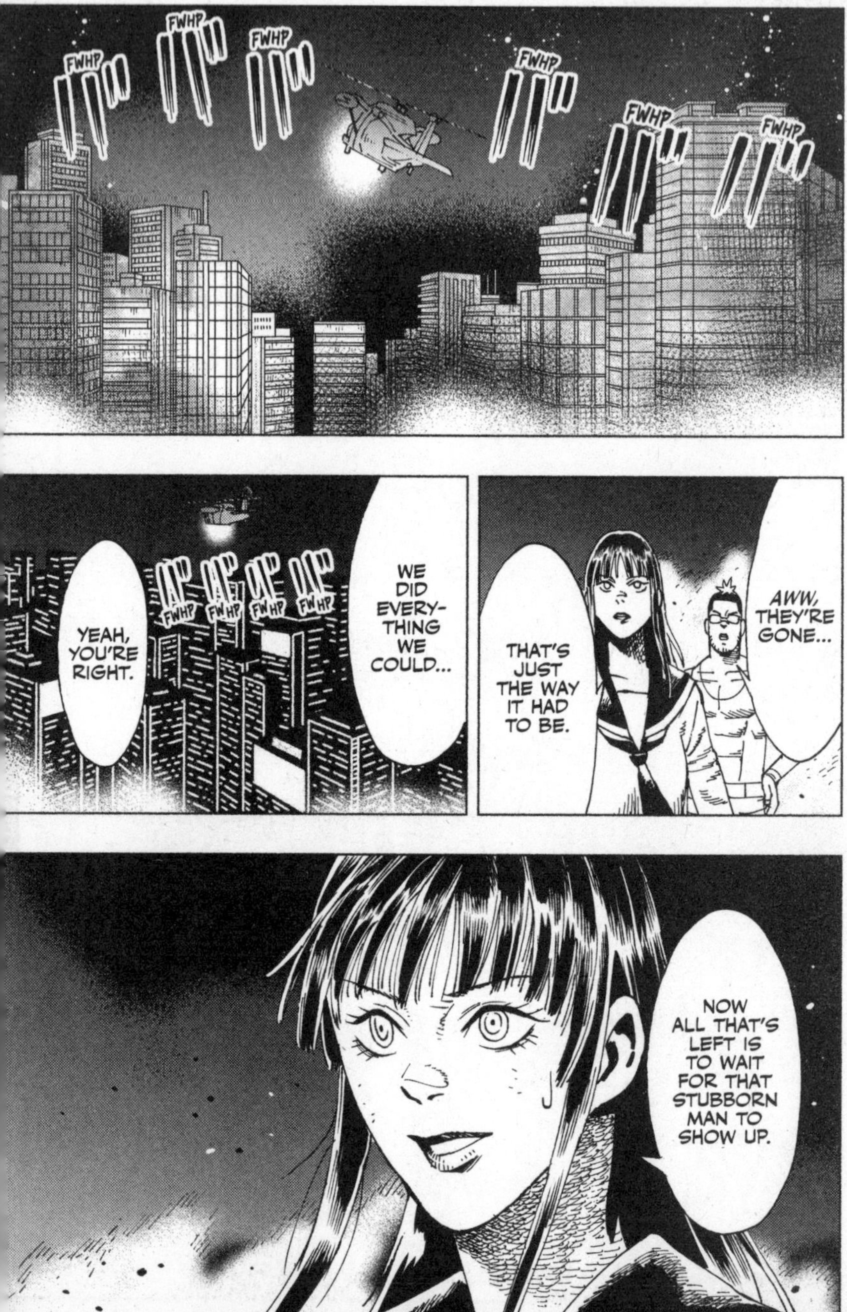
FWHP
FWHP
FWHP
FWHP
FWHP
FWHP
AWW, THEY'RE GONE...
THAT'S JUST THE WAY IT HAD TO BE.
WE DID EVERY-THING WE COULD...
FWHP
FWHP
FWHP
FWHP
YEAH, YOU'RE RIGHT.
NOW ALL THAT'S LEFT IS TO WAIT FOR THAT STUBBORN MAN TO SHOW UP.

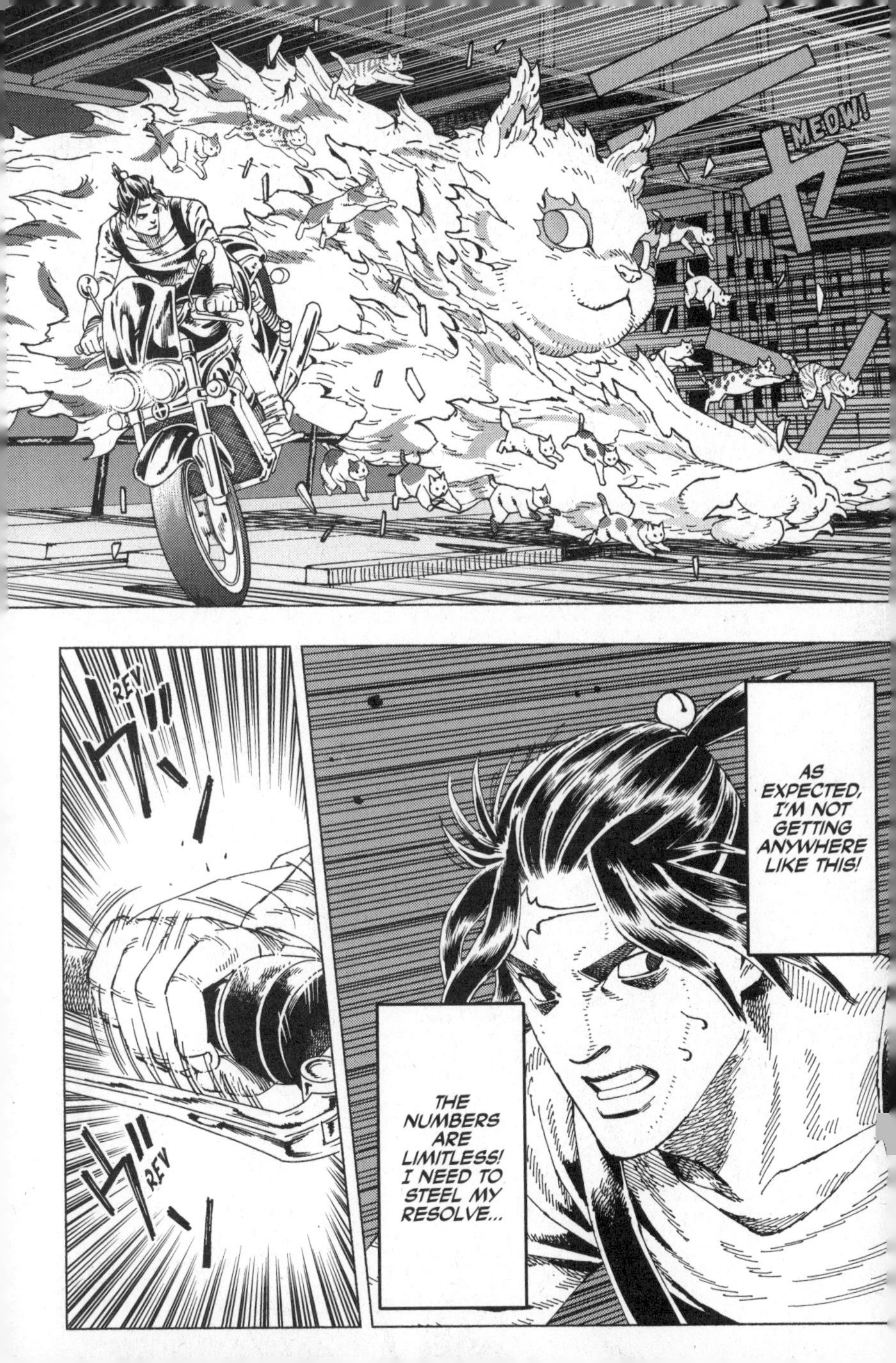
MEOW!
AS EXPECTED, I'M NOT GETTING ANYWHERE LIKE THIS!
THE NUMBERS ARE LIMITLESS! I NEED TO STEEL MY RESOLVE...
REV
REV

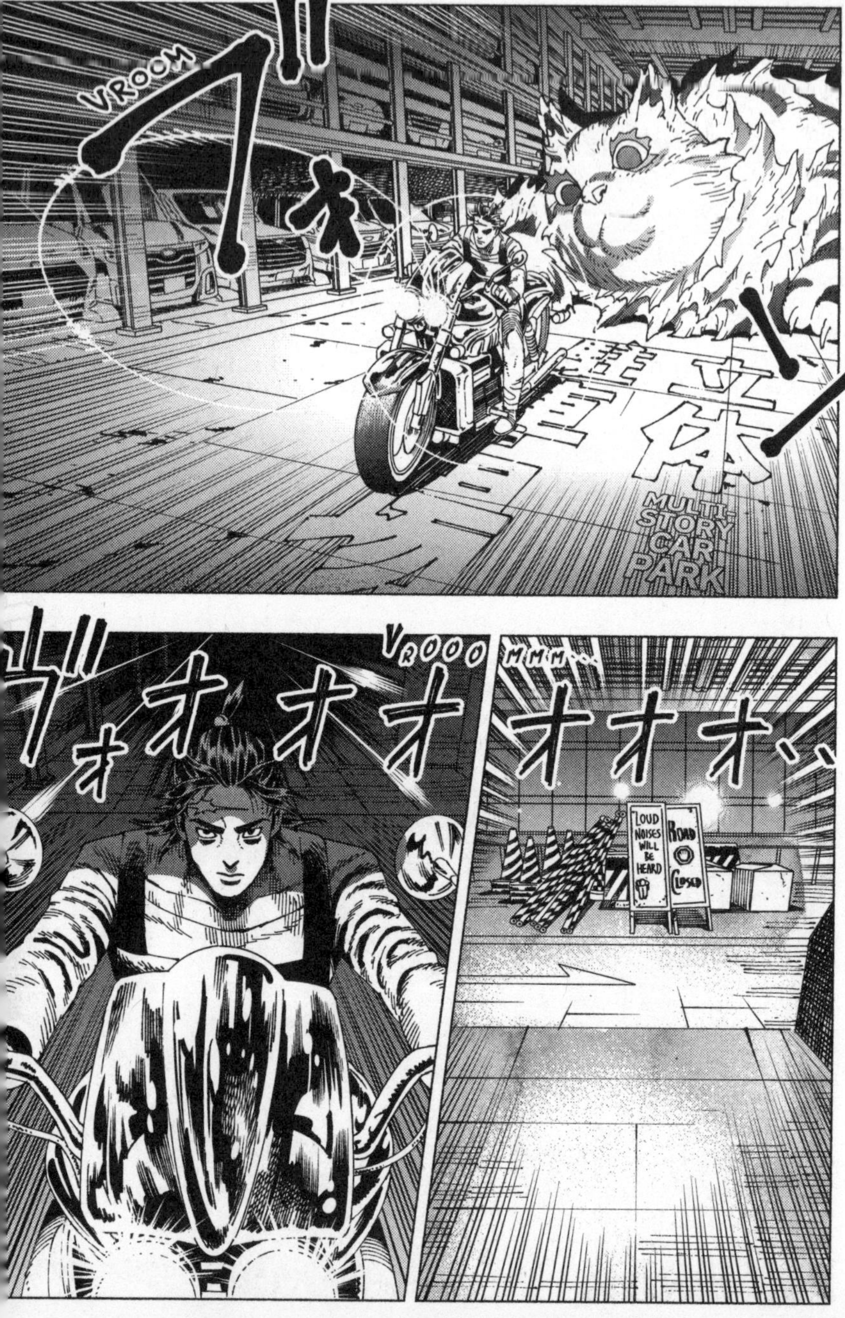
ブォ!!
VROOM
立体
MULTI-STORY CAR PARK
ヴォオオオオオオ…
VROOOMMM…
LOUD NOISES WILL BE HEARD
ROAD CLOSED

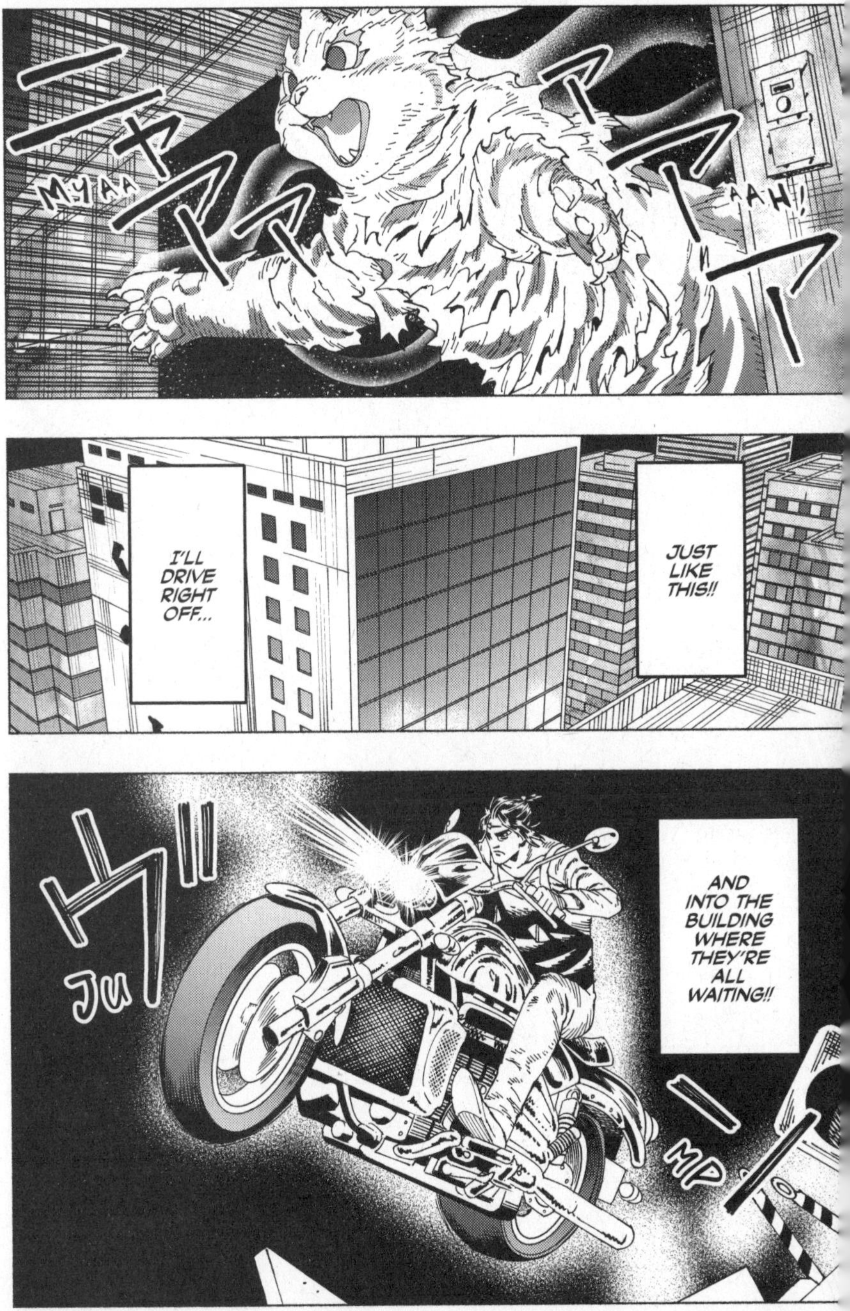
MYAA
AAH!
I'LL DRIVE RIGHT OFF...
JUST LIKE THIS!!
AND INTO THE BUILDING WHERE THEY'RE ALL WAITING!!
JU
MP

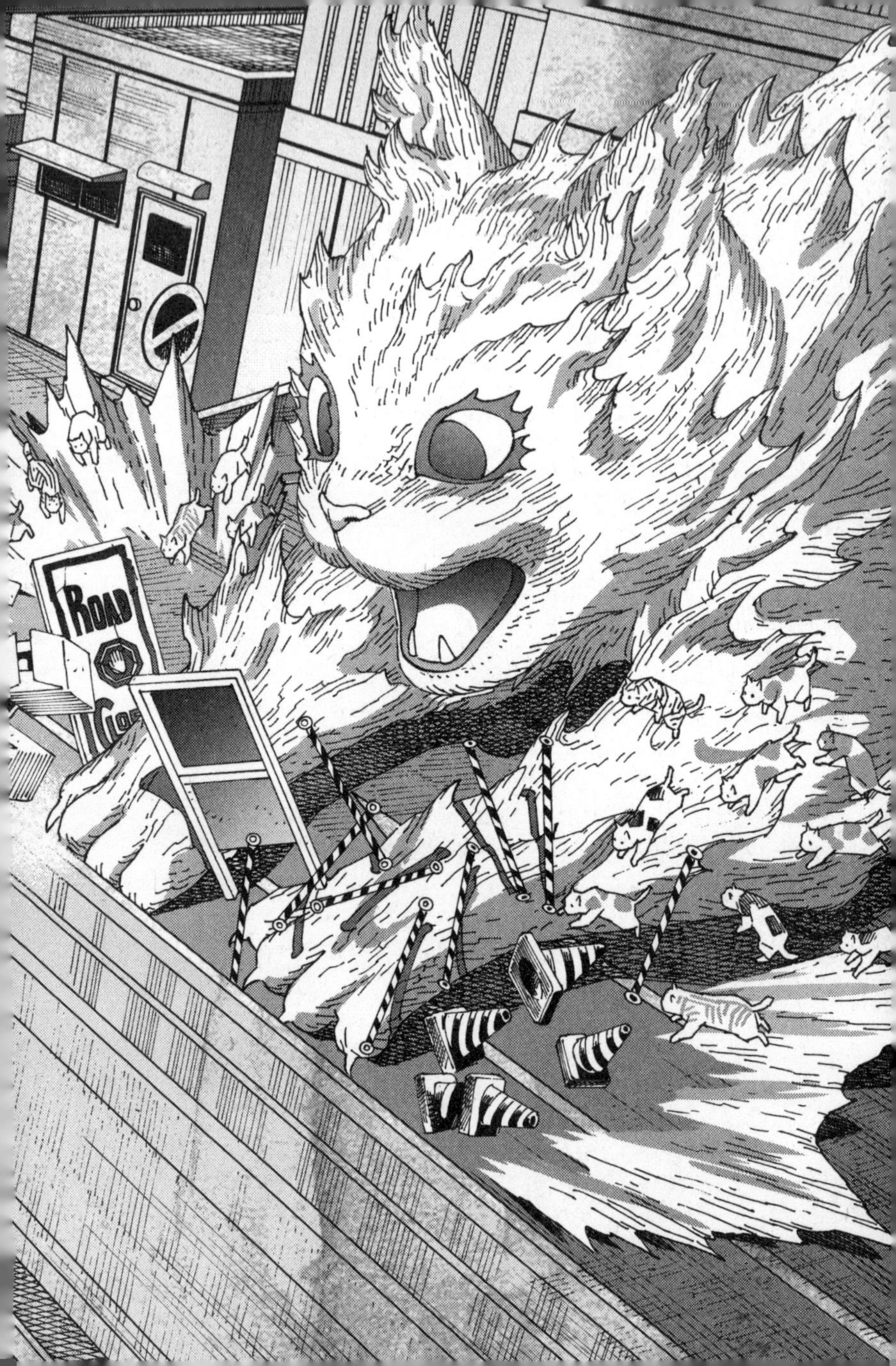
ROAD

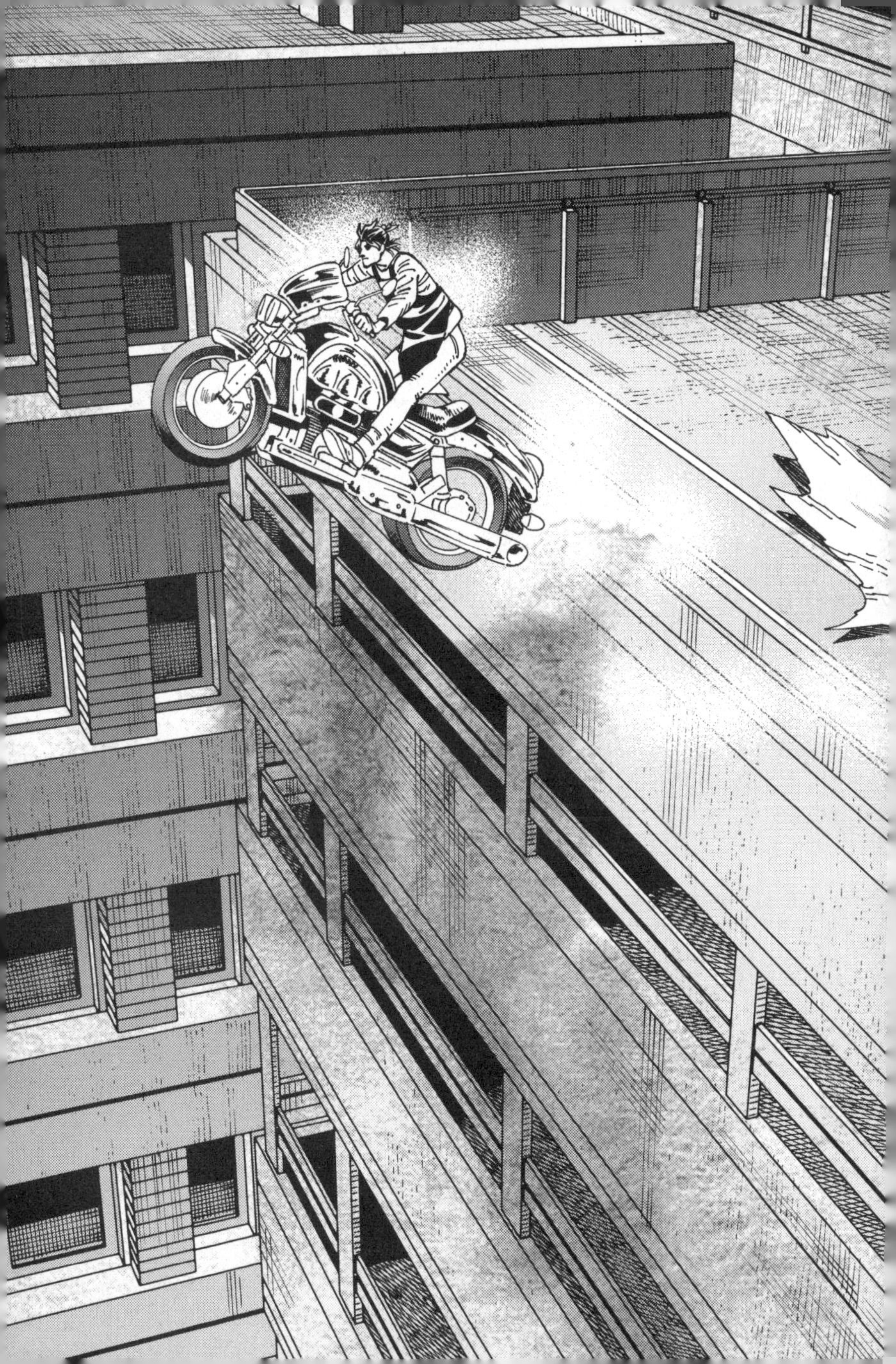

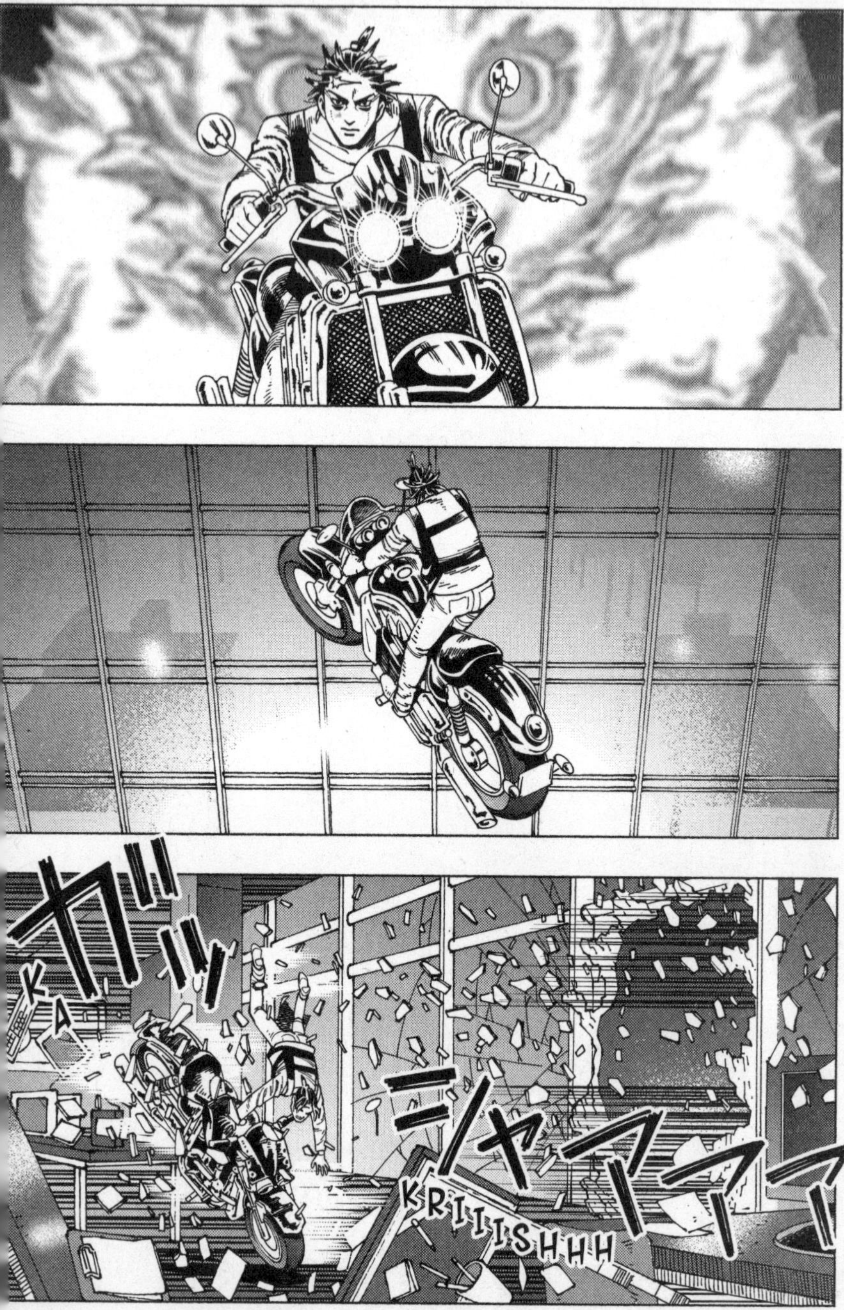
ガッ
KA
KRIIIISHHH

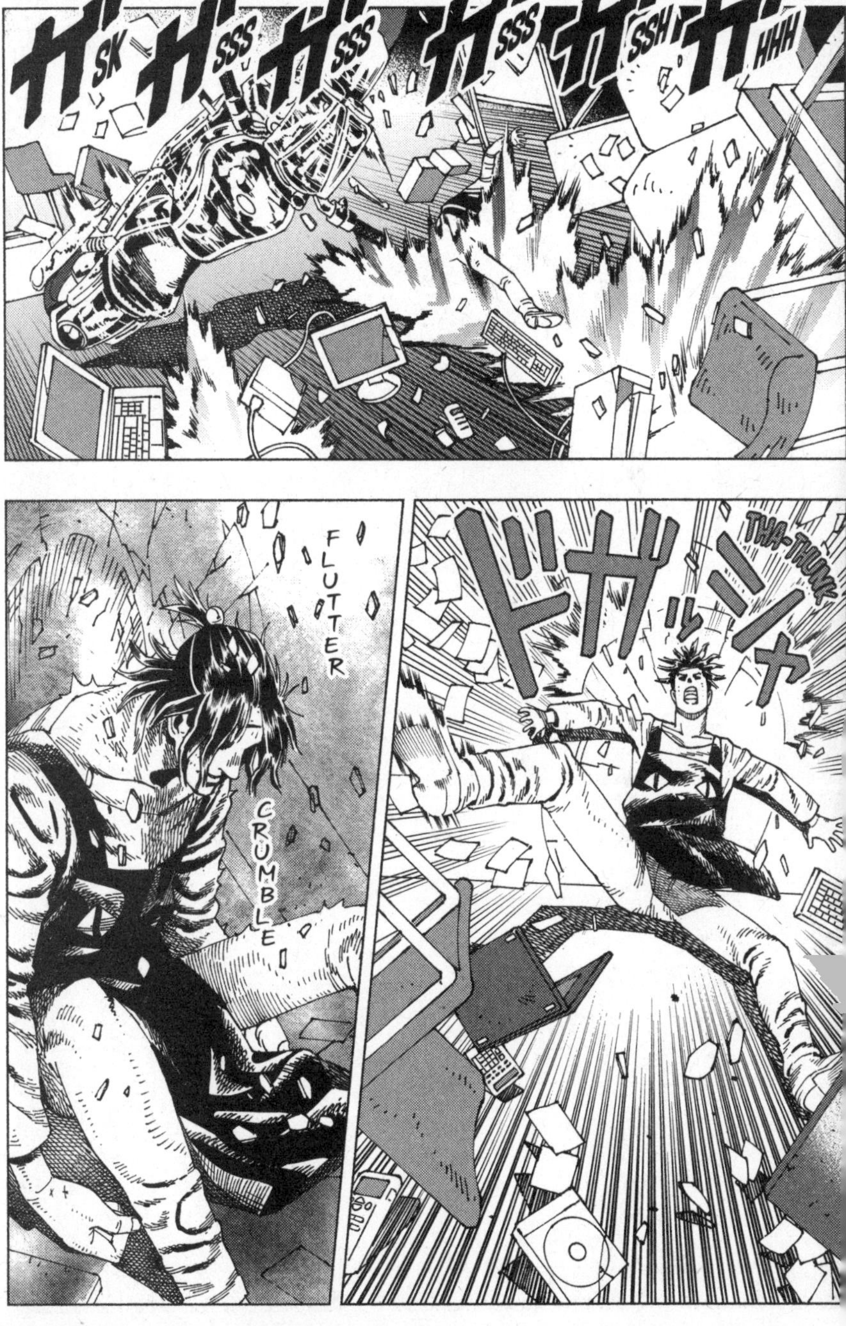
ガガガガガガ
SK SSS SSS SSS SSH HHH
ドガッシャ
THA-THUNK
FLUTTER
CRUMBLE

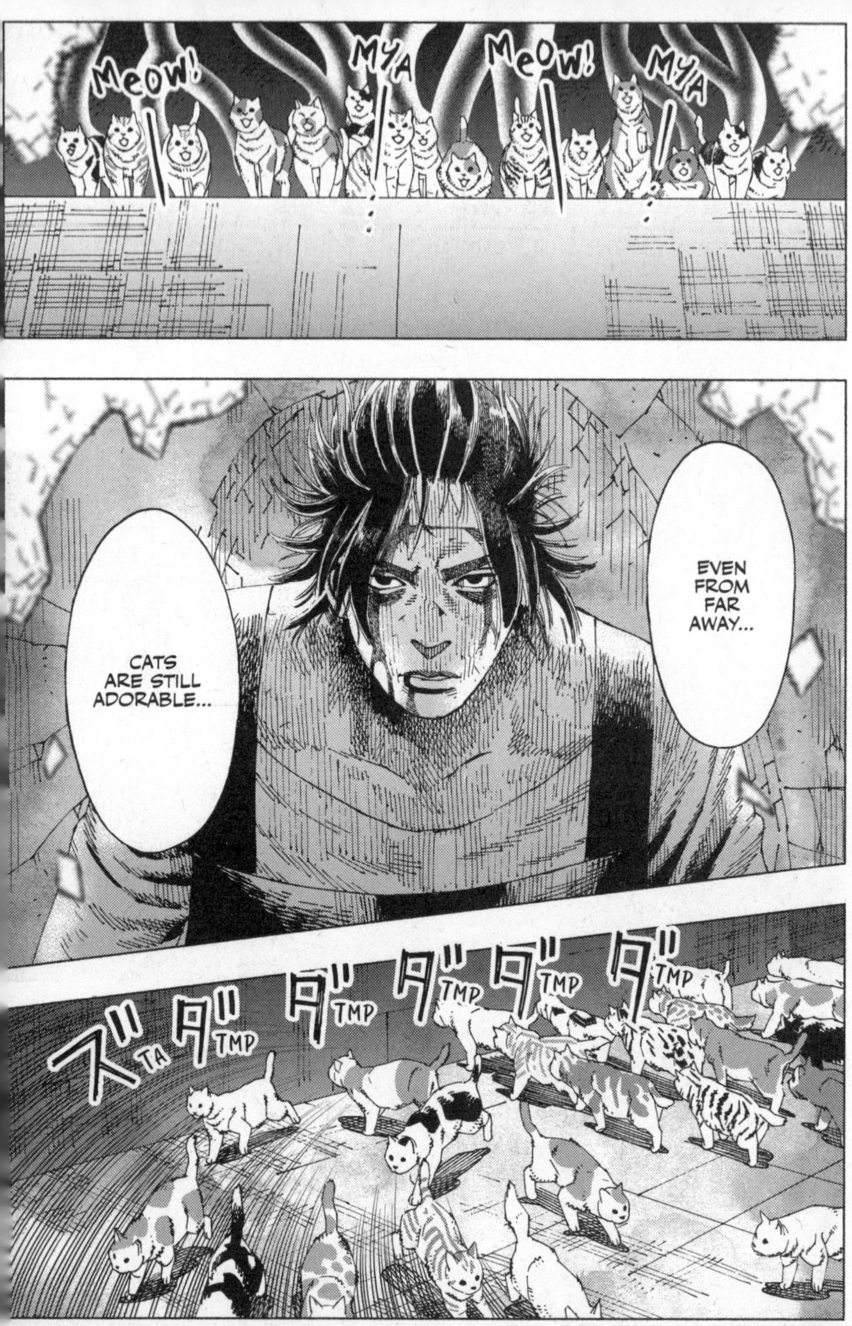
MYA
MeOW!
MYA
MeOW!
EVEN FROM FAR AWAY...
CATS ARE STILL ADORABLE...
TA
TMP
TMP
TMP
TMP
TMP

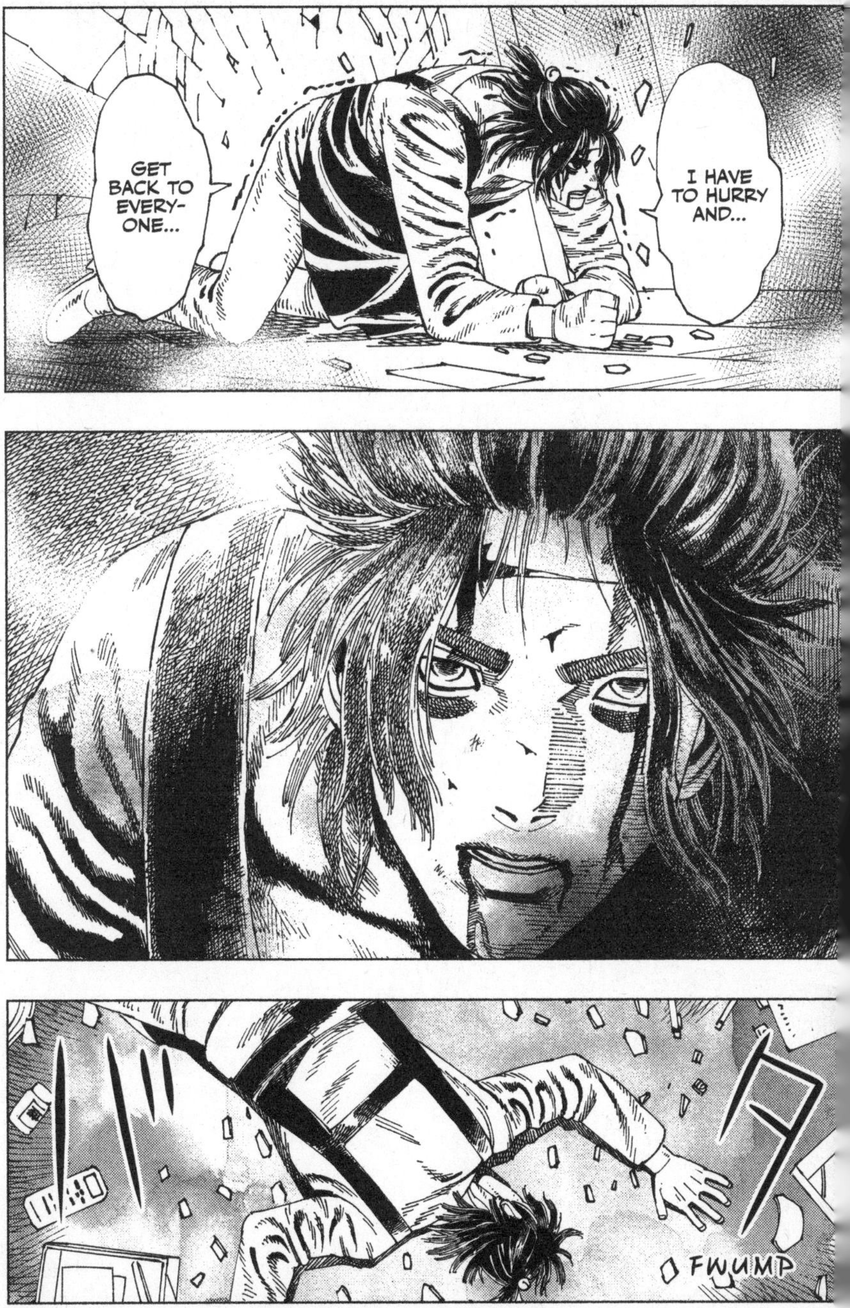
I HAVE TO HURRY AND...
GET BACK TO EVERY-ONE...
FWUMP

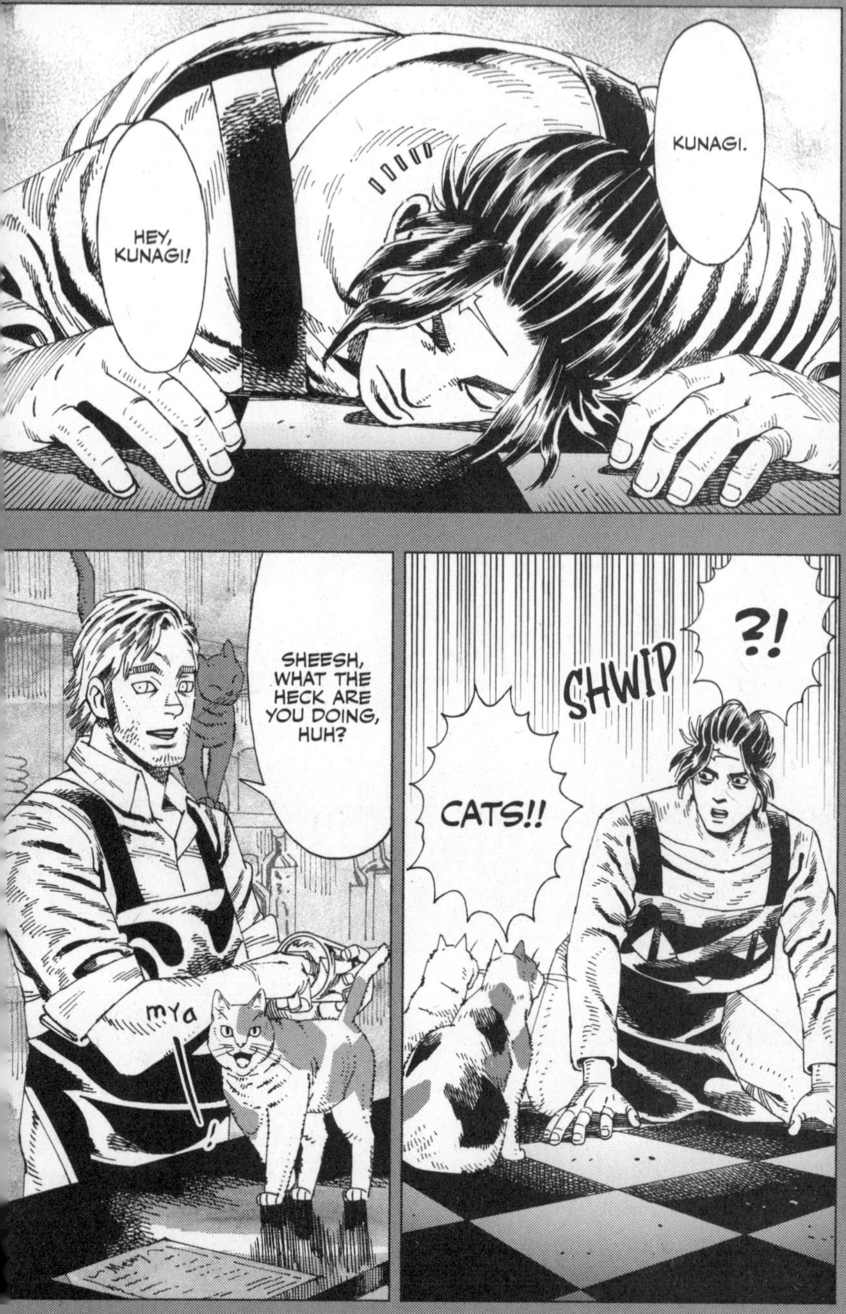
KUNAGI.
HEY, KUNAGI!
?!
SHWIP
CATS!!
SHEESH, WHAT THE HECK ARE YOU DOING, HUH?
mya

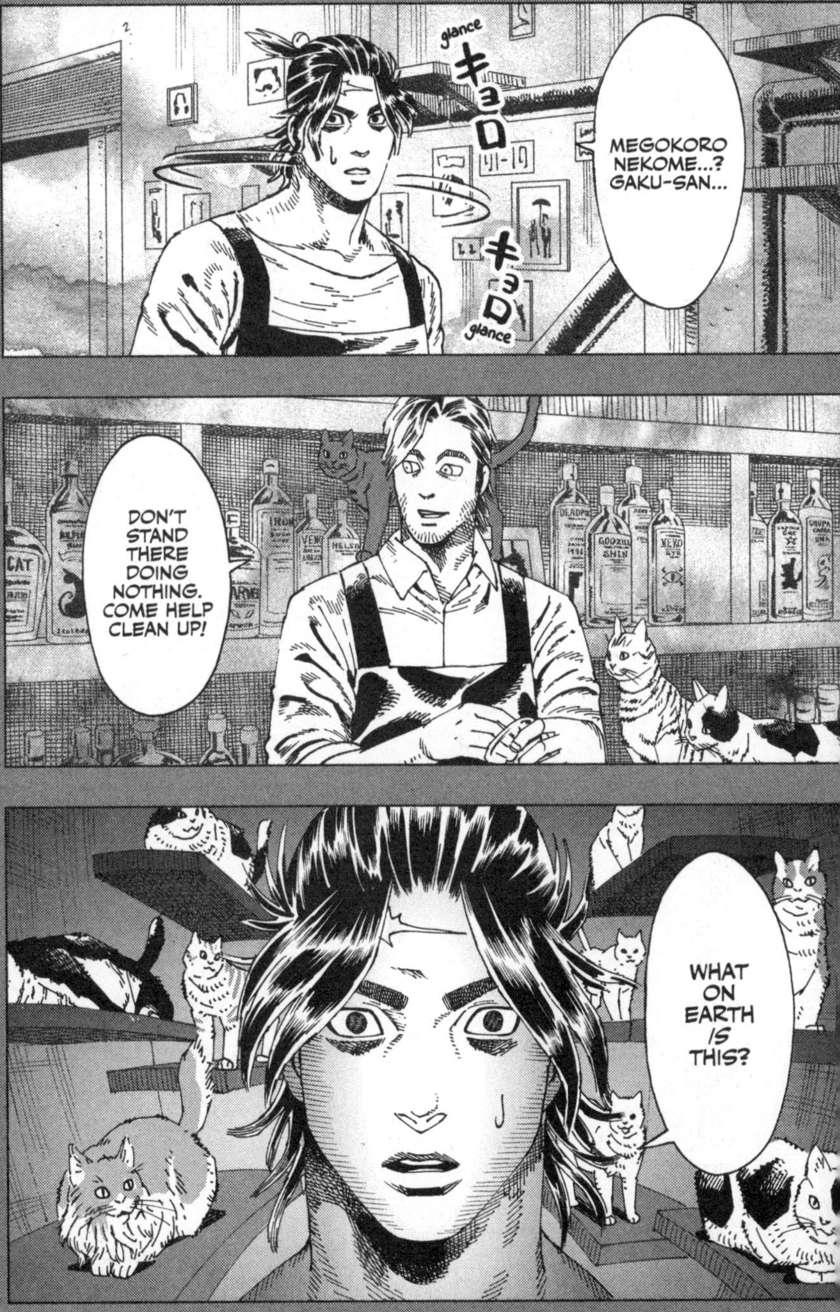

MEGOKORO NEKOME...? GAKU-SAN...
glance キョロ
キョロ glance
DON'T STAND THERE DOING NOTHING. COME HELP CLEAN UP!
WHAT ON EARTH *IS* THIS?

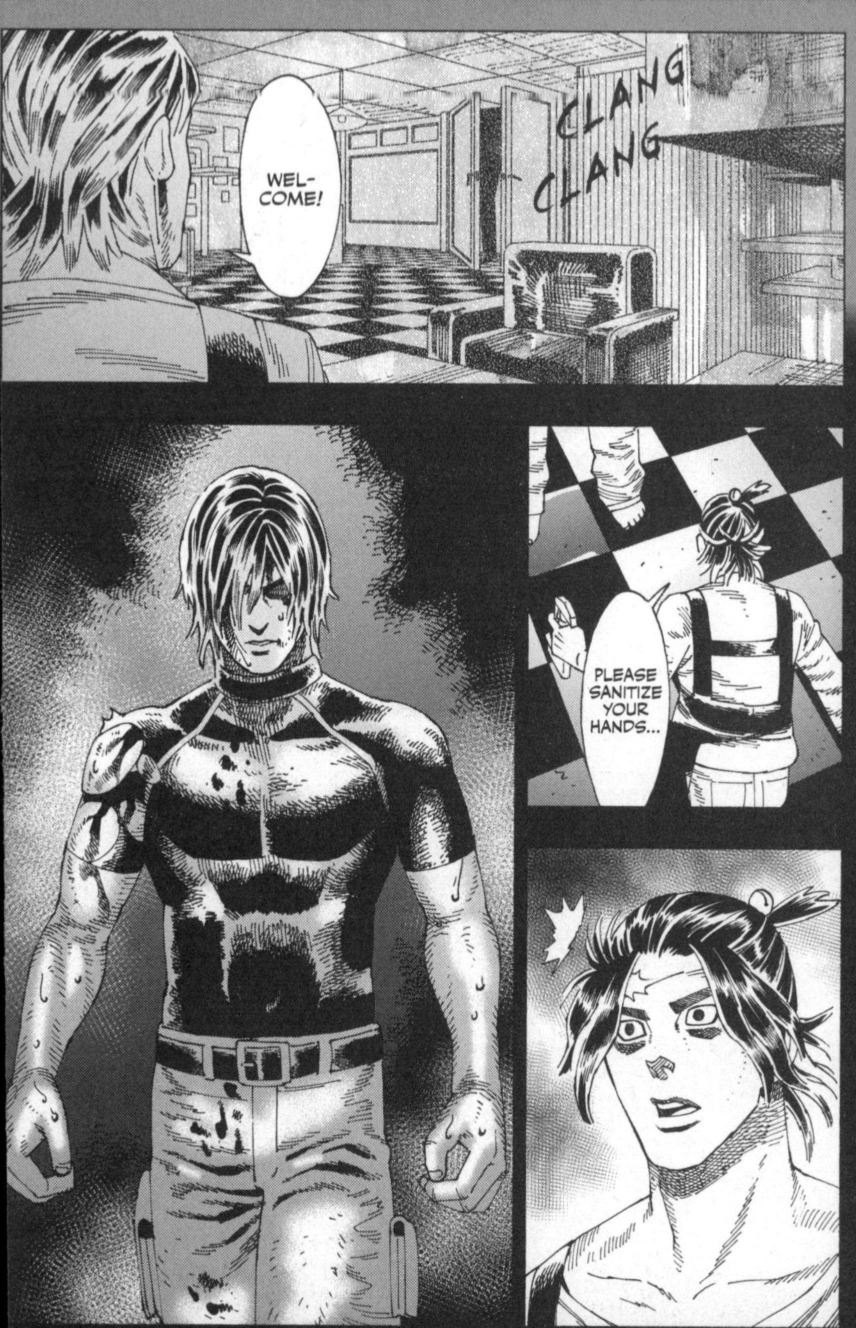
CLANG CLANG
WEL-COME!
PLEASE SANITIZE YOUR HANDS...

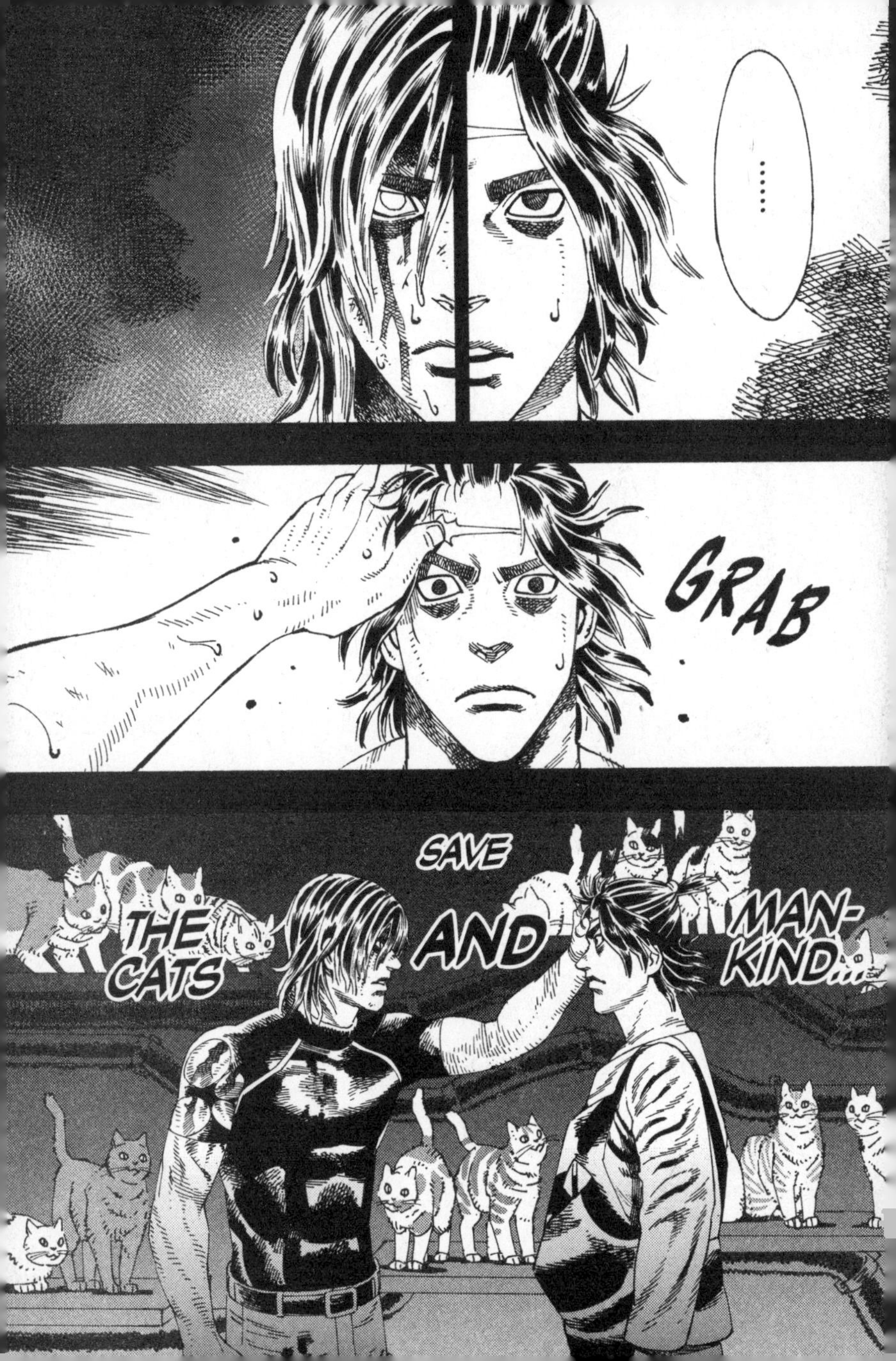
......
GRAB
MAN-KIND...
SAVE
AND
THE CATS

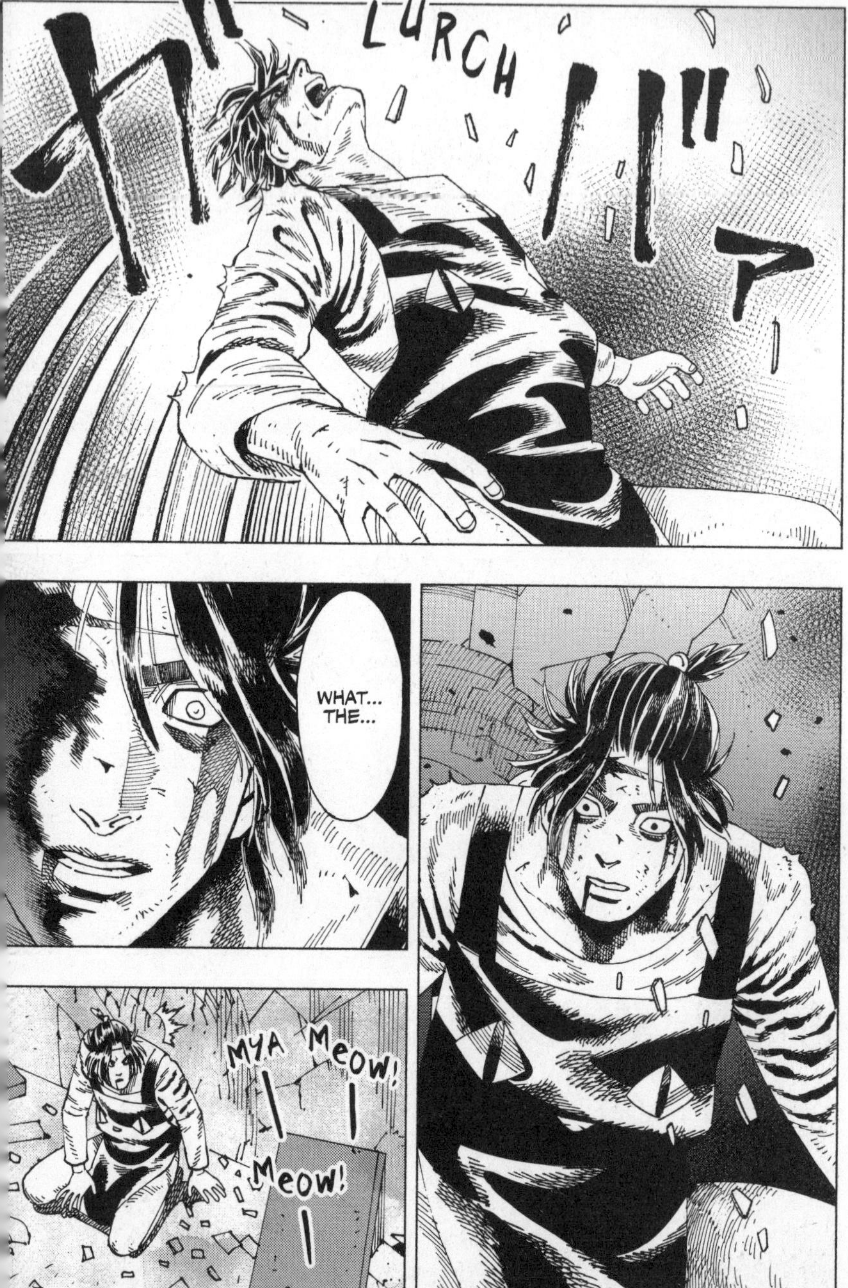
LURCH
WHAT... THE...
Meow!
MYA
Meow!

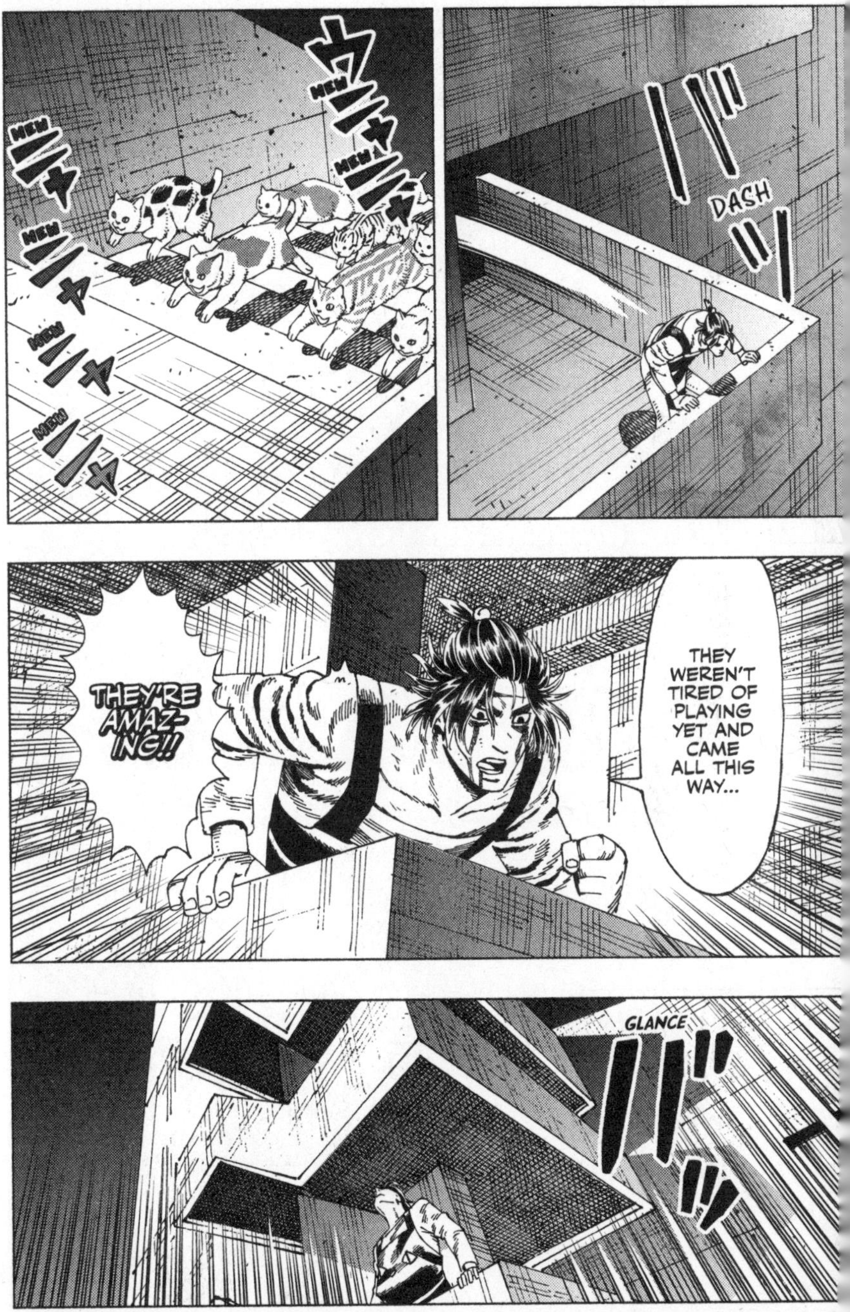
DASH
MEW
MEW
MEW
MEW
MEW
MEW
THEY WEREN'T TIRED OF PLAYING YET AND CAME ALL THIS WAY...
THEY'RE AMAZ-ING!!
GLANCE

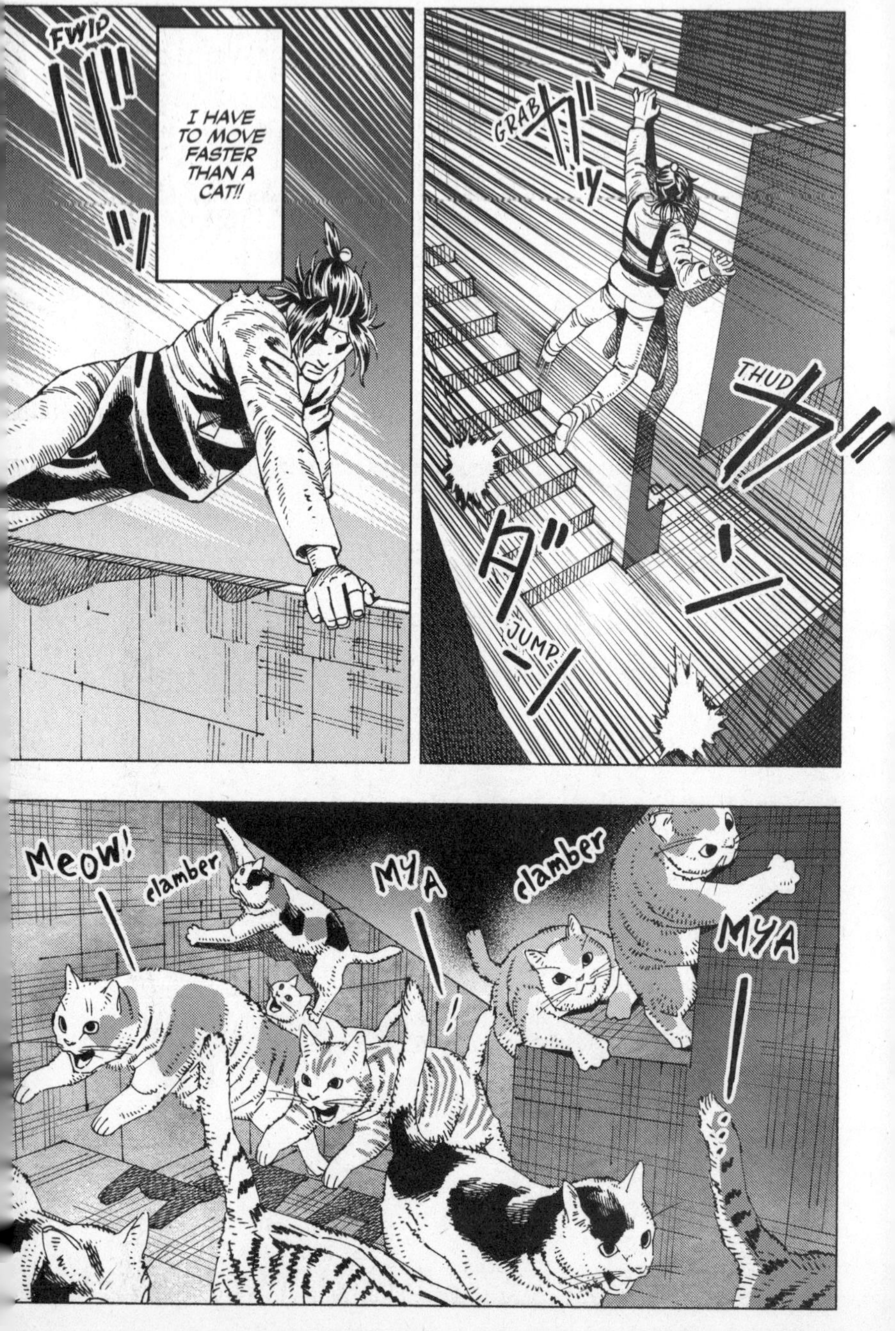
GRAB
THUD
JUMP
FWIP
I HAVE TO MOVE FASTER THAN A CAT!!
MYA
clamber
MYA
clamber
Meow!

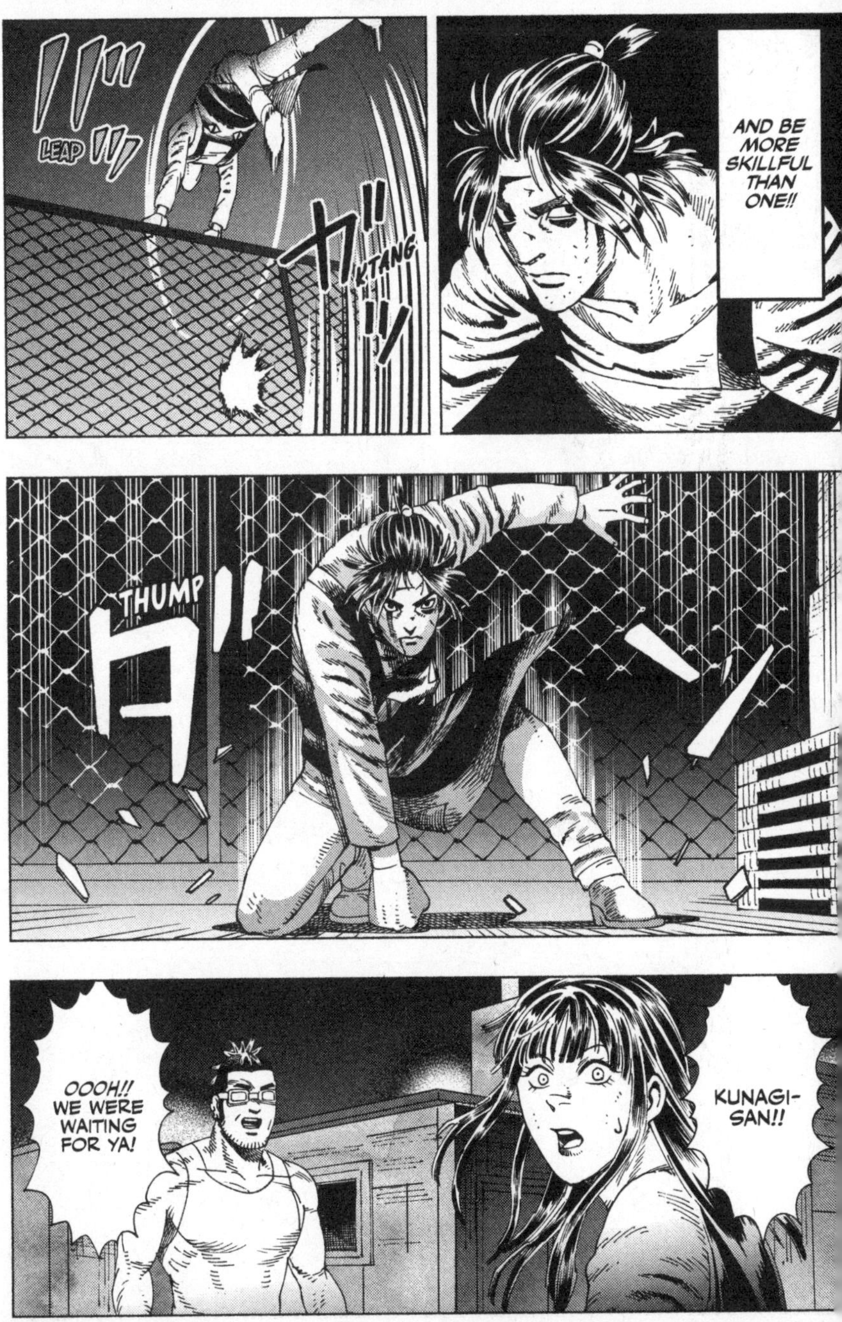
AND BE MORE SKILLFUL THAN ONE!!
LEAP
KTANG
THUMP
KUNAGI-SAN!!
OOOH!! WE WERE WAITING FOR YA!

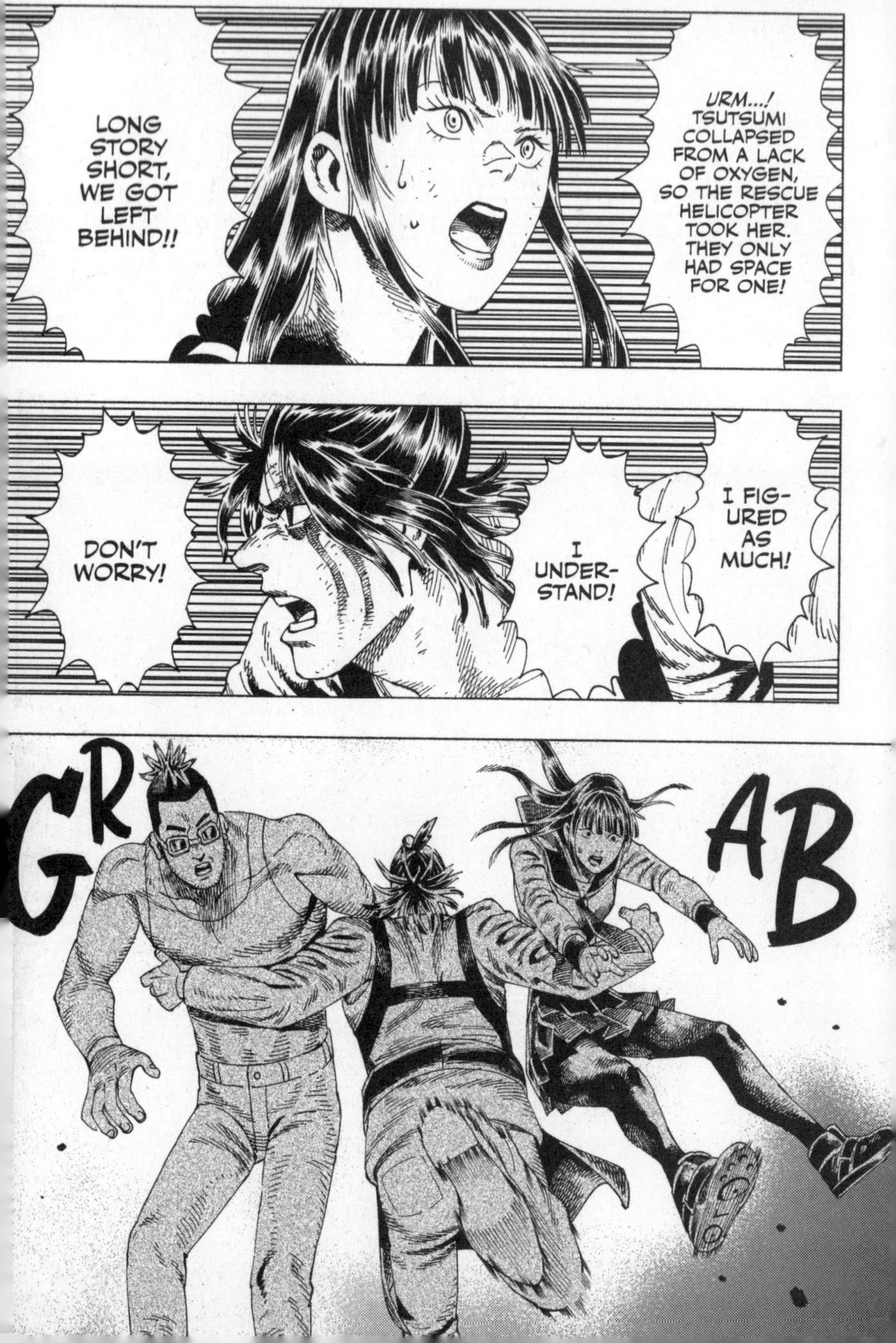
URM...! TSUTSUMI COLLAPSED FROM A LACK OF OXYGEN, SO THE RESCUE HELICOPTER TOOK HER. THEY ONLY HAD SPACE FOR ONE!
LONG STORY SHORT, WE GOT LEFT BEHIND!!
I FIG-URED AS MUCH!
I UNDER-STAND!
DON'T WORRY!
GRAB

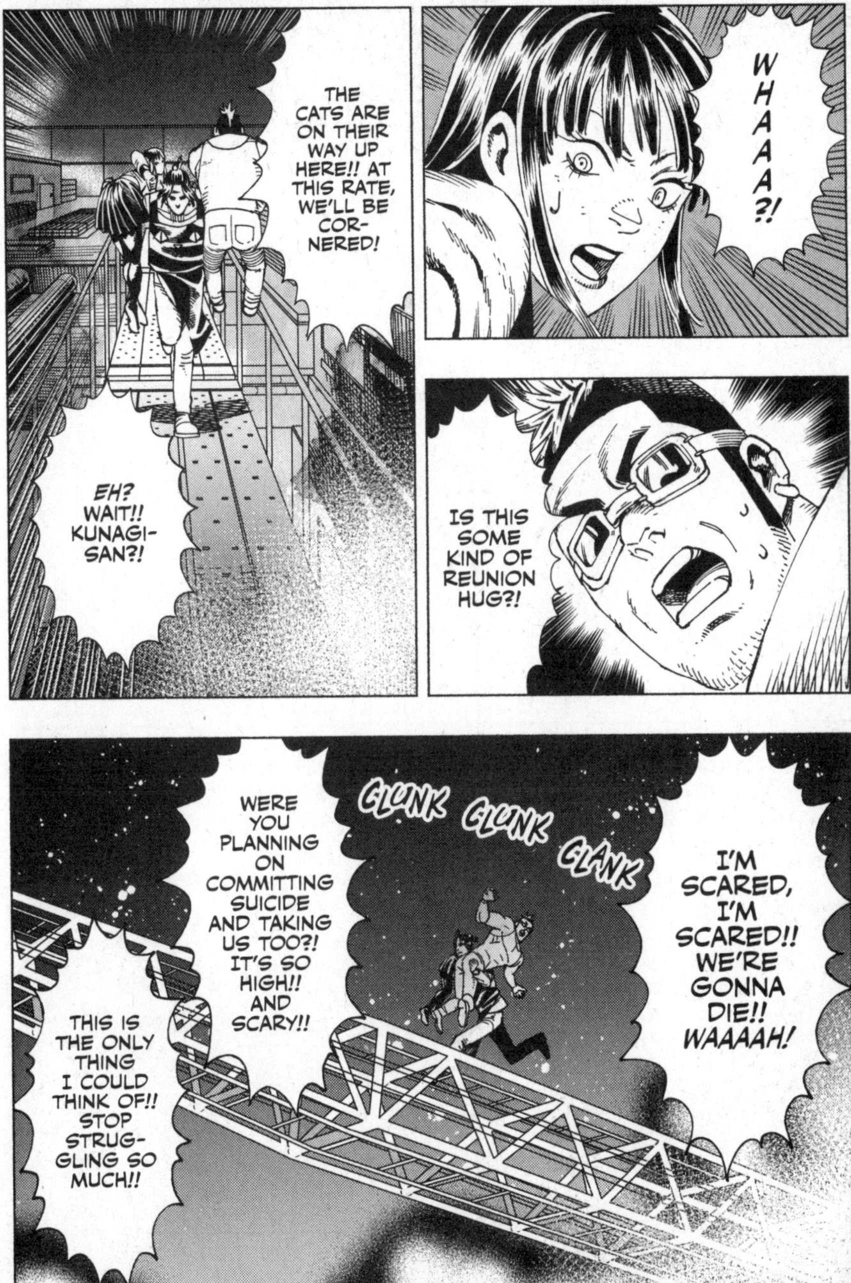
WHAAAA?!
IS THIS SOME KIND OF REUNION HUG?!
THE CATS ARE ON THEIR WAY UP HERE!! AT THIS RATE, WE'LL BE COR-NERED!
EH? WAIT!! KUNAGI-SAN?!
CLANK
CLUNK
CLUNK
I'M SCARED, I'M SCARED!! WE'RE GONNA DIE!! WAAAAH!
WERE YOU PLANNING ON COMMITTING SUICIDE AND TAKING US TOO?! IT'S SO HIGH!! AND SCARY!!
THIS IS THE ONLY THING I COULD THINK OF!! STOP STRUG-GLING SO MUCH!!

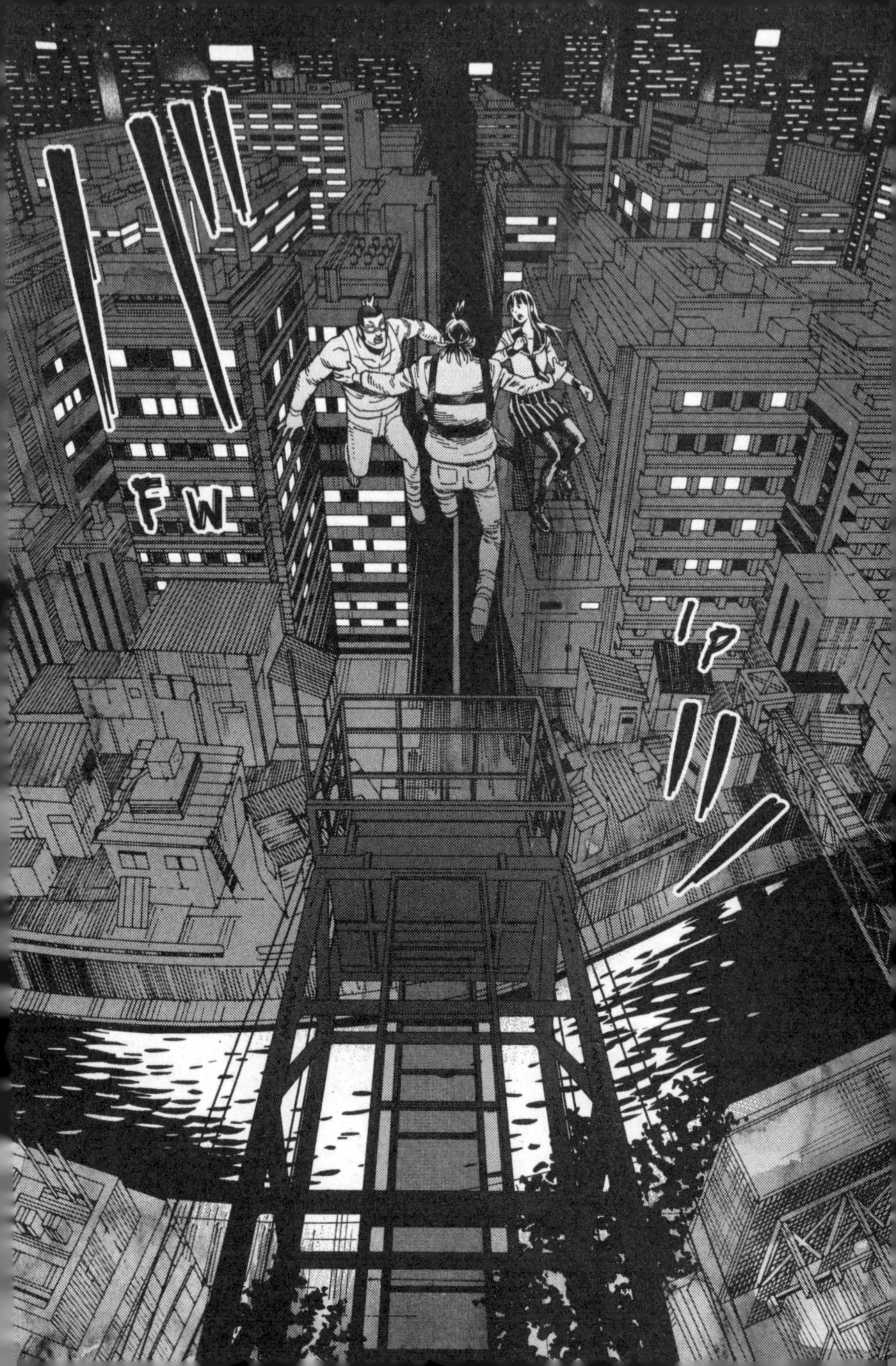
FW
IP

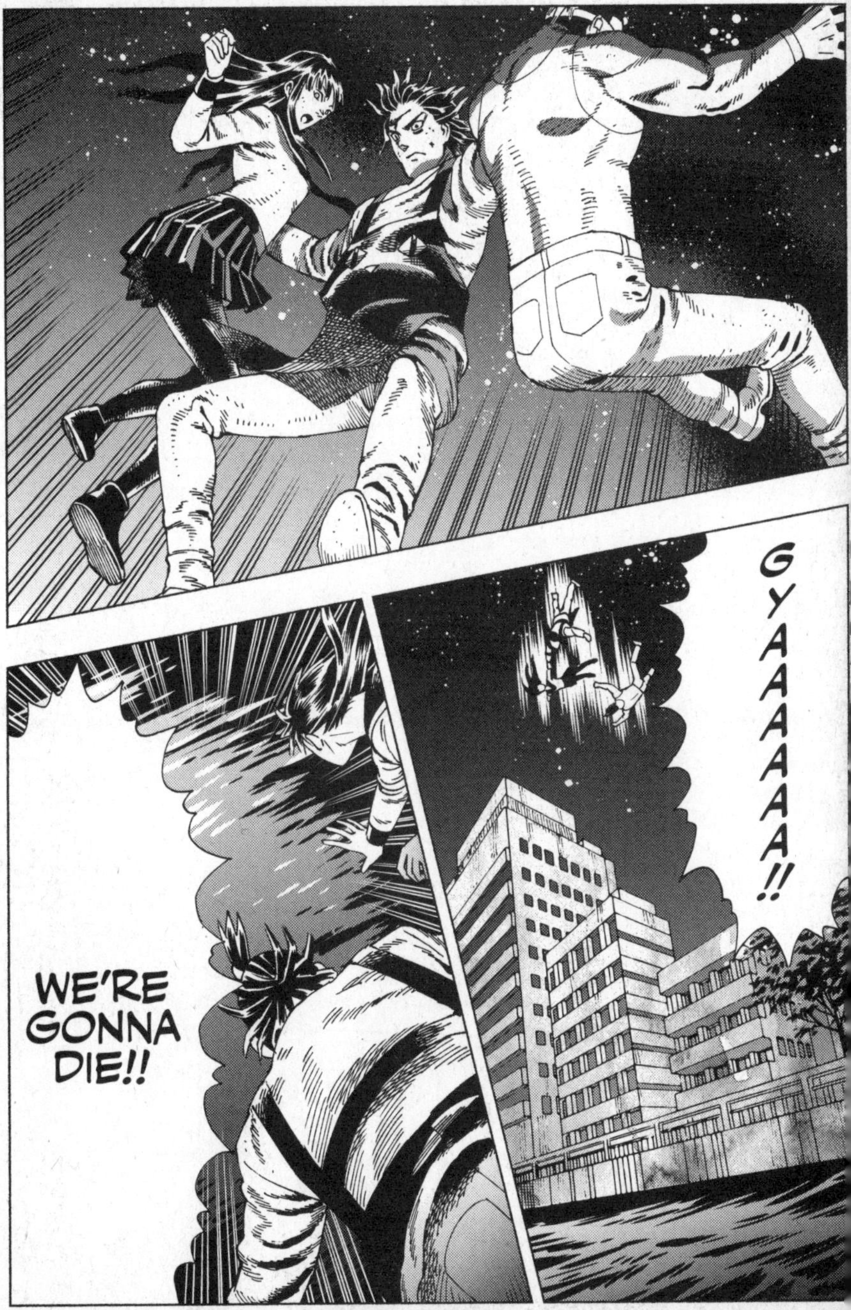

GYAAAAAAA!!
WE'RE GONNA DIE!!

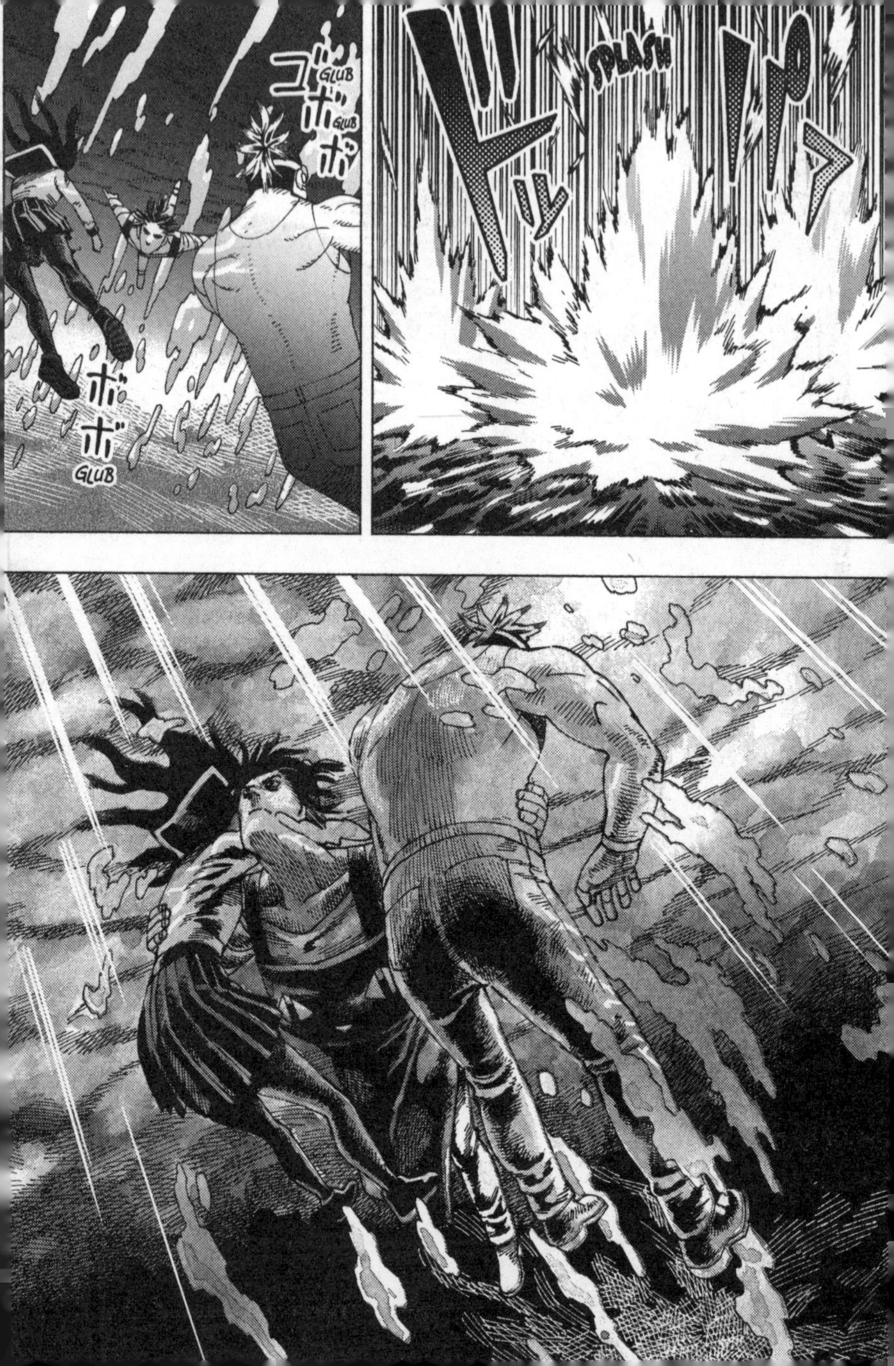

SPLASH
ゴボボ
GLUB GLUB
ボボ
GLUB

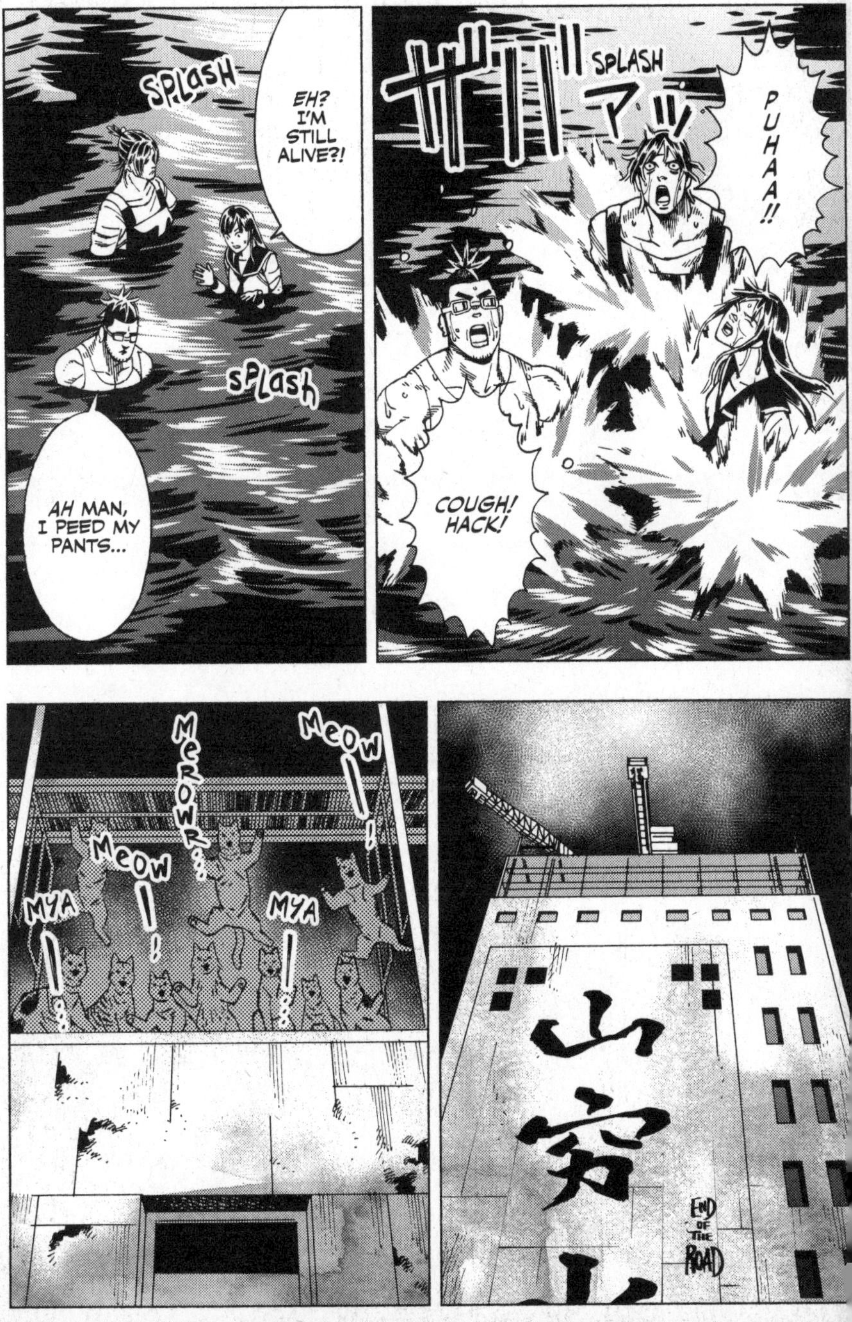
SPLASH
PUHAAA!!
COUGH! HACK!
SPLASH
EH? I'M STILL ALIVE?!
SPLASH
AH MAN, I PEED MY PANTS...
END OF THE ROAD
Meow!
MEROWR...
Meow!
MYA!...
MYA!...

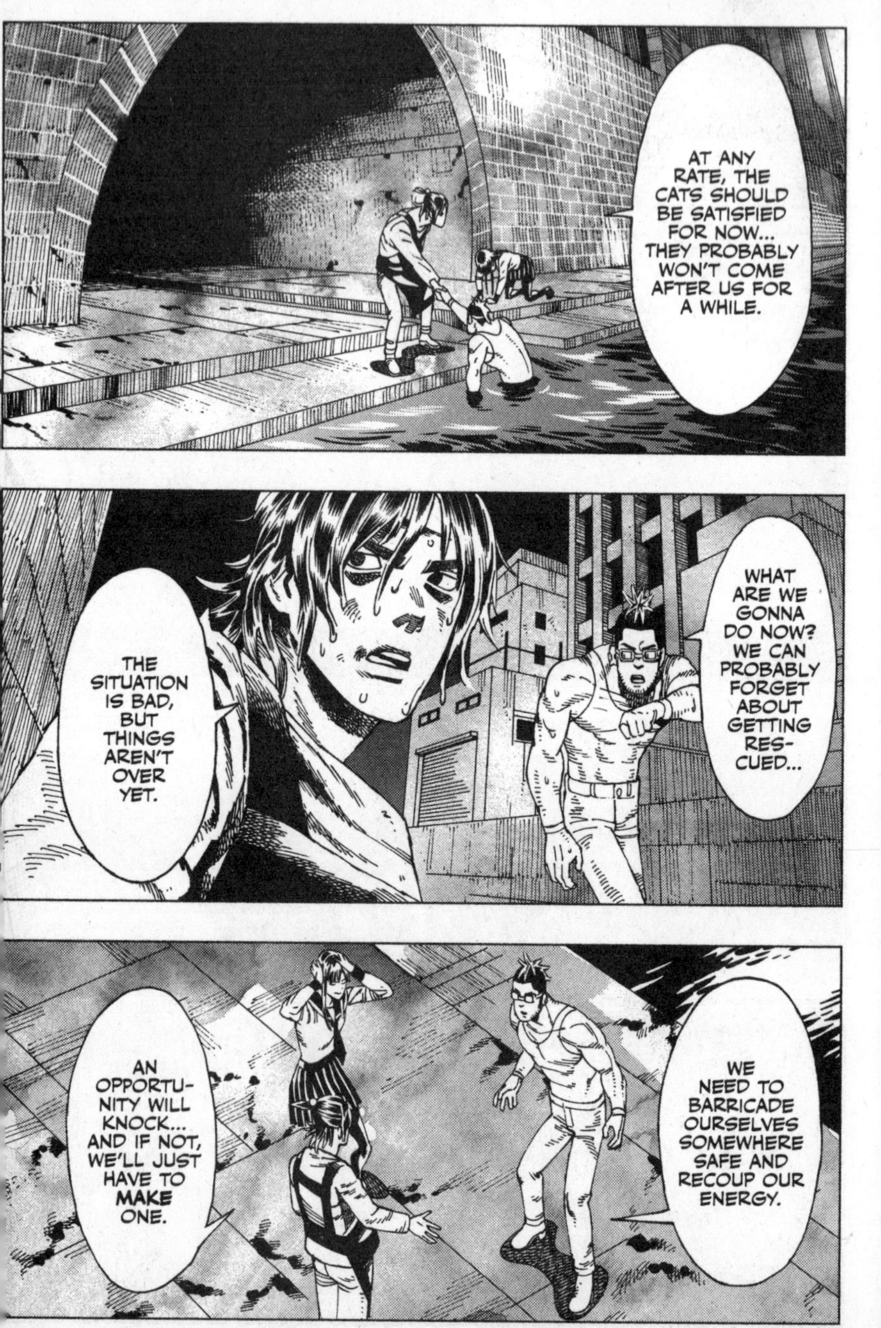
AT ANY RATE, THE CATS SHOULD BE SATISFIED FOR NOW... THEY PROBABLY WON'T COME AFTER US FOR A WHILE.
WHAT ARE WE GONNA DO NOW? WE CAN PROBABLY FORGET ABOUT GETTING RES-CUED...
THE SITUATION IS BAD, BUT THINGS AREN'T OVER YET.
WE NEED TO BARRICADE OURSELVES SOMEWHERE SAFE AND RECOUP OUR ENERGY.
AN OPPORTU-NITY WILL KNOCK... AND IF NOT, WE'LL JUST HAVE TO **MAKE** ONE.

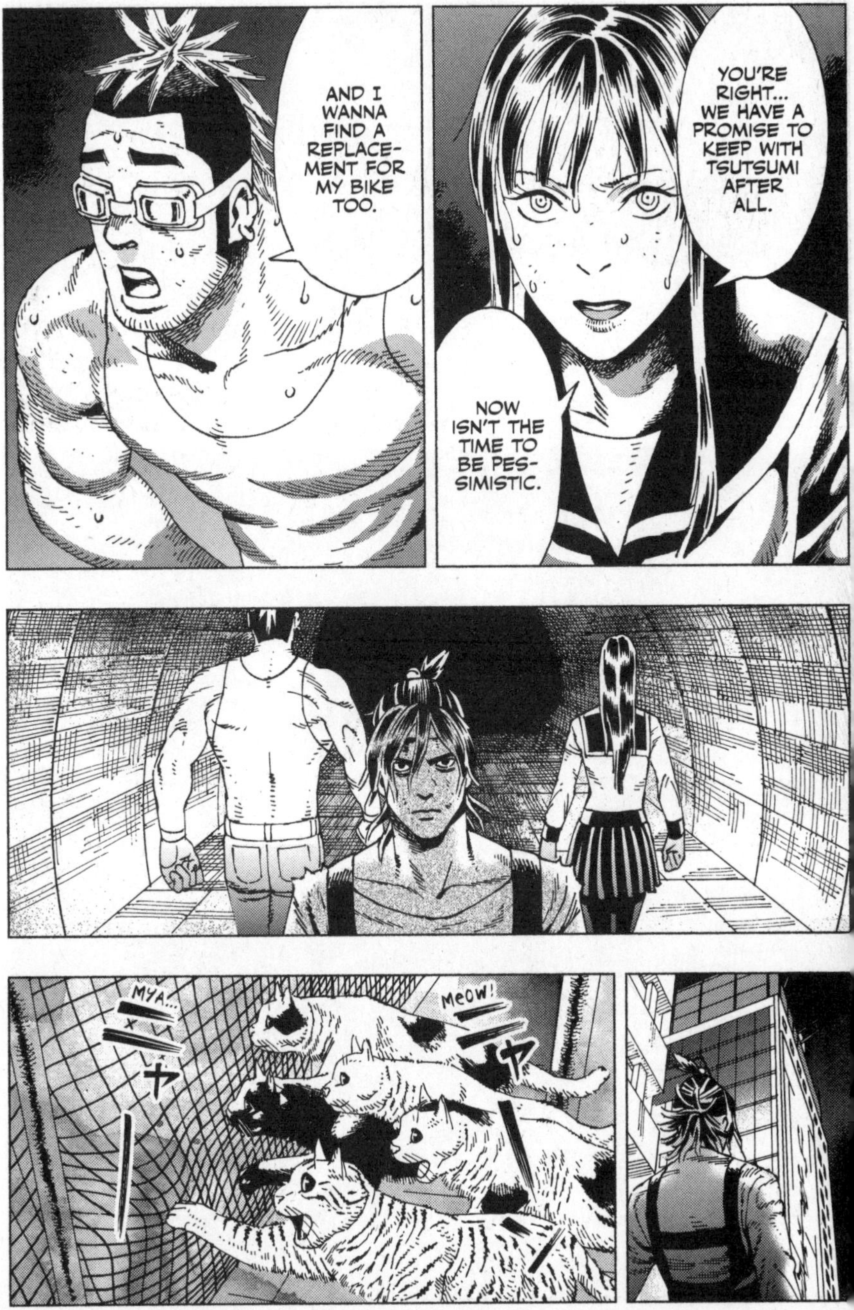
YOU'RE RIGHT... WE HAVE A PROMISE TO KEEP WITH TSUTSUMI AFTER ALL.
NOW ISN'T THE TIME TO BE PES-SIMISTIC.
AND I WANNA FIND A REPLACE-MENT FOR MY BIKE TOO.
MEOW!
MYA...

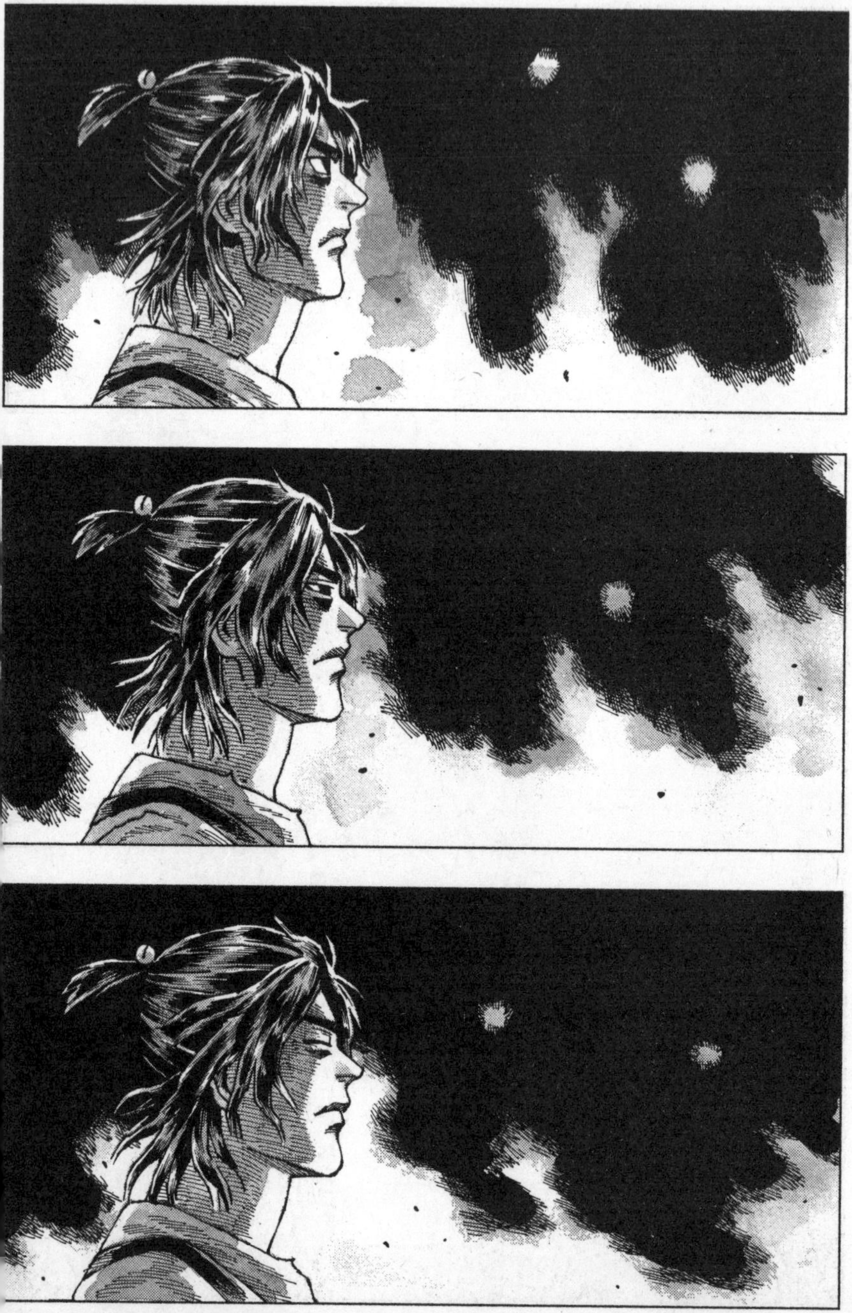

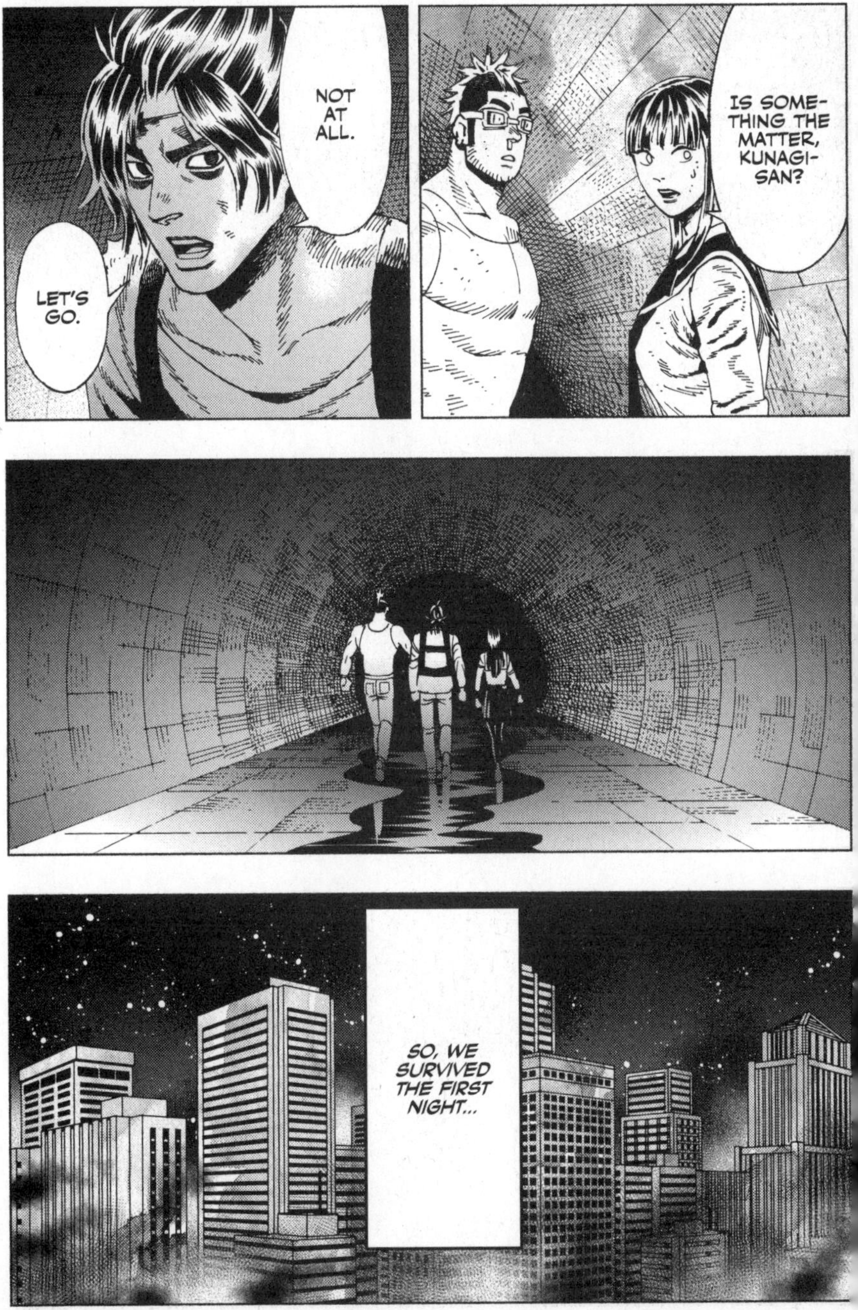
IS SOME-THING THE MATTER, KUNAGI-SAN?
NOT AT ALL.
LET'S GO.
SO, WE SURVIVED THE FIRST NIGHT...

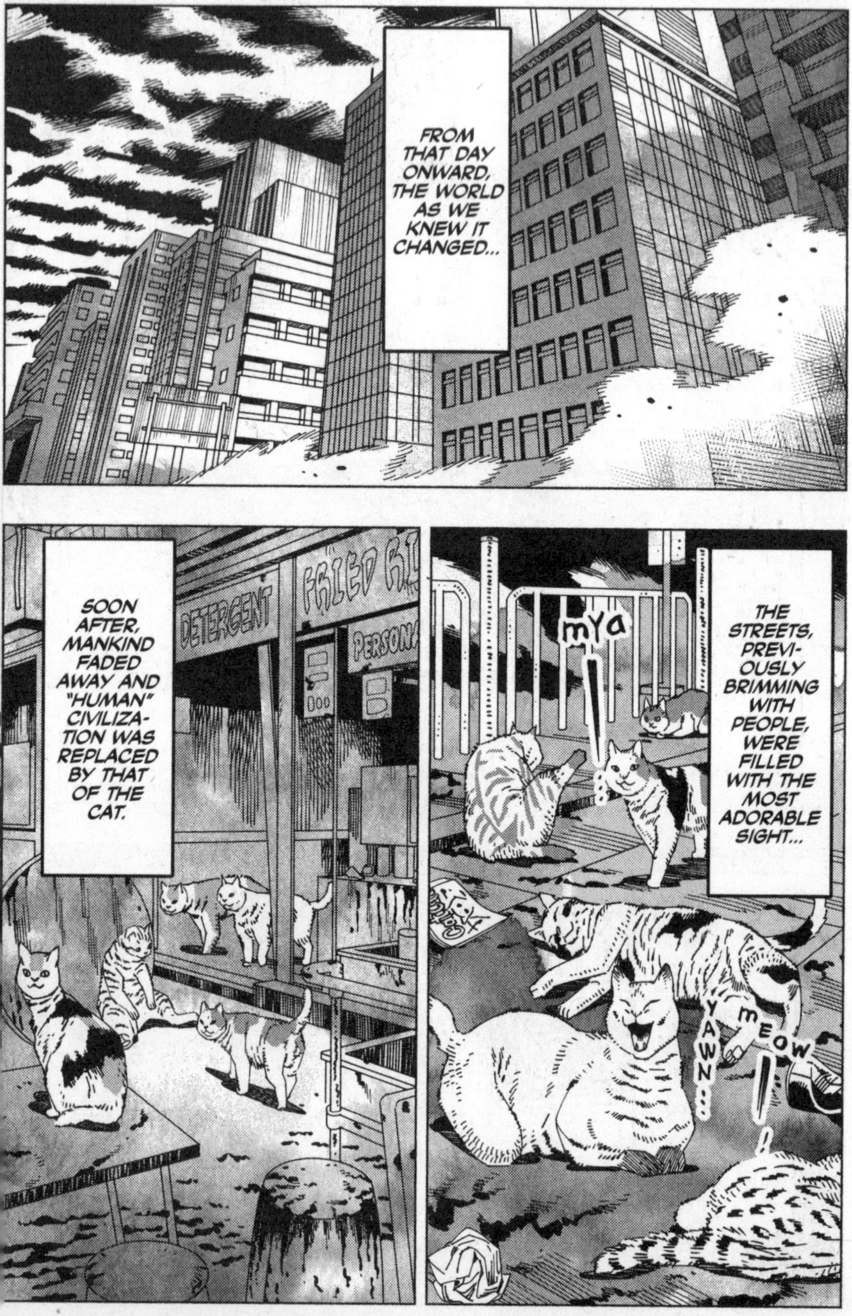
FROM THAT DAY ONWARD, THE WORLD AS WE KNEW IT CHANGED...
THE STREETS, PREVIOUSLY BRIMMING WITH PEOPLE, WERE FILLED WITH THE MOST ADORABLE SIGHT...
mYa
MEOW
YAWN...
SOON AFTER, MANKIND FADED AWAY AND "HUMAN" CIVILIZATION WAS REPLACED BY THAT OF THE CAT.
DETERGENT

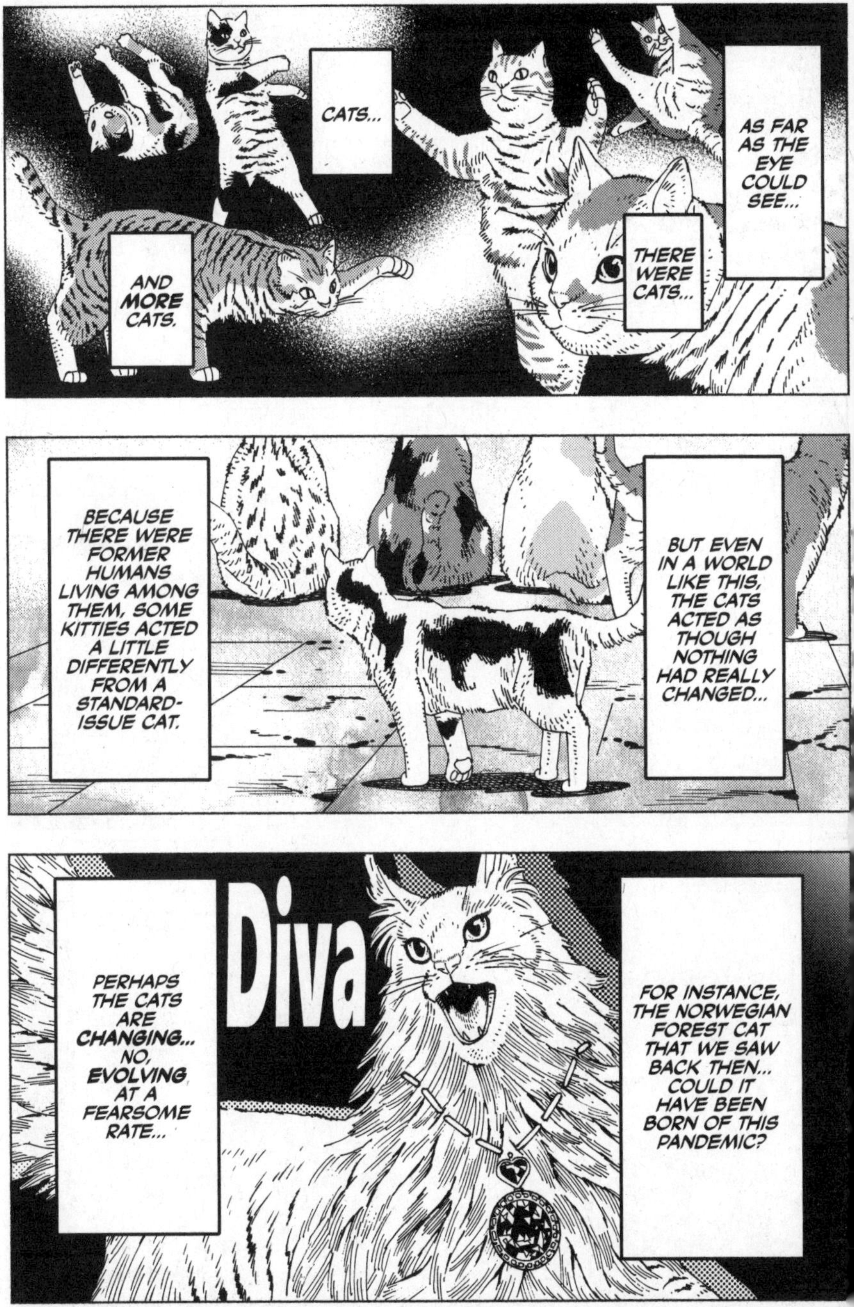
AS FAR AS THE EYE COULD SEE...
THERE WERE CATS...
CATS...
AND MORE CATS.
BUT EVEN IN A WORLD LIKE THIS, THE CATS ACTED AS THOUGH NOTHING HAD REALLY CHANGED...
BECAUSE THERE WERE FORMER HUMANS LIVING AMONG THEM, SOME KITTIES ACTED A LITTLE DIFFERENTLY FROM A STANDARD-ISSUE CAT.
FOR INSTANCE, THE NORWEGIAN FOREST CAT THAT WE SAW BACK THEN... COULD IT HAVE BEEN BORN OF THIS PANDEMIC?
Diva
PERHAPS THE CATS ARE CHANGING... NO, EVOLVING AT A FEARSOME RATE...

WHILE EVADING THE WATCHFUL EYE OF THE CATS, WE FOUND PROVISIONS...

AND GATHERED TOOLS AND EQUIPMENT...

IN PREPARATION FOR OUR ESCAPE.

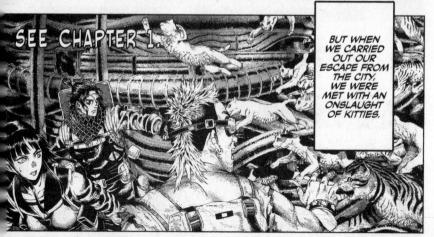

SEE CHAPTER 1.

BUT WHEN WE CARRIED OUT OUR ESCAPE FROM THE CITY, WE WERE MET WITH AN ONSLAUGHT OF KITTIES.

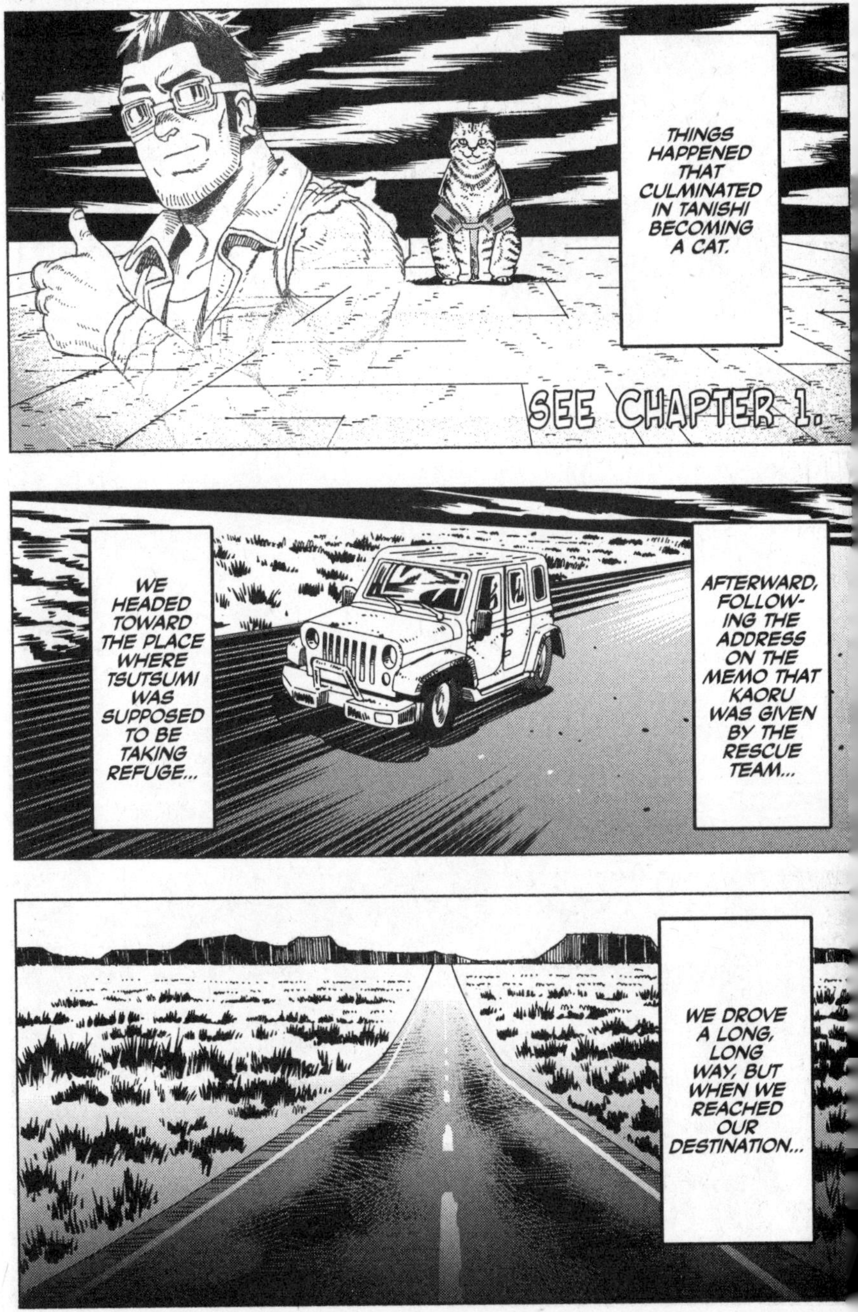
THINGS HAPPENED THAT CULMINATED IN TANISHI BECOMING A CAT.
SEE CHAPTER 1.
AFTERWARD, FOLLOWING THE ADDRESS ON THE MEMO THAT KAORU WAS GIVEN BY THE RESCUE TEAM...
WE HEADED TOWARD THE PLACE WHERE TSUTSUMI WAS SUPPOSED TO BE TAKING REFUGE...
WE DROVE A LONG, LONG WAY, BUT WHEN WE REACHED OUR DESTINATION...

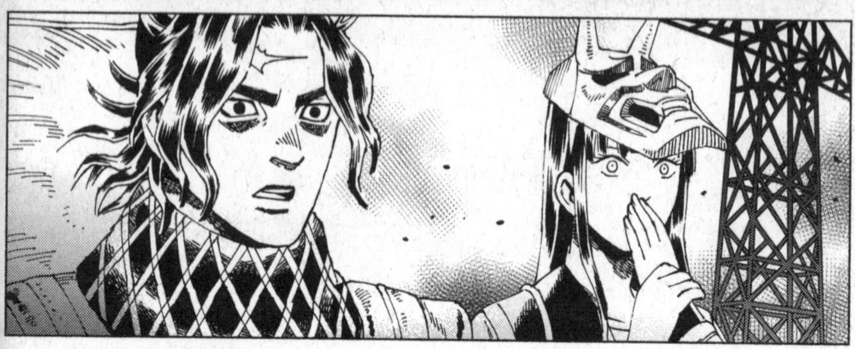

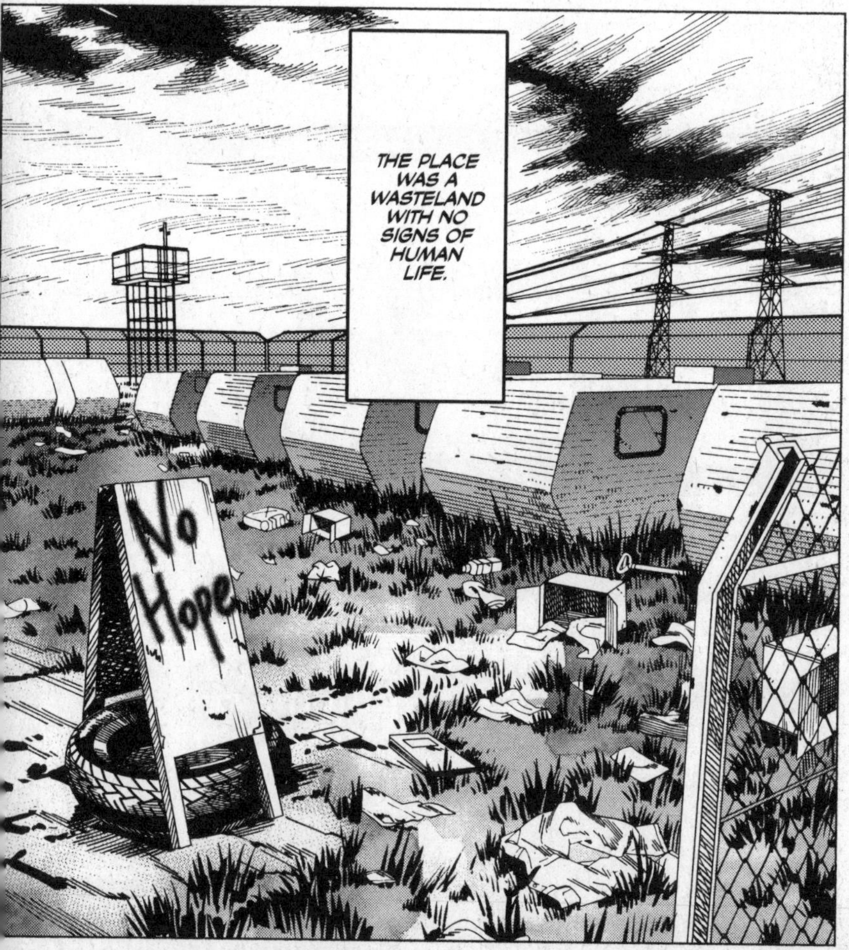
THE PLACE WAS A WASTELAND WITH NO SIGNS OF HUMAN LIFE.
No Hope

A FEW MONTHS LATER
MANKIND HAS FALLEN

To be continued...

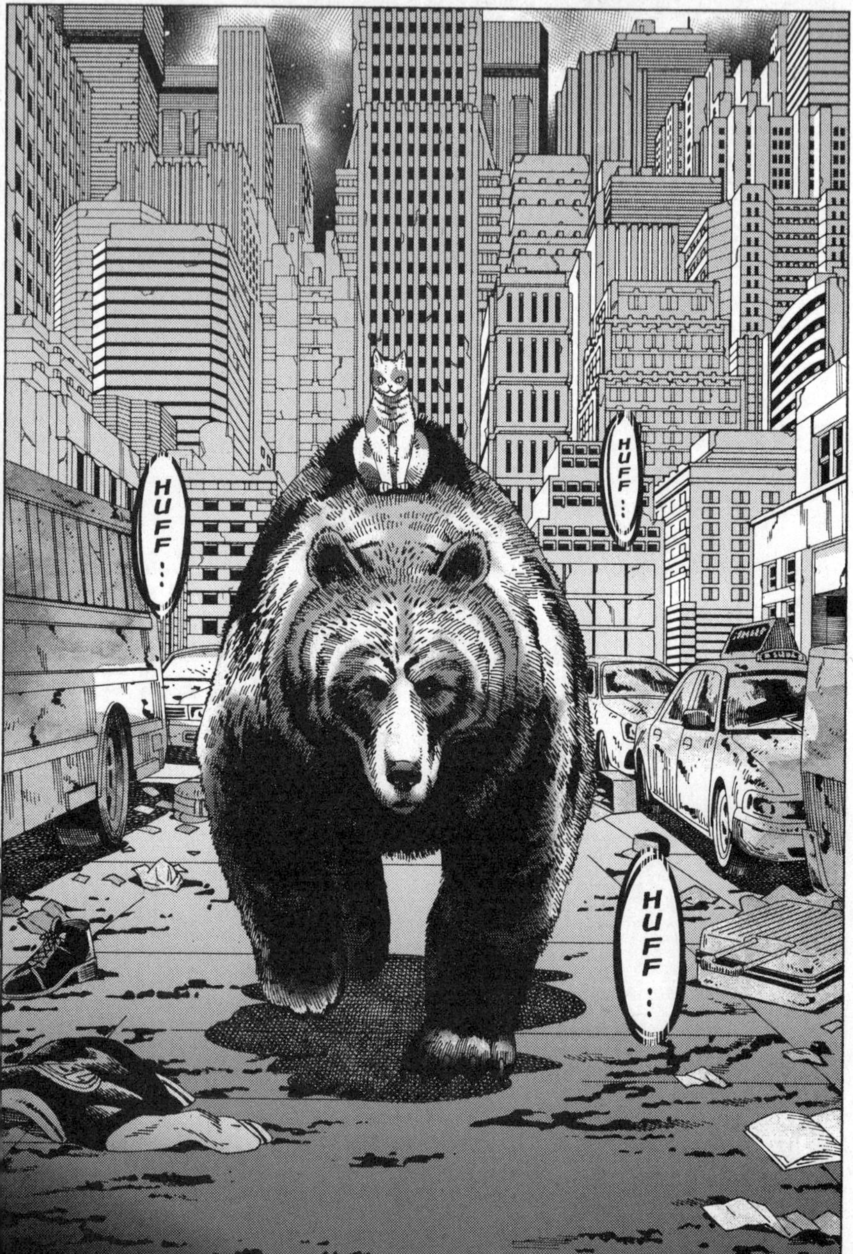
HUFF...
HUFF...
HUFF...

Diva

A cat with an ear-piercing cry that is music to cats and serves to gather them together. A cat's cry has a unique timbre, which allows them to easily do things like toy with humans.

NYAIGHT OF THE LIVING CAT 2

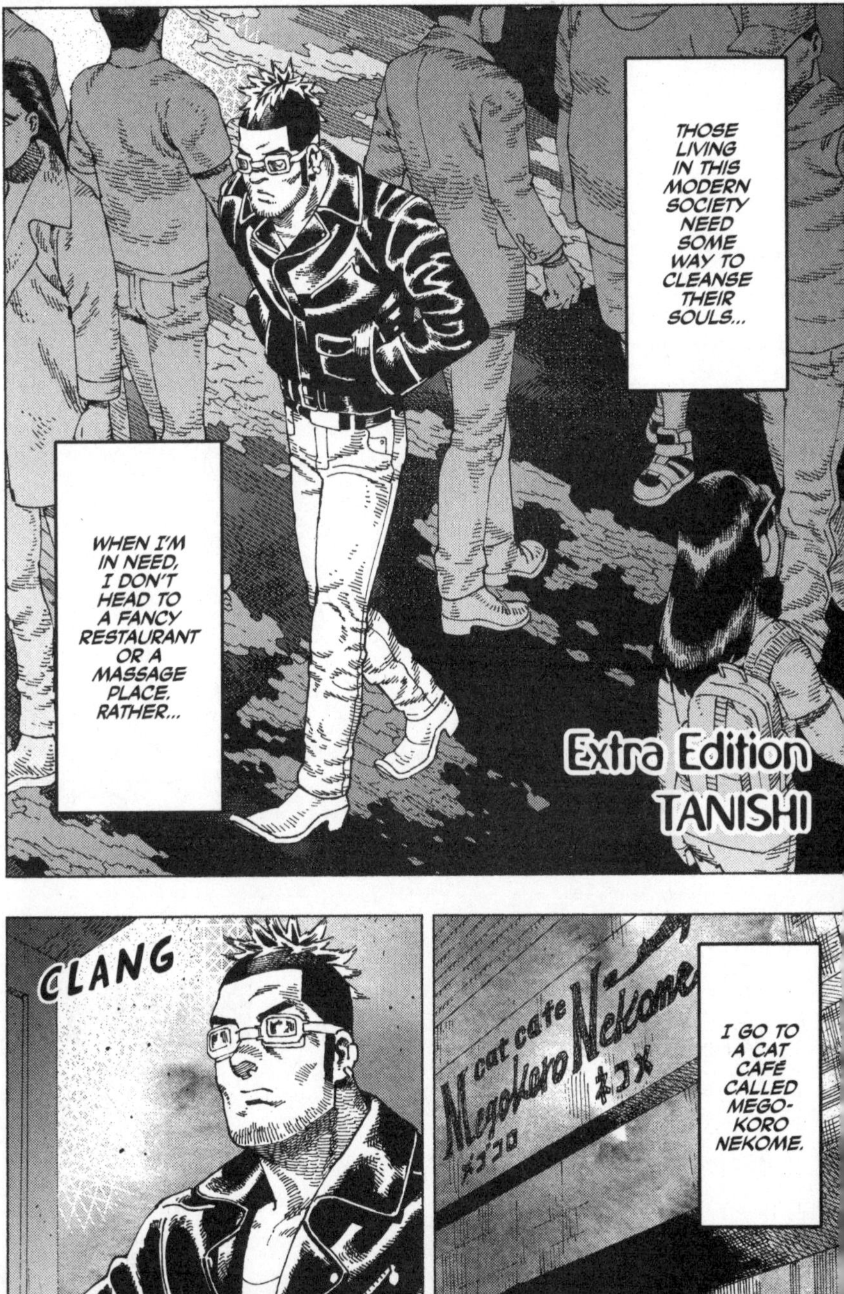
THOSE LIVING IN THIS MODERN SOCIETY NEED SOME WAY TO CLEANSE THEIR SOULS...
WHEN I'M IN NEED, I DON'T HEAD TO A FANCY RESTAURANT OR A MASSAGE PLACE. RATHER...
Extra Edition
TANISHI
cat cafe
Megokoro Nekome
ネコメ
メゴコロ
I GO TO A CAT CAFÉ CALLED MEGO-KORO NEKOME.
CLANG

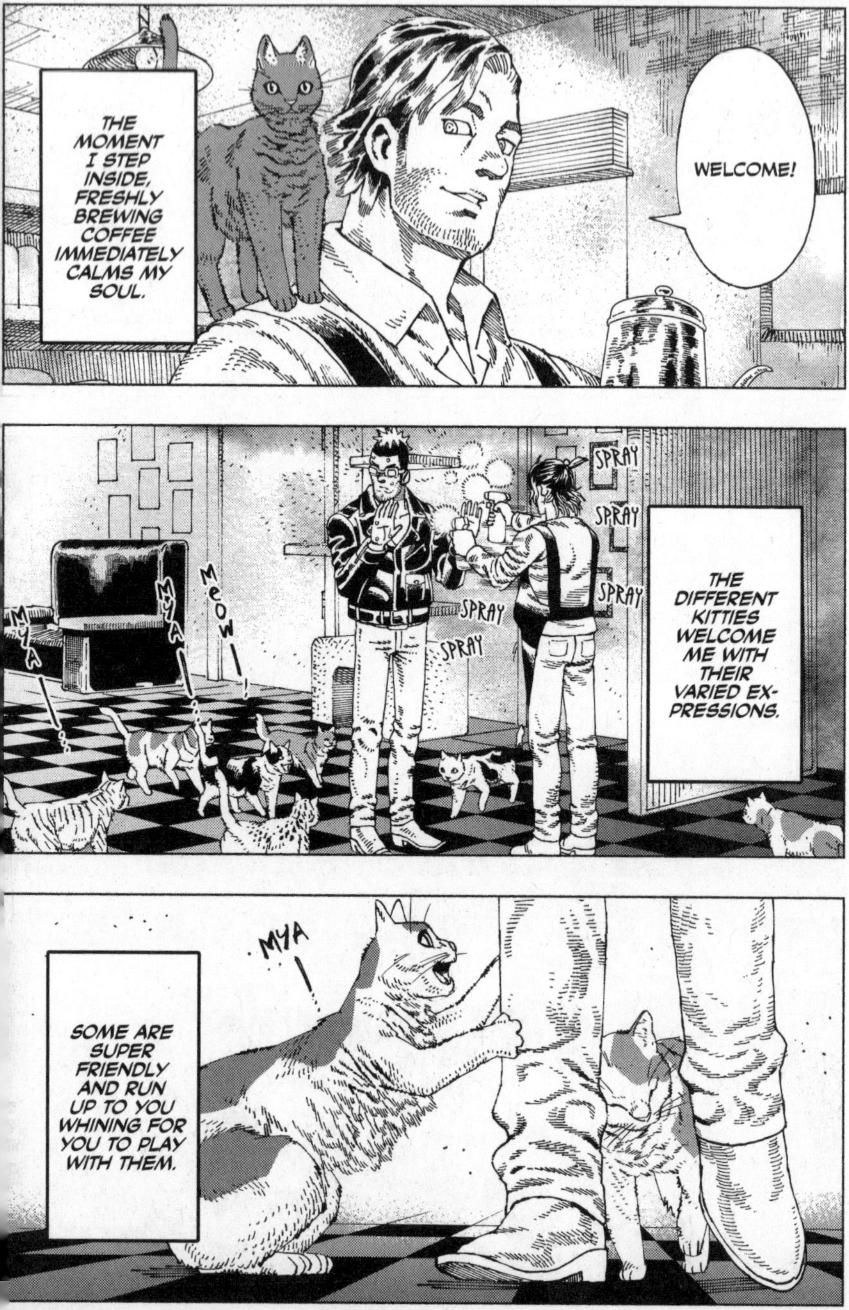
WELCOME!
THE MOMENT I STEP INSIDE, FRESHLY BREWING COFFEE IMMEDIATELY CALMS MY SOUL.
THE DIFFERENT KITTIES WELCOME ME WITH THEIR VARIED EX-PRESSIONS.
SPRAY
SPRAY
SPRAY
SPRAY
SPRAY
MEOW!
MYA!...
MYA!...
MYA!
SOME ARE SUPER FRIENDLY AND RUN UP TO YOU WHINING FOR YOU TO PLAY WITH THEM.

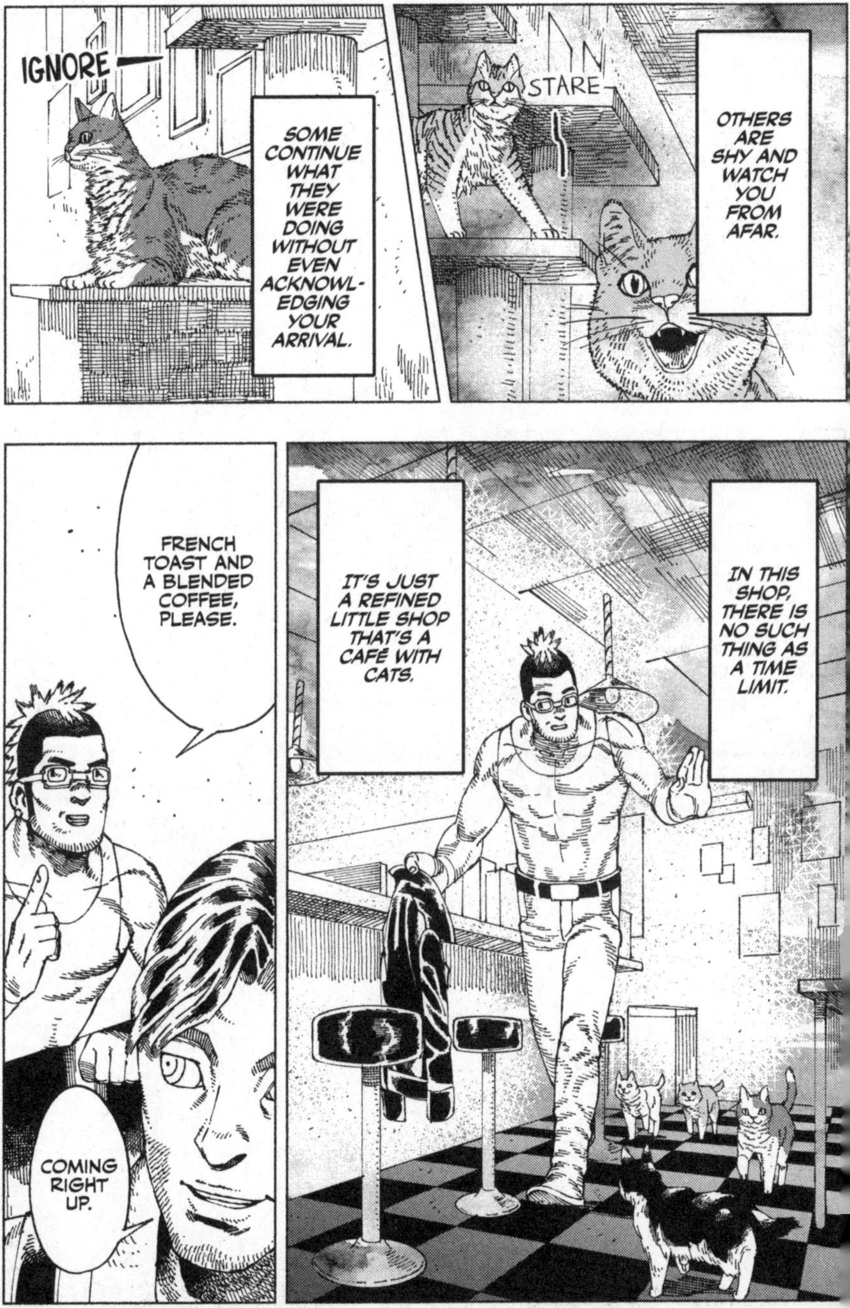
OTHERS ARE SHY AND WATCH YOU FROM AFAR.
STARE
SOME CONTINUE WHAT THEY WERE DOING WITHOUT EVEN ACKNOWL-EDGING YOUR ARRIVAL.
IGNORE
IN THIS SHOP, THERE IS NO SUCH THING AS A TIME LIMIT.
IT'S JUST A REFINED LITTLE SHOP THAT'S A CAFÉ WITH CATS.
FRENCH TOAST AND A BLENDED COFFEE, PLEASE.
COMING RIGHT UP.

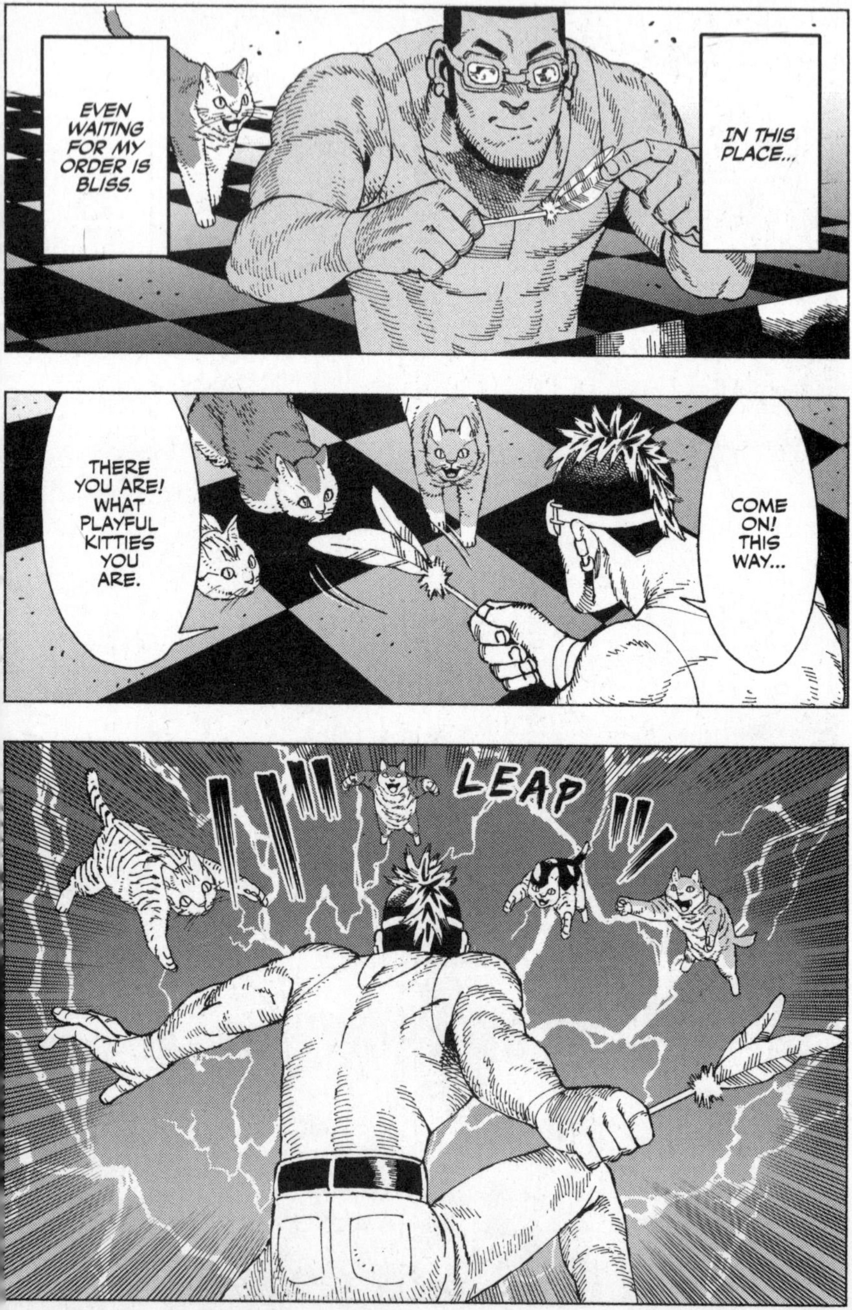
IN THIS PLACE...
EVEN WAITING FOR MY ORDER IS BLISS.
COME ON! THIS WAY...
THERE YOU ARE! WHAT PLAYFUL KITTIES YOU ARE.
LEAP

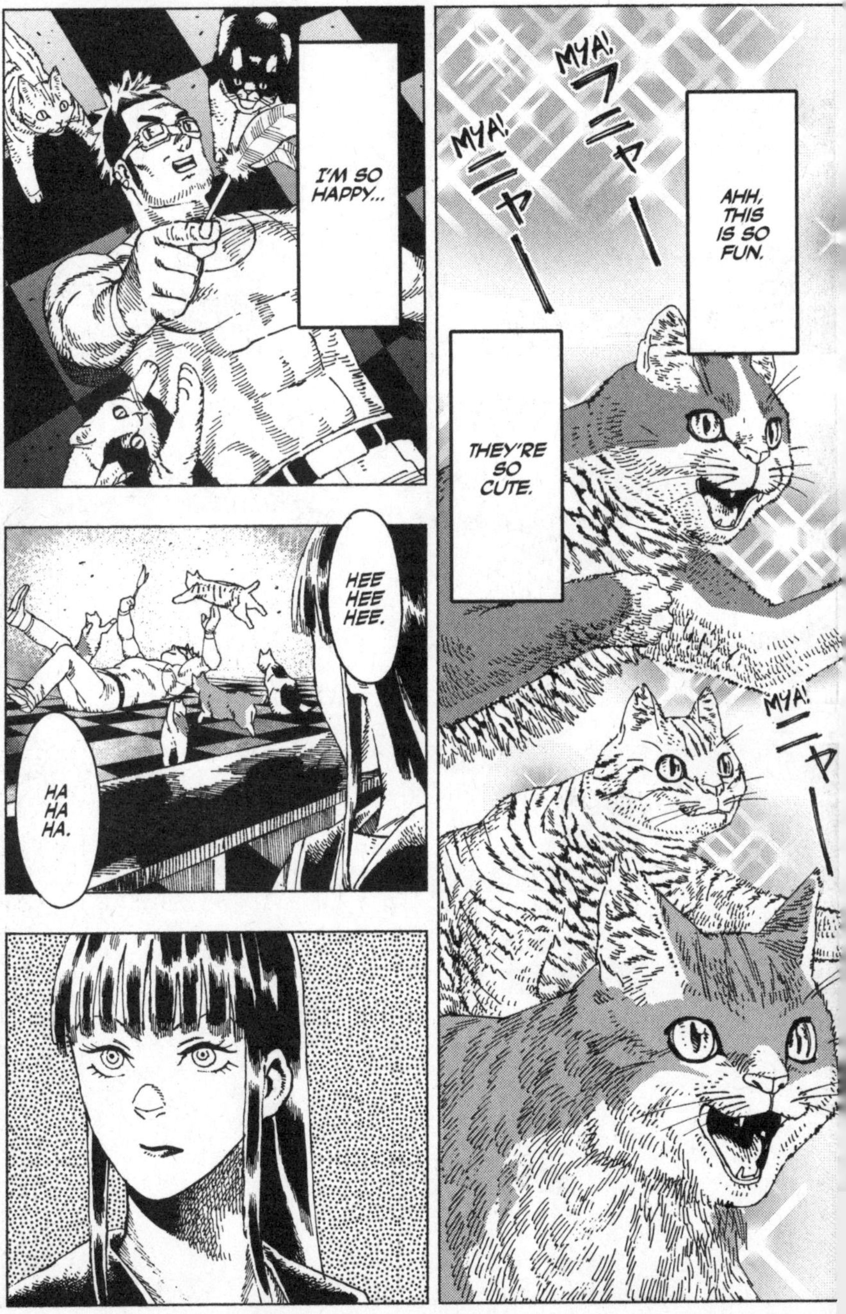
MYA! フニャー
MYA! ニャー
AHH, THIS IS SO FUN.
THEY'RE SO CUTE.
MYA! ニャー
I'M SO HAPPY...
HEE HEE HEE.
HA HA HA.

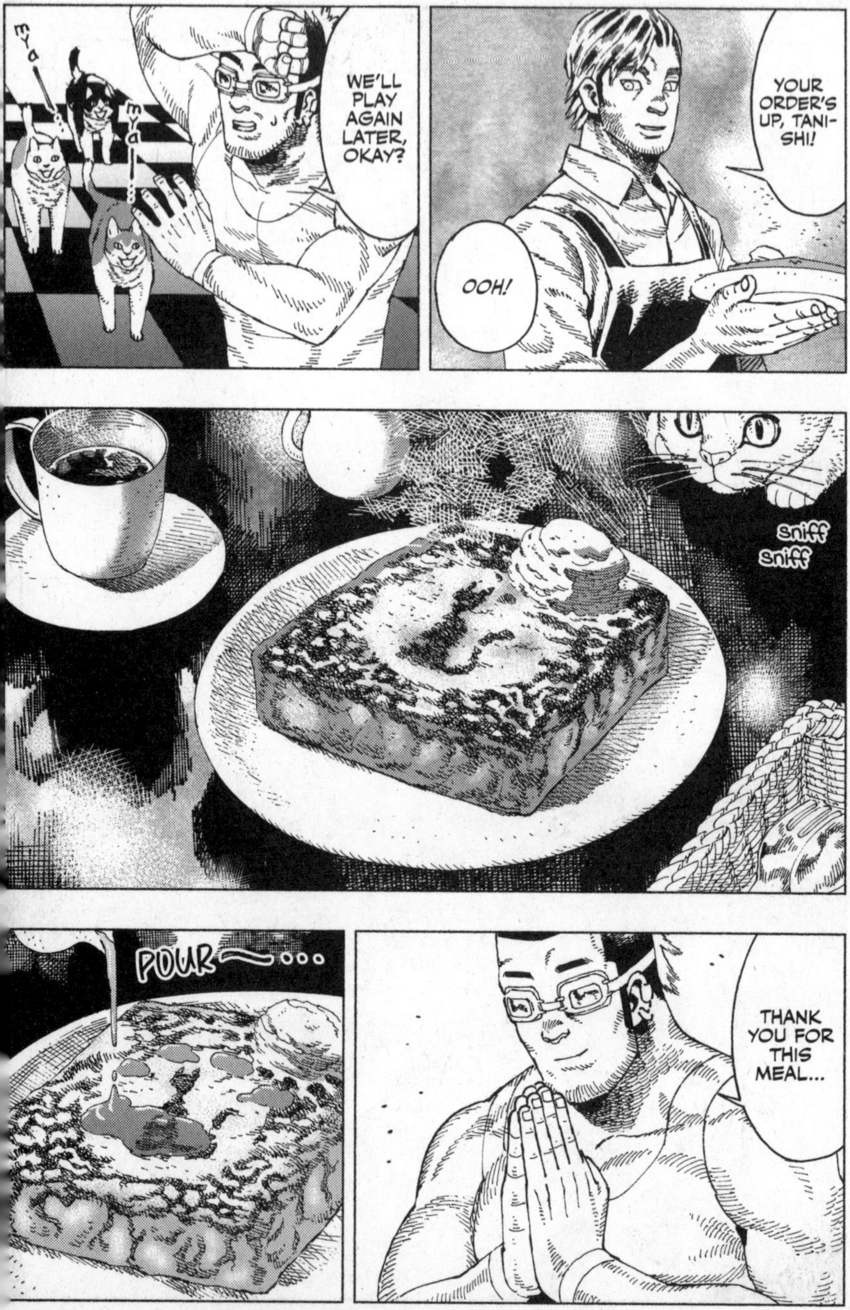
YOUR ORDER'S UP, TANI-SHI!
OOH!
WE'LL PLAY AGAIN LATER, OKAY?
mya
mya
sniff sniff
THANK YOU FOR THIS MEAL...
POUR~...

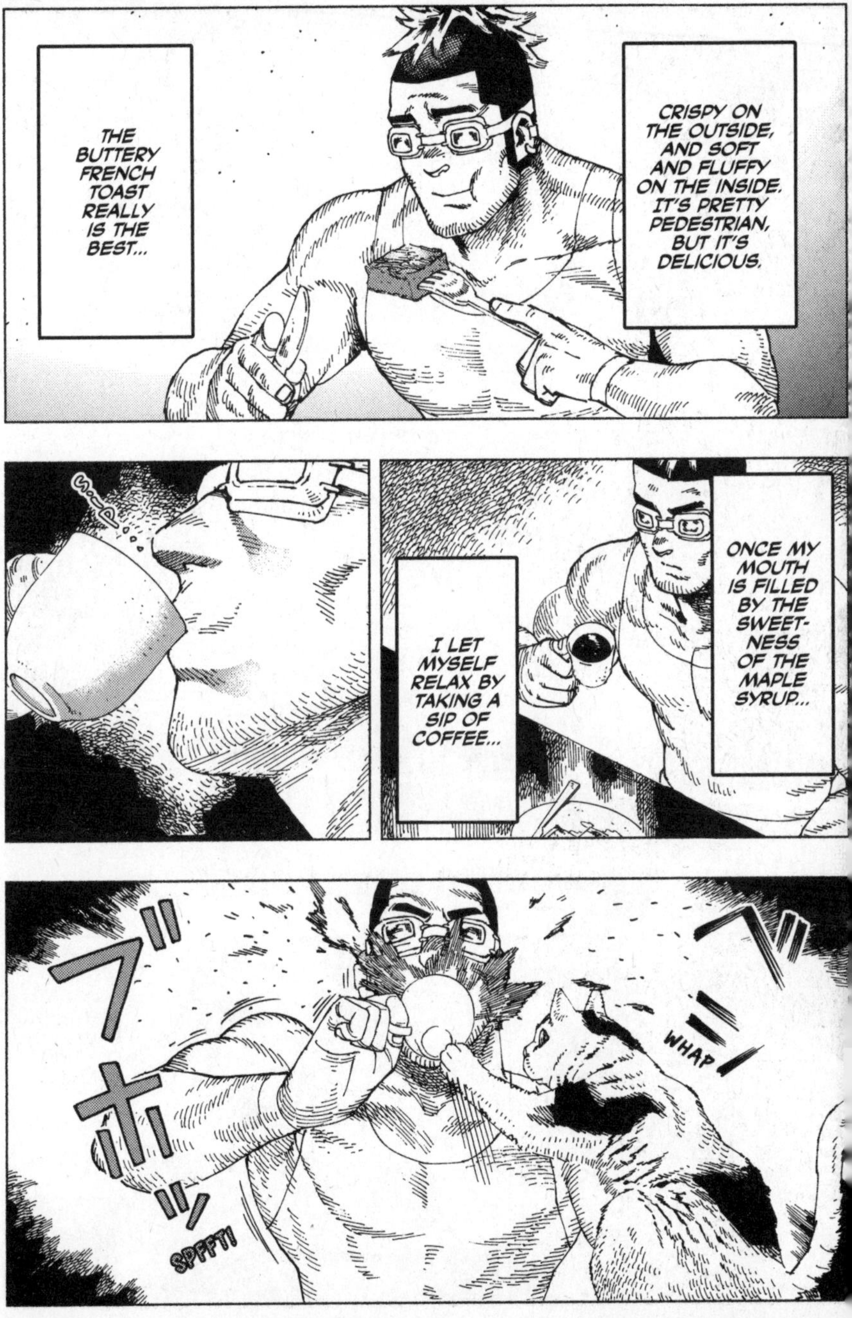
CRISPY ON THE OUTSIDE, AND SOFT AND FLUFFY ON THE INSIDE. IT'S PRETTY PEDESTRIAN, BUT IT'S DELICIOUS.
THE BUTTERY FRENCH TOAST REALLY IS THE BEST...
ONCE MY MOUTH IS FILLED BY THE SWEET-NESS OF THE MAPLE SYRUP...
I LET MYSELF RELAX BY TAKING A SIP OF COFFEE...
WHAP!
SPFFT!

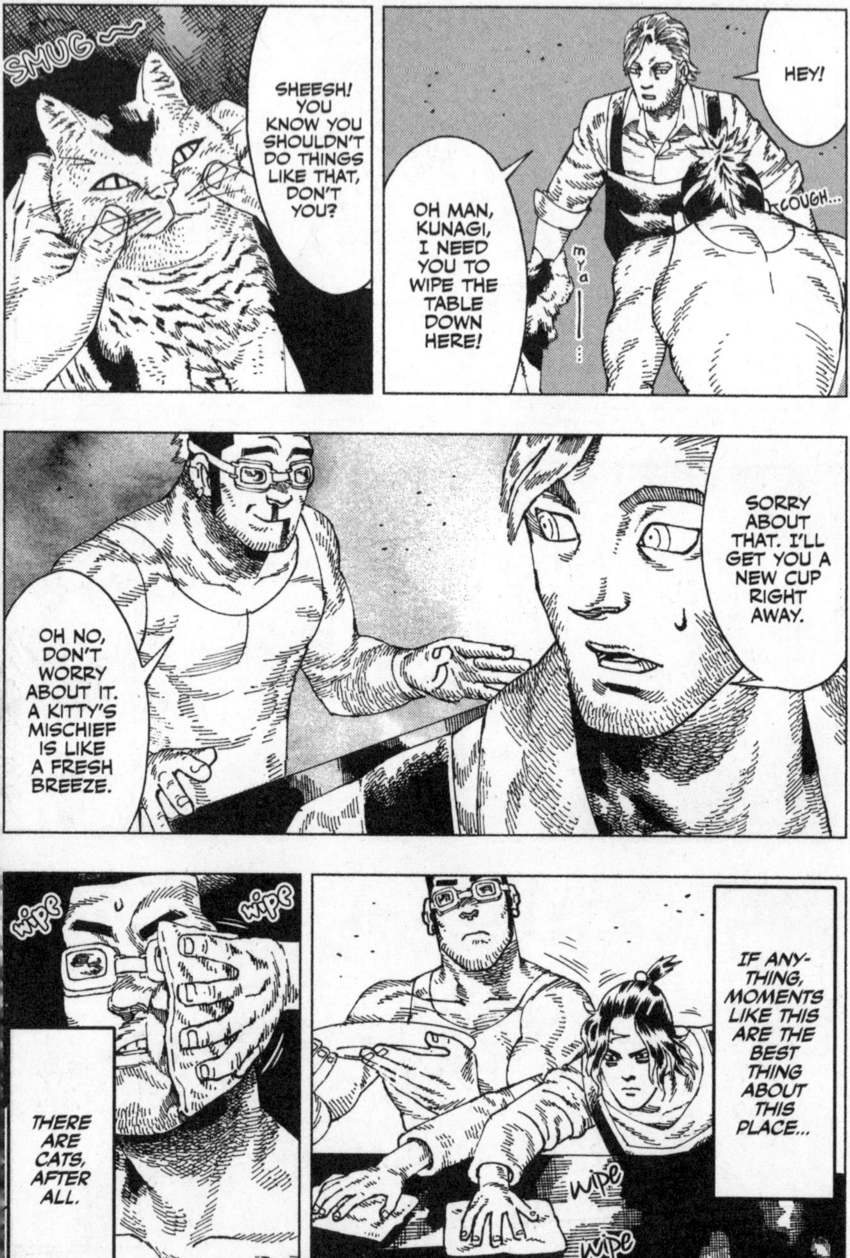
HEY!
OH MAN, KUNAGI, I NEED YOU TO WIPE THE TABLE DOWN HERE!
COUGH...
mya—...
SMUG~
SHEESH! YOU KNOW YOU SHOULDN'T DO THINGS LIKE THAT, DON'T YOU?
SORRY ABOUT THAT. I'LL GET YOU A NEW CUP RIGHT AWAY.
OH NO, DON'T WORRY ABOUT IT. A KITTY'S MISCHIEF IS LIKE A FRESH BREEZE.
IF ANYTHING, MOMENTS LIKE THIS ARE THE BEST THING ABOUT THIS PLACE...
wipe
wipe
wipe
wipe
THERE ARE CATS, AFTER ALL.

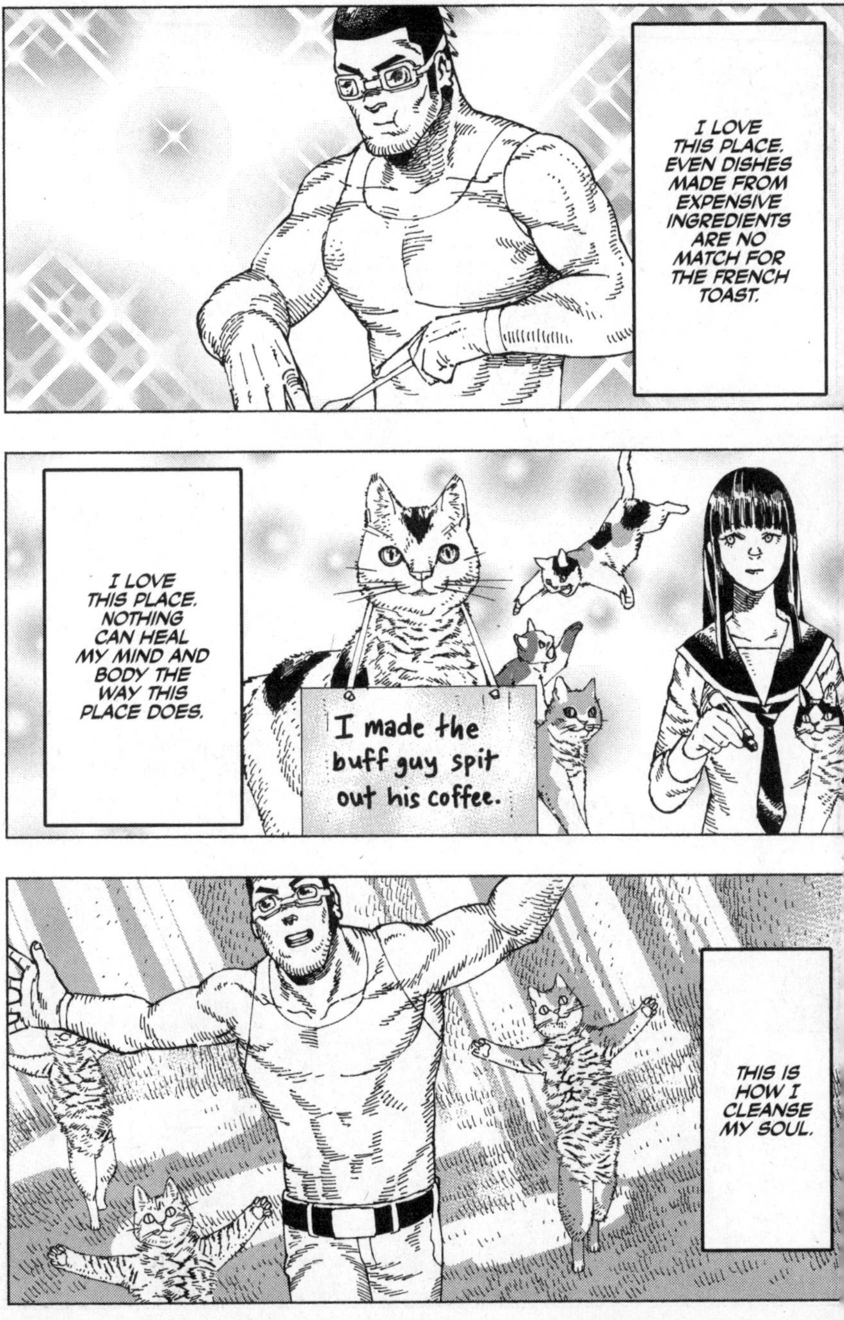
I LOVE THIS PLACE. EVEN DISHES MADE FROM EXPENSIVE INGREDIENTS ARE NO MATCH FOR THE FRENCH TOAST.
I LOVE THIS PLACE. NOTHING CAN HEAL MY MIND AND BODY THE WAY THIS PLACE DOES.
I made the buff guy spit out his coffee.
THIS IS HOW I CLEANSE MY SOUL.

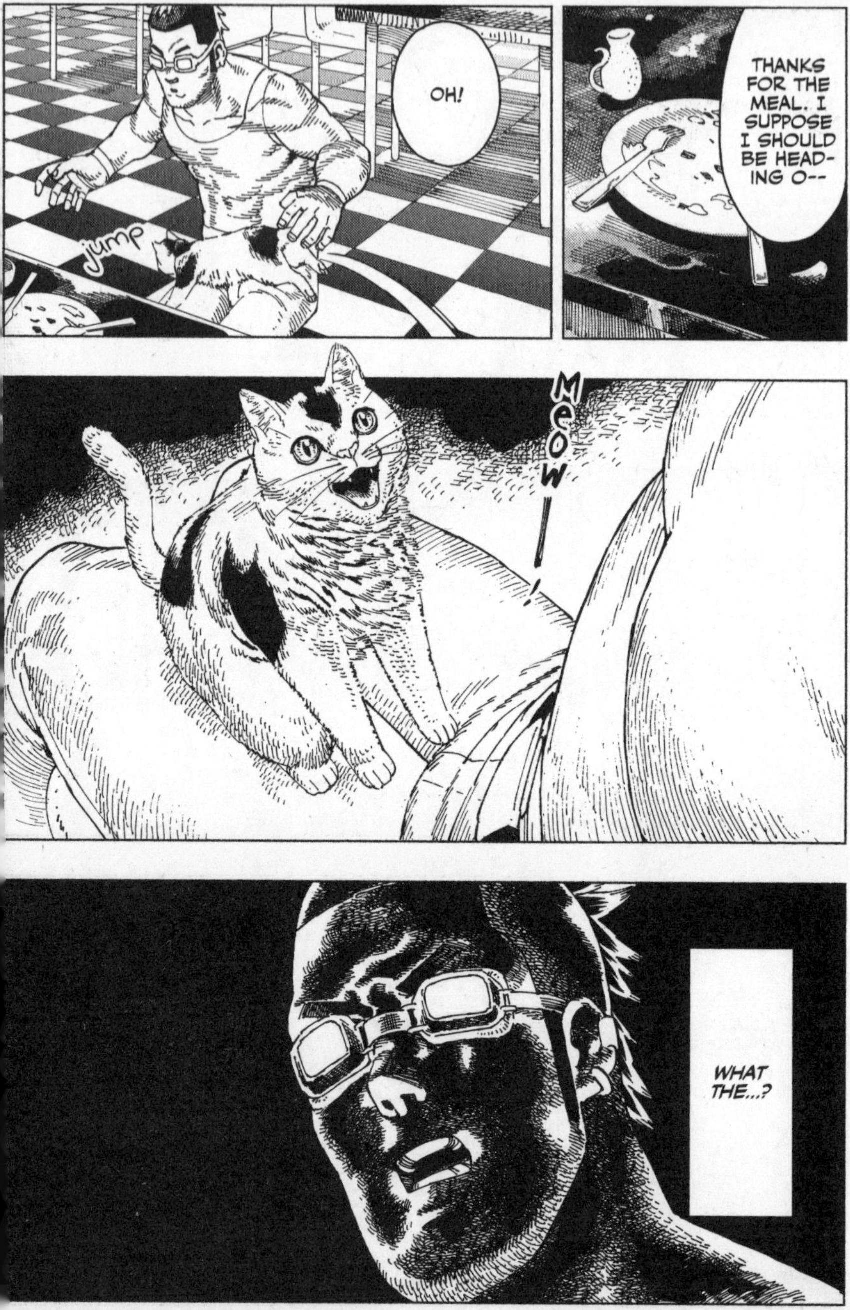
THANKS FOR THE MEAL. I SUPPOSE I SHOULD BE HEAD-ING O--
OH!
jump
MEOW!!
WHAT THE...?

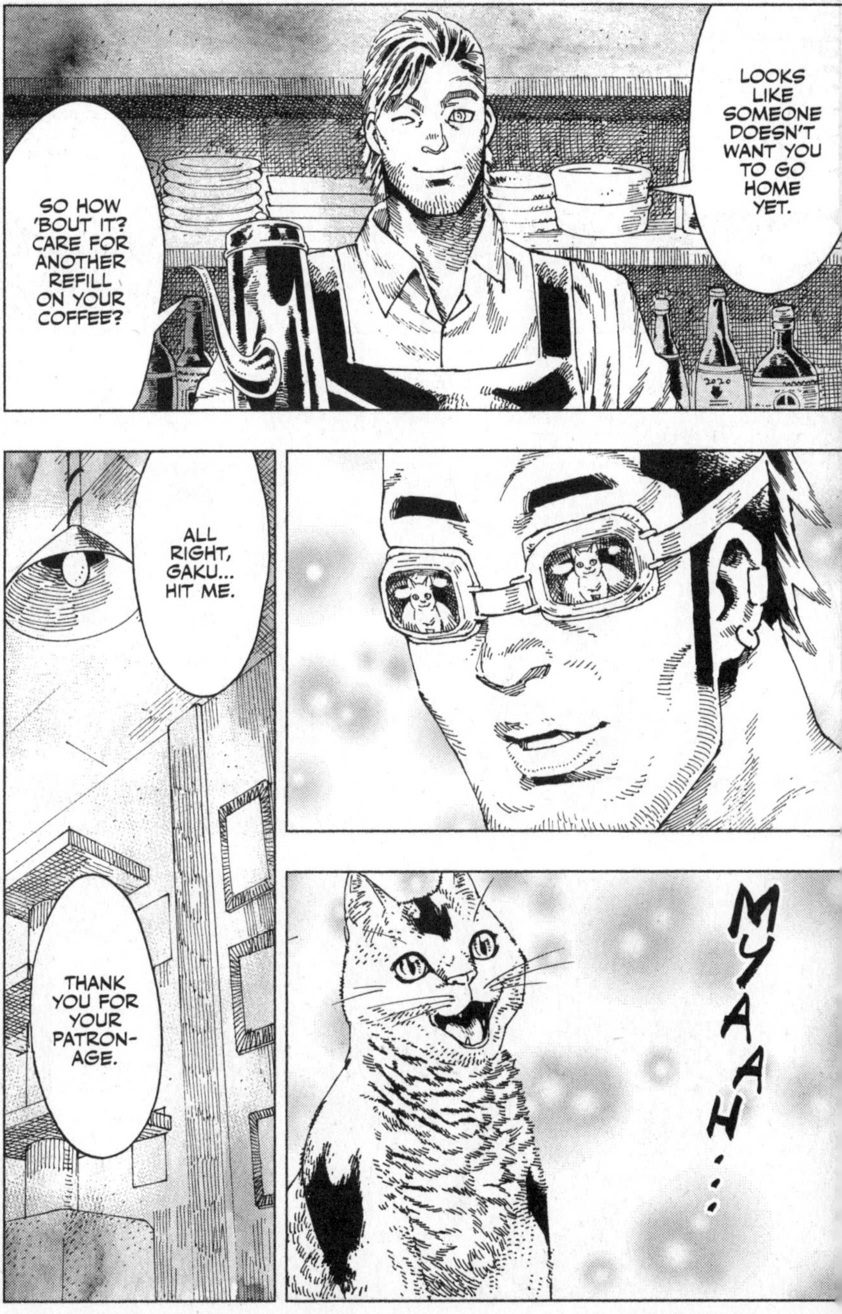
LOOKS LIKE SOMEONE DOESN'T WANT YOU TO GO HOME YET.
SO HOW 'BOUT IT? CARE FOR ANOTHER REFILL ON YOUR COFFEE?
MYAAH...
ALL RIGHT, GAKU... HIT ME.
THANK YOU FOR YOUR PATRON-AGE.

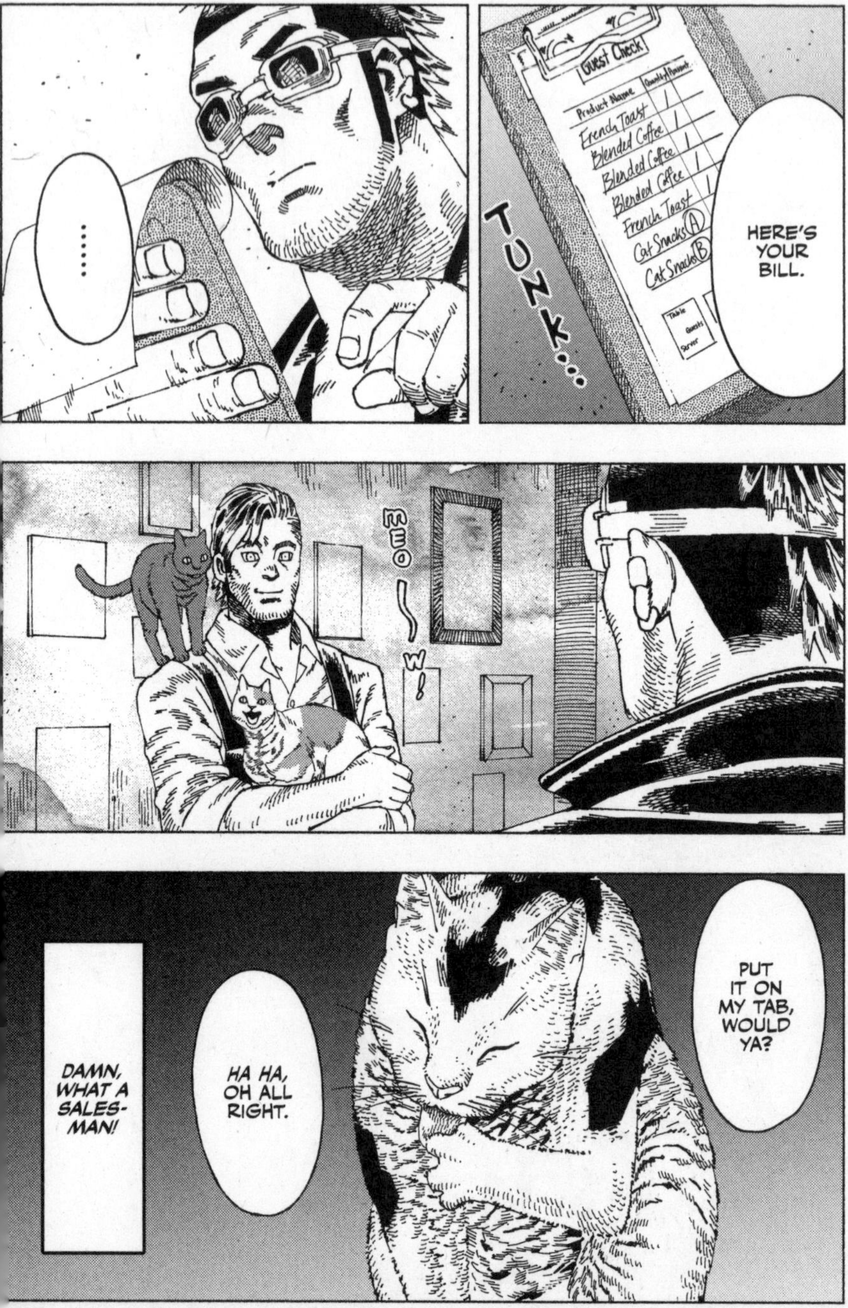
HERE'S YOUR BILL.
TUNK...
Guest Check
Product Name
French Toast
Blended Coffee
Blended Coffee
Blended Coffee
French Toast
Cat Snacks (A)
Cat Snacks (B)
Table
Guests
Server
......
MEO~~W!
PUT IT ON MY TAB, WOULD YA?
HA HA, OH ALL RIGHT.
DAMN, WHAT A SALES-MAN!

Aura

A giant mass of cat energy from hundreds upon thousands of cats that gathered and converged. Not just *a* cat, but all cats at once. Effortlessly surpasses the realm of mere human potential.

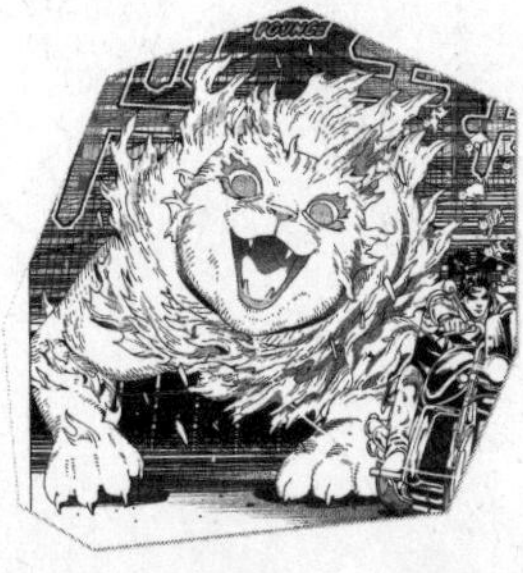
POUNCE

Extra 1: Before/After

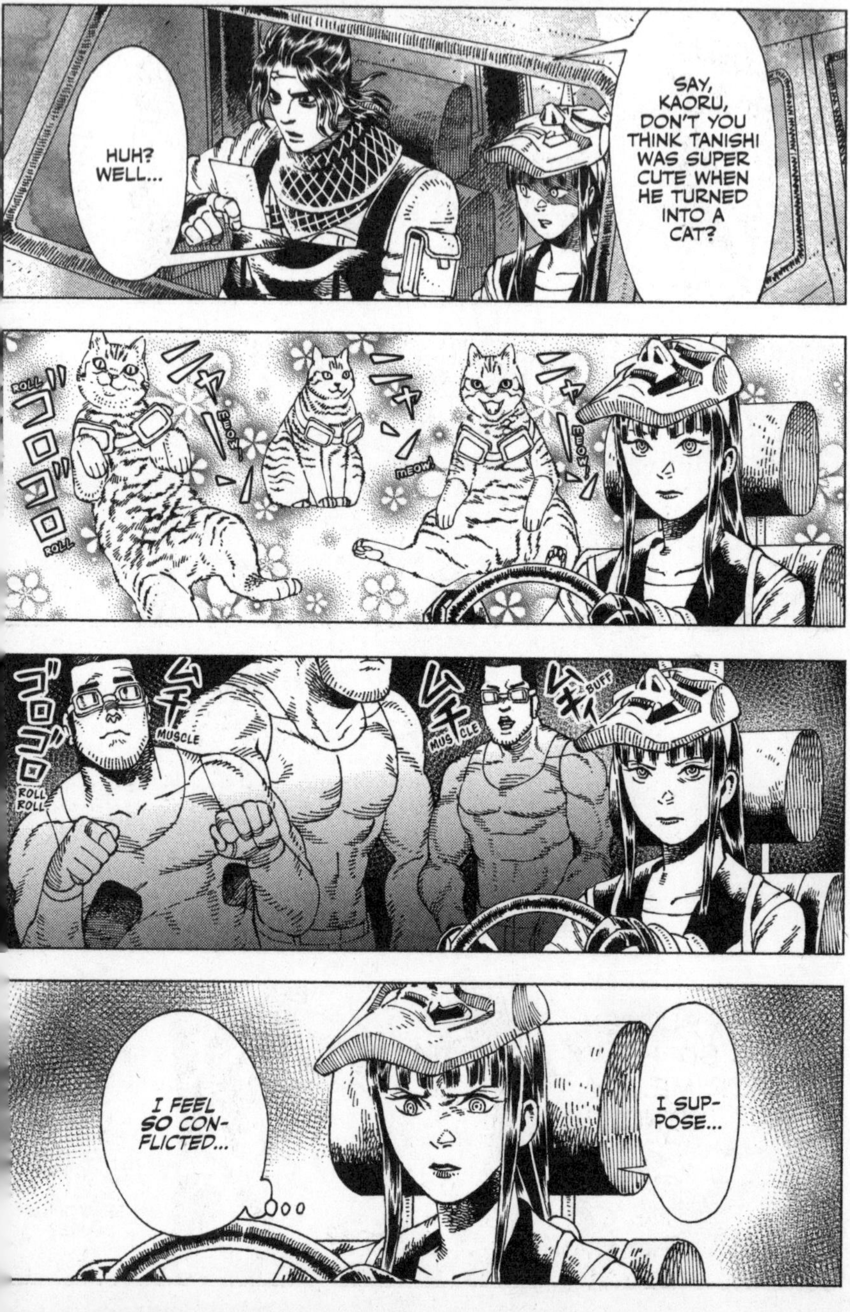

SAY, KAORU, DON'T YOU THINK TANISHI WAS SUPER CUTE WHEN HE TURNED INTO A CAT?
HUH? WELL...
MEOW
MEOW!
MEOW
ROLL ROLL
BUFF
MUSCLE
MUSCLE
ROLL ROLL
I SUP-POSE...
I FEEL SO CON-FLICTED...

Extra 2: Your Name

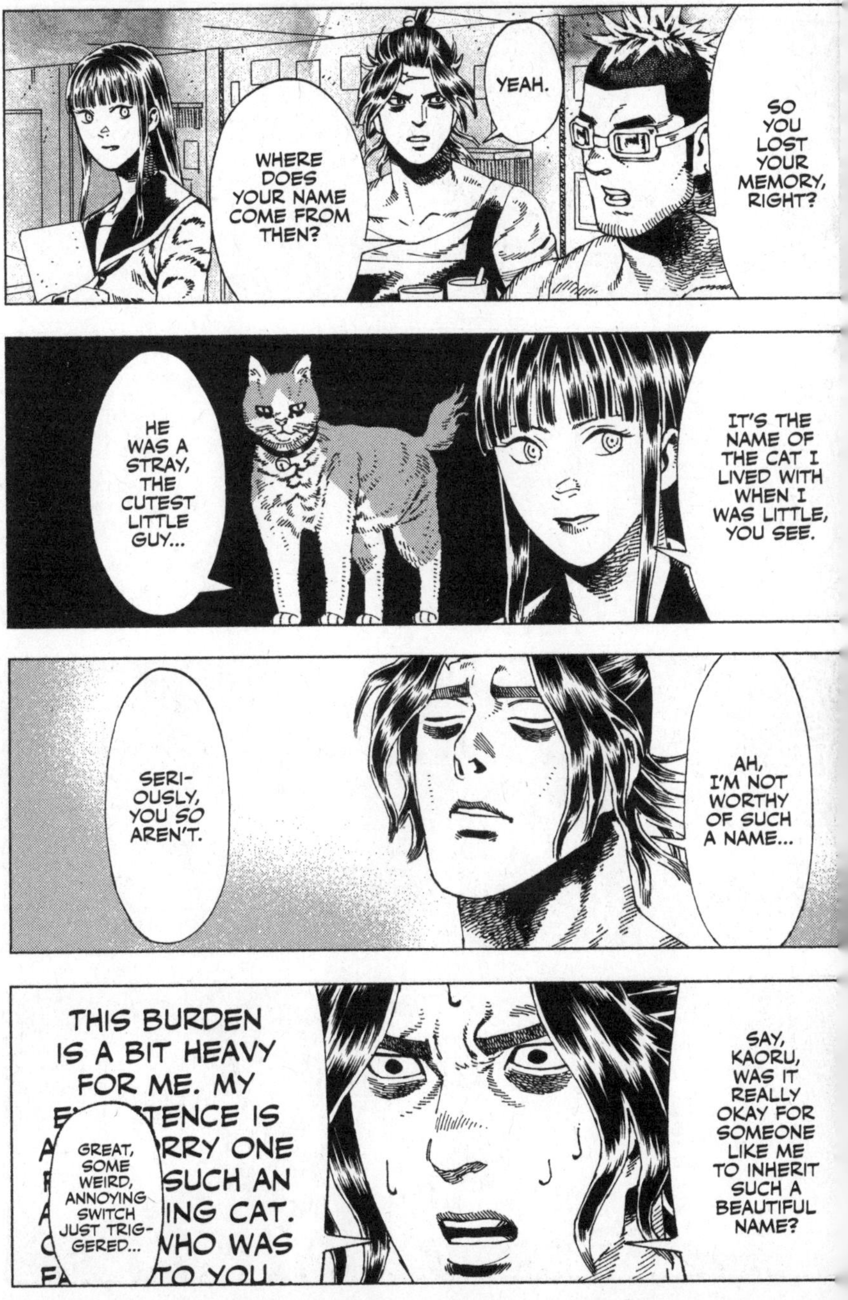
SO YOU LOST YOUR MEMORY, RIGHT?
YEAH.
WHERE DOES YOUR NAME COME FROM THEN?
IT'S THE NAME OF THE CAT I LIVED WITH WHEN I WAS LITTLE, YOU SEE.
HE WAS A STRAY, THE CUTEST LITTLE GUY...
AH, I'M NOT WORTHY OF SUCH A NAME...
SERI-OUSLY, YOU *SO* AREN'T.
SAY, KAORU, WAS IT REALLY OKAY FOR SOMEONE LIKE ME TO INHERIT SUCH A BEAUTIFUL NAME?
THIS BURDEN IS A BIT HEAVY FOR ME. MY
TENCE IS
RRY ONE
SUCH AN
ING CAT.
WHO WAS
TO YOU...
GREAT, SOME WEIRD, ANNOYING SWITCH JUST TRIG-GERED...

Extra 3: First Mission

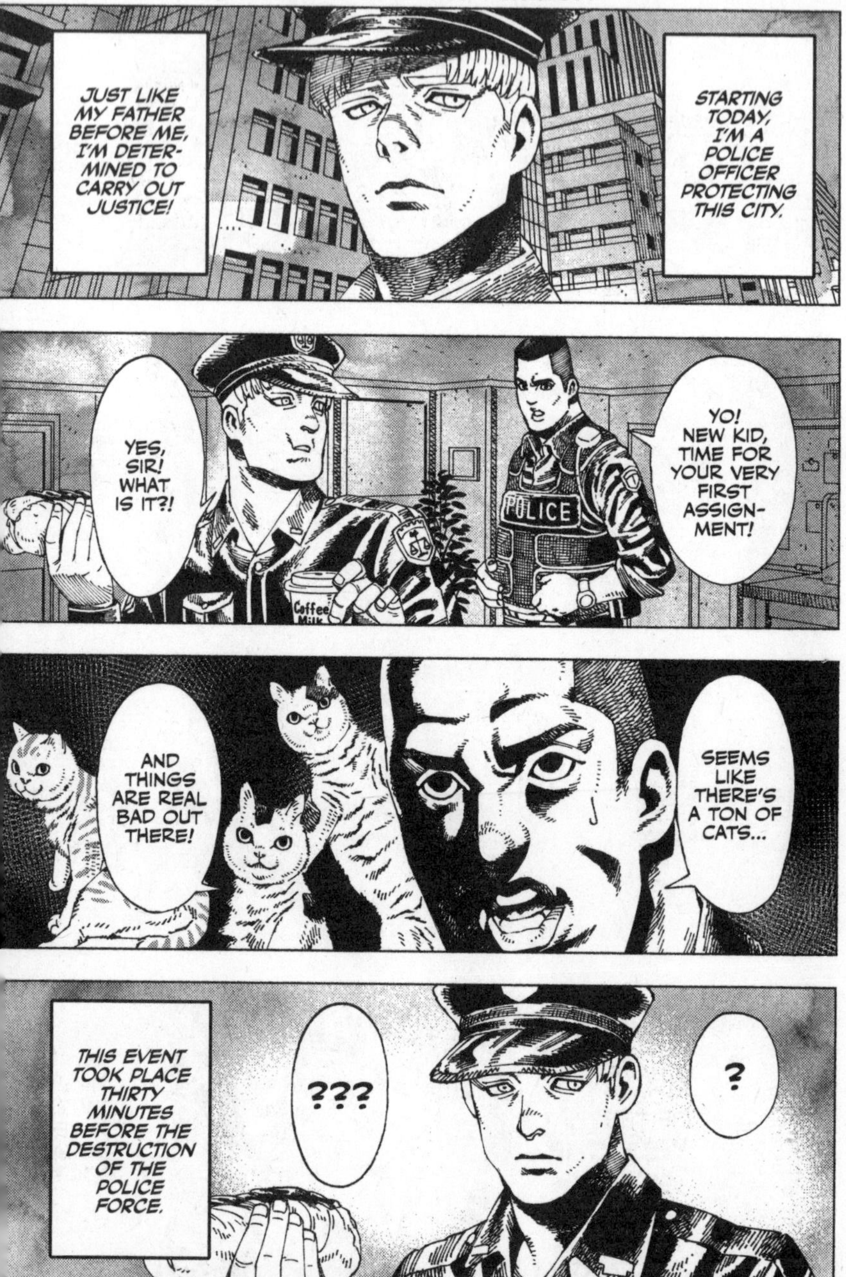
STARTING TODAY, I'M A POLICE OFFICER PROTECTING THIS CITY.
JUST LIKE MY FATHER BEFORE ME, I'M DETERMINED TO CARRY OUT JUSTICE!
YO! NEW KID, TIME FOR YOUR VERY FIRST ASSIGNMENT!
POLICE
YES, SIR! WHAT IS IT?!
Coffee Milk
SEEMS LIKE THERE'S A TON OF CATS...
AND THINGS ARE REAL BAD OUT THERE!
?
???
THIS EVENT TOOK PLACE THIRTY MINUTES BEFORE THE DESTRUCTION OF THE POLICE FORCE.

Extra 4: Collector

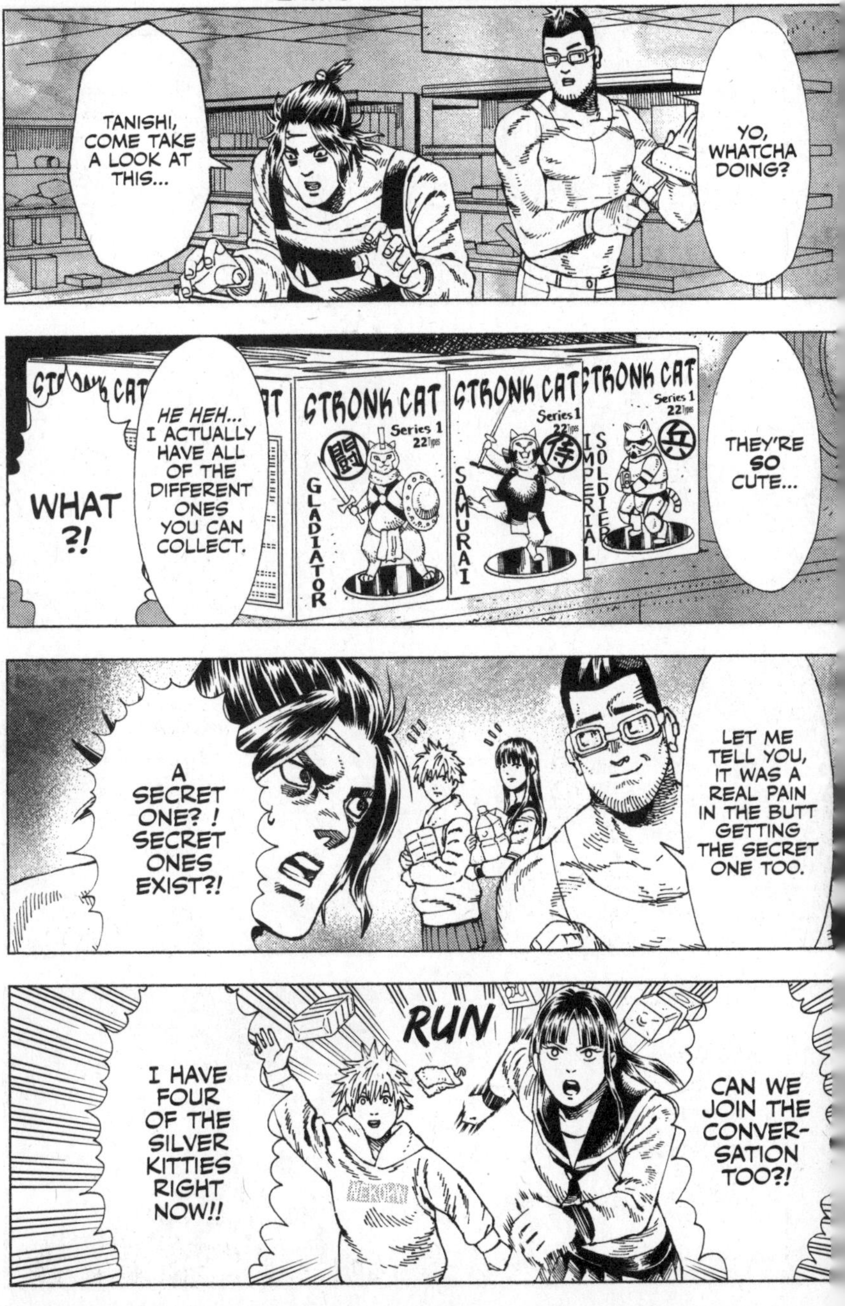

YO, WHATCHA DOING?
TANISHI, COME TAKE A LOOK AT THIS...
THEY'RE SO CUTE...
STRONK CAT
Series 1
22 Types
IMPERIAL SOLDIER
STRONK CAT
Series 1
22 Types
SAMURAI
STRONK CAT
Series 1
22 Types
GLADIATOR
HE HEH... I ACTUALLY HAVE ALL OF THE DIFFERENT ONES YOU CAN COLLECT.
WHAT?!
LET ME TELL YOU, IT WAS A REAL PAIN IN THE BUTT GETTING THE SECRET ONE TOO.
A SECRET ONE?! SECRET ONES EXIST?!
CAN WE JOIN THE CONVER-SATION TOO?!
RUN
I HAVE FOUR OF THE SILVER KITTIES RIGHT NOW!!

Extra 5: Amazing Tool

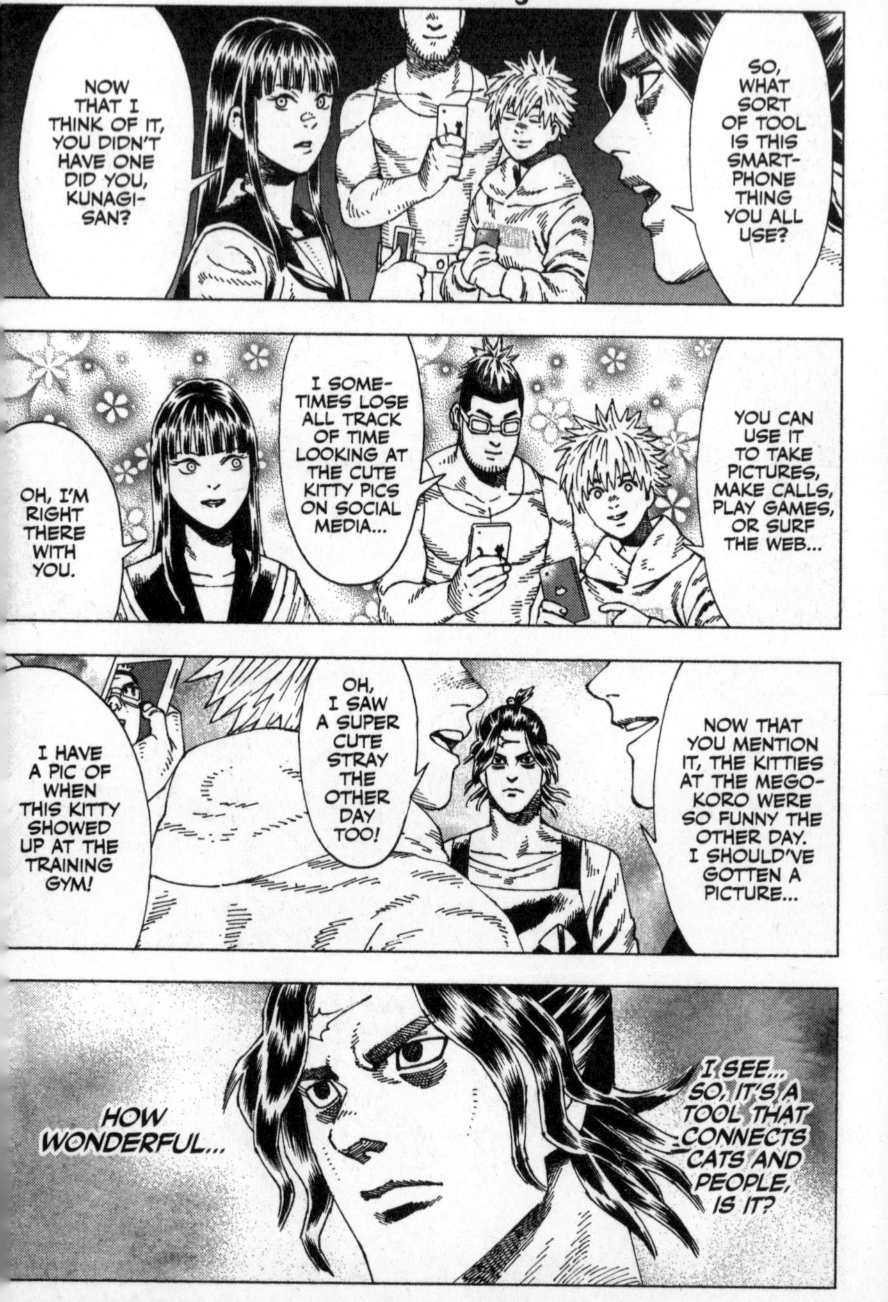
SO, WHAT SORT OF TOOL IS THIS SMARTPHONE THING YOU ALL USE?
NOW THAT I THINK OF IT, YOU DIDN'T HAVE ONE DID YOU, KUNAGI-SAN?
YOU CAN USE IT TO TAKE PICTURES, MAKE CALLS, PLAY GAMES, OR SURF THE WEB...
I SOMETIMES LOSE ALL TRACK OF TIME LOOKING AT THE CUTE KITTY PICS ON SOCIAL MEDIA...
OH, I'M RIGHT THERE WITH YOU.
NOW THAT YOU MENTION IT, THE KITTIES AT THE MEGOKORO WERE SO FUNNY THE OTHER DAY. I SHOULD'VE GOTTEN A PICTURE...
OH, I SAW A SUPER CUTE STRAY THE OTHER DAY TOO!
I HAVE A PIC OF WHEN THIS KITTY SHOWED UP AT THE TRAINING GYM!
I SEE... SO, IT'S A TOOL THAT CONNECTS CATS AND PEOPLE, IS IT?
HOW WONDERFUL...

Extra 6: Will

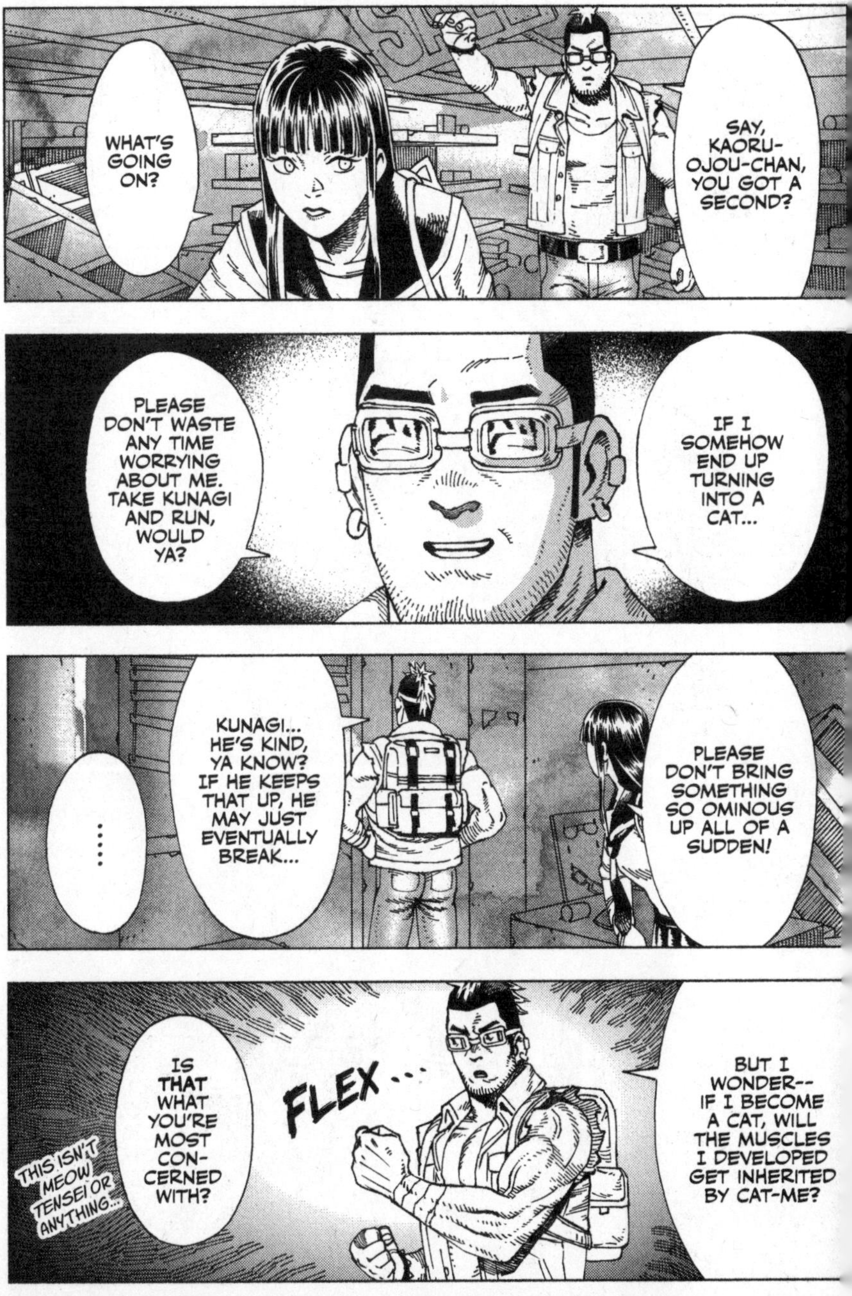
SAY, KAORU-OJOU-CHAN, YOU GOT A SECOND?
WHAT'S GOING ON?
IF I SOMEHOW END UP TURNING INTO A CAT...
PLEASE DON'T WASTE ANY TIME WORRYING ABOUT ME. TAKE KUNAGI AND RUN, WOULD YA?
PLEASE DON'T BRING SOMETHING SO OMINOUS UP ALL OF A SUDDEN!
KUNAGI... HE'S KIND, YA KNOW? IF HE KEEPS THAT UP, HE MAY JUST EVENTUALLY BREAK...
.....
BUT I WONDER-- IF I BECOME A CAT, WILL THE MUSCLES I DEVELOPED GET INHERITED BY CAT-ME?
FLEX...
IS **THAT** WHAT YOU'RE MOST CON-CERNED WITH?
THIS ISN'T MEOW TENSEI OR ANYTHING...

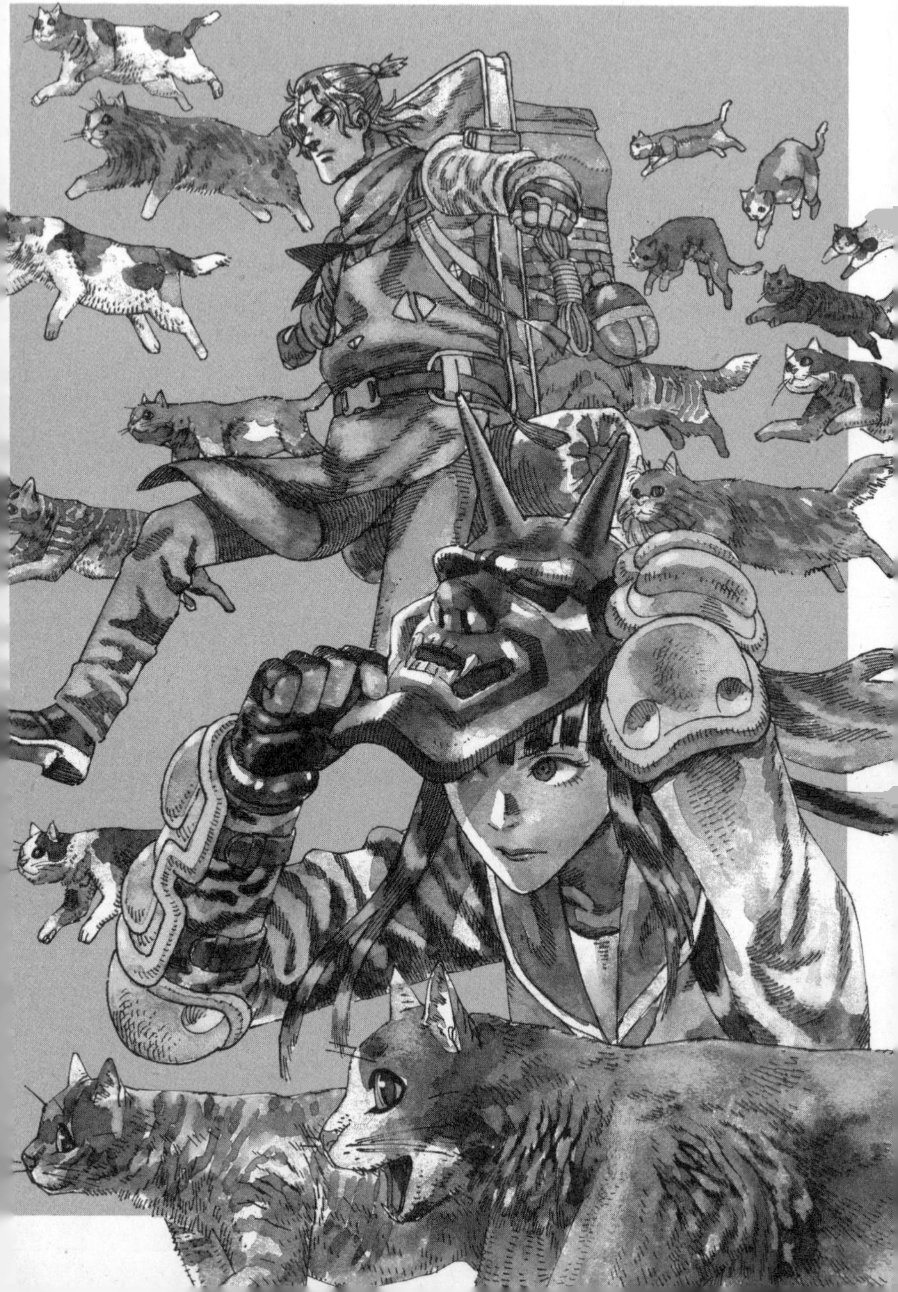

Special THANKS

スペシャルサンクス

〈 Pet Cat Appearances 〉*

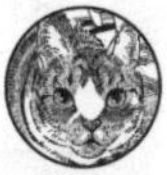

Satsuki-chan from Honda-san's Household.

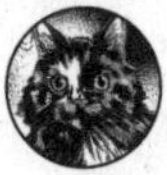

Ayame-chan from Ajiko-san's Household.

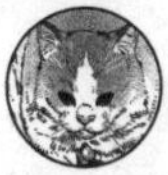

Chappy-kun from Ehara-san's Household.

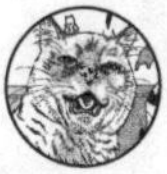

Kinjiro-kun from Shigii-san's Household.

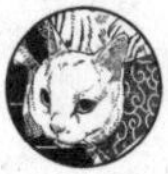

Ren-kun from Seraku Miyachi-san's Household.

*In order of appearance.

〈 Data Collection Assistance 〉

Cat Café Latte

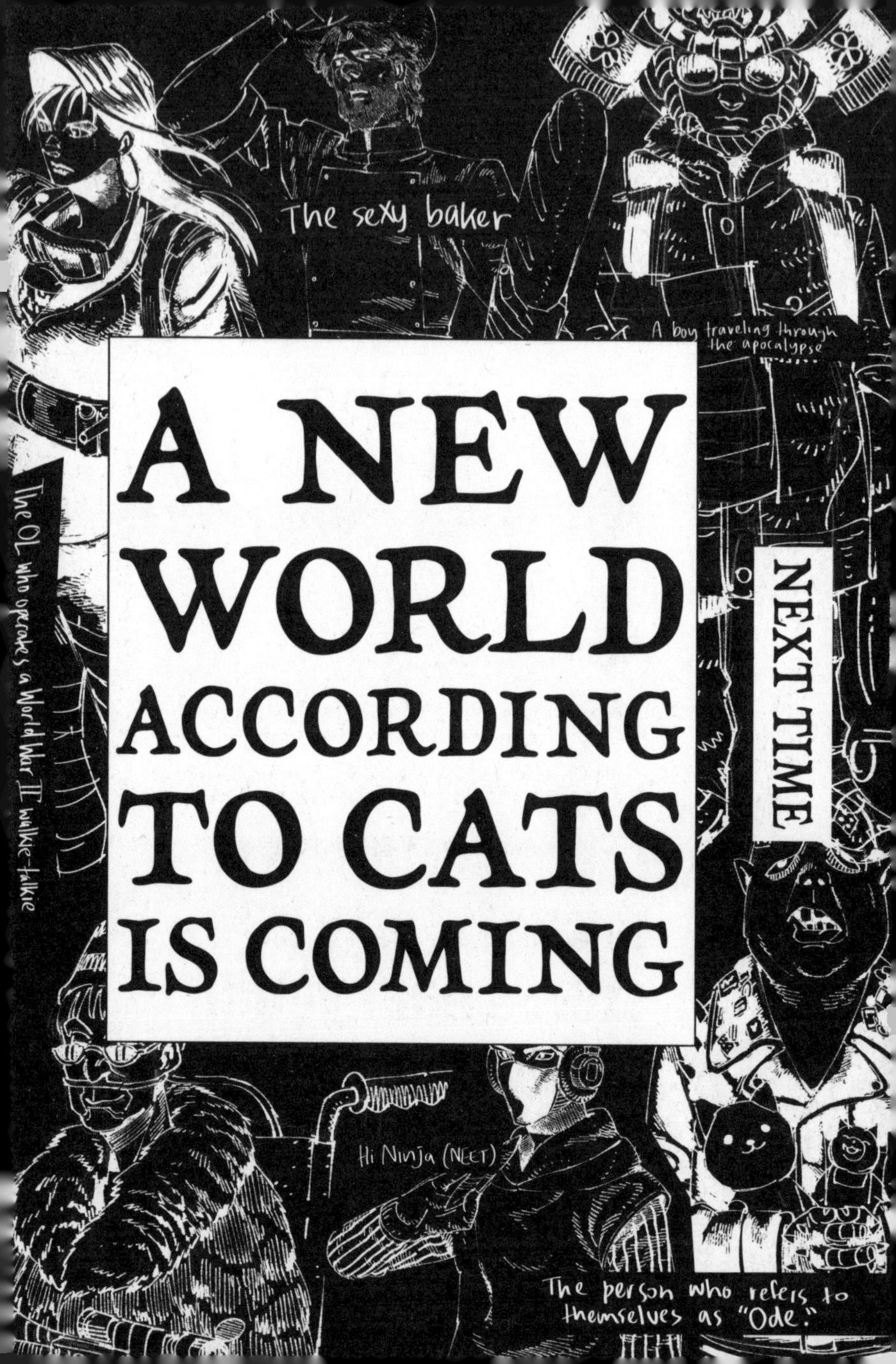
NEXT TIME
A NEW WORLD ACCORDING TO CATS IS COMING
The sexy baker
A boy traveling through the apocalypse
The OL who operates a World War II walkie-talkie
Hi Ninja (NEET)
The person who refers to themselves as "Ode."

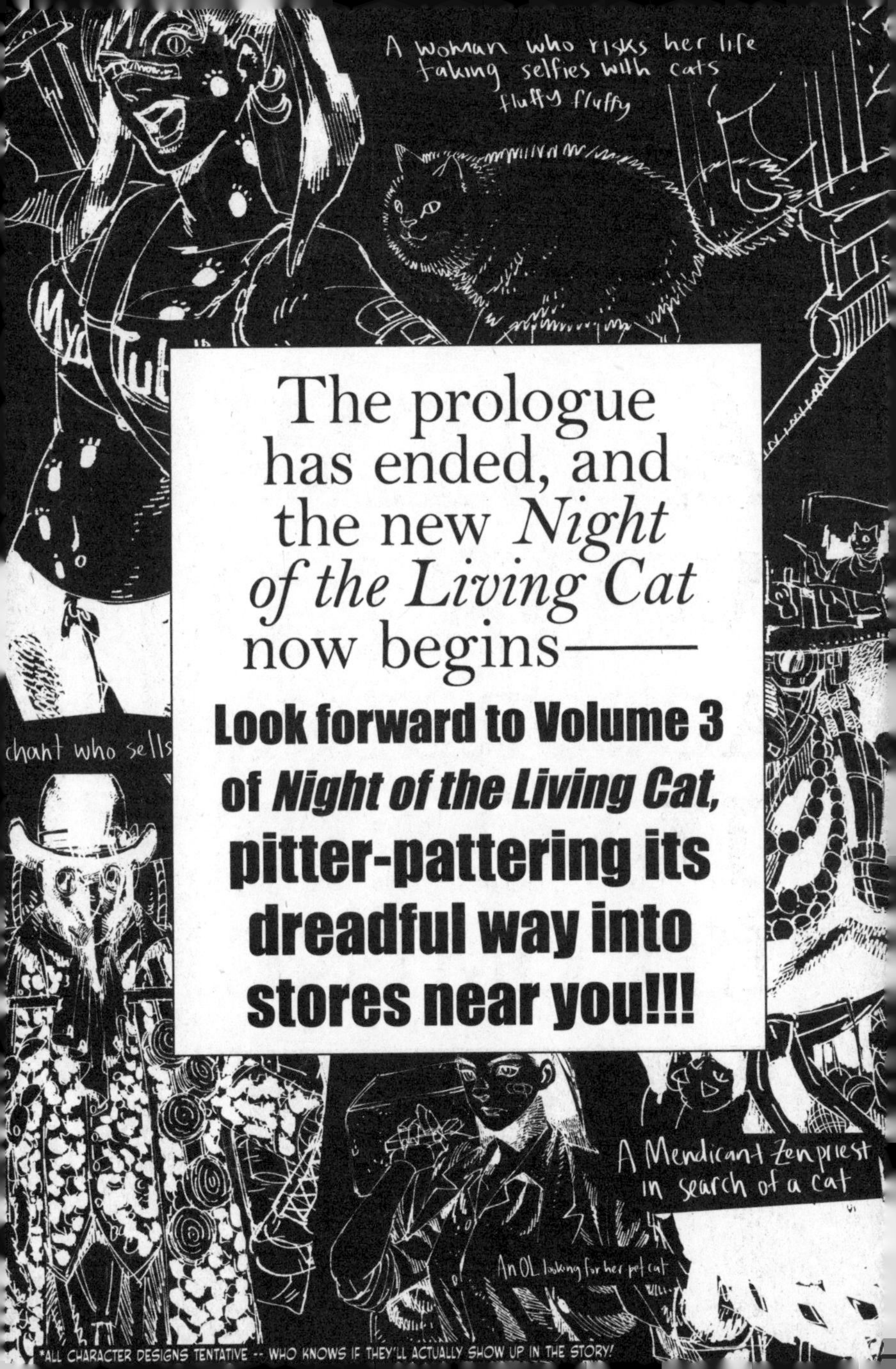
A woman who risks her life taking selfies with cats
fluffy fluffy
chant who sells
A Mendicant Zen priest in search of a cat
An OL looking for her pet cat
*ALL CHARACTER DESIGNS TENTATIVE -- WHO KNOWS IF THEY'LL ACTUALLY SHOW UP IN THE STORY!

The prologue has ended, and the new *Night of the Living Cat* now begins——

Look forward to Volume 3 of *Night of the Living Cat*, pitter-pattering its dreadful way into stores near you!!!

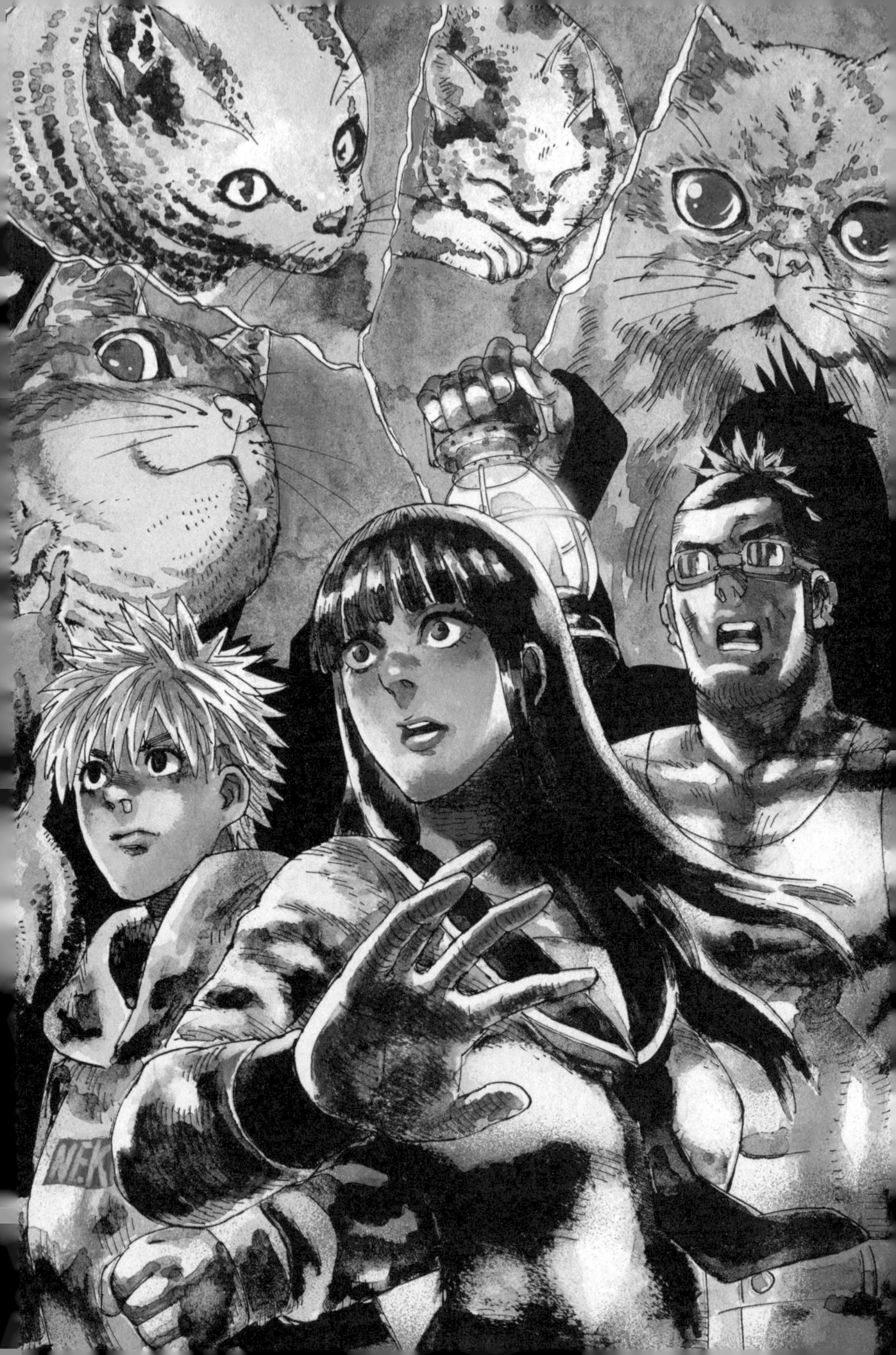

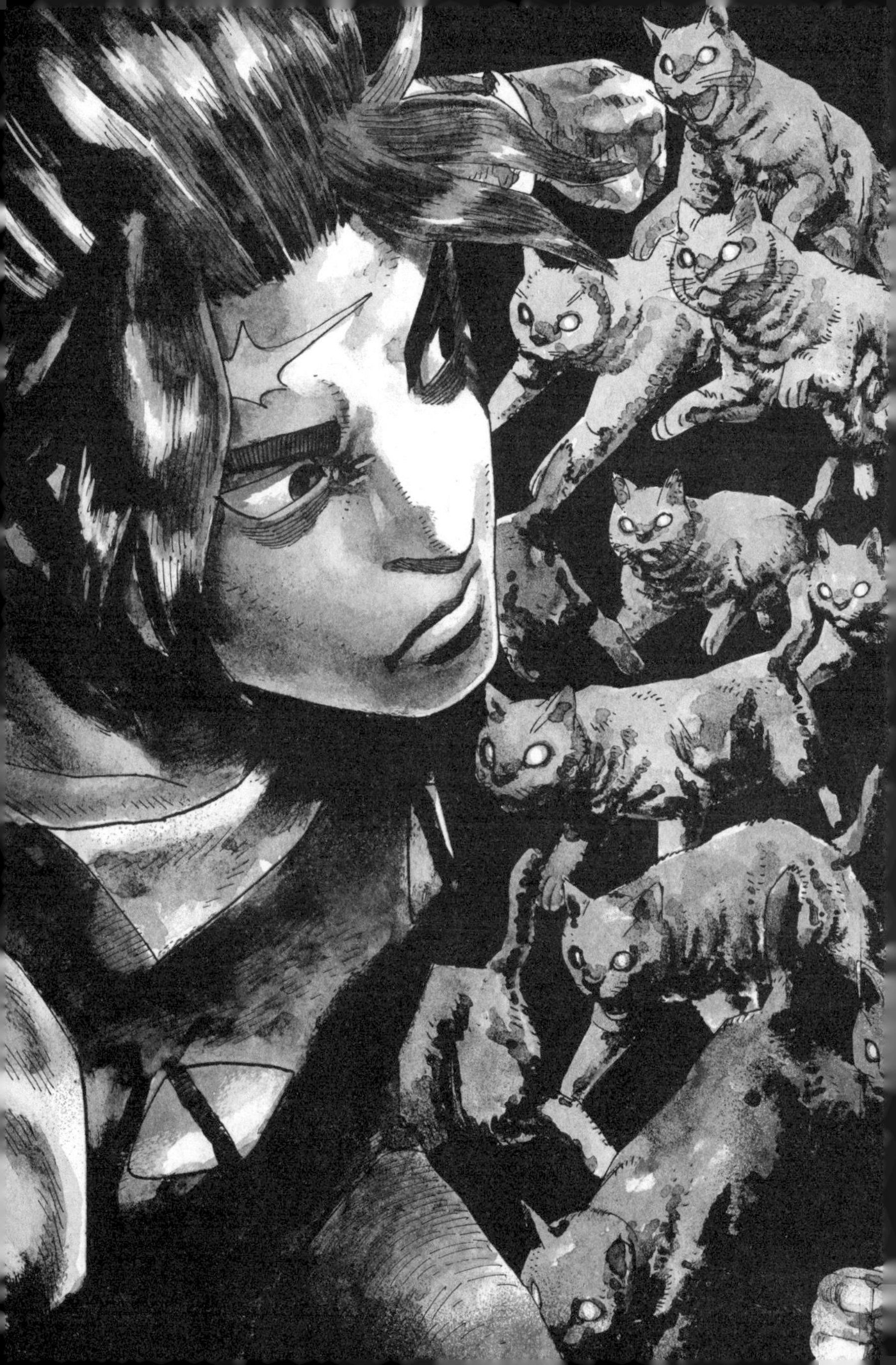

NYAIGHT
OF THE
LIVING
CAT
2

SEVEN SEAS ENTERTAINMENT PRESENTS

NIGHT OF THE LIVING CAT

story by HAWKMAN   art by MECHA-ROOTS   VOLUME TWO

TRANSLATION
Nan Rymer

ADAPTATION
Asha Bardon

LETTERING
Jaewon Ha

COVER DESIGN
Nicky Lim

EDITOR
Abby Lehrke

SENIOR EDITOR
Jack Sullivan

COPY EDITOR
Leighanna DeRouen

PRODUCTION DESIGNER
Christa Miesner

PRODUCTION MANAGER
Lissa Pattillo

PREPRESS TECHNICIAN
Melanie Ujimori
Jules Valera

EDITOR-IN-CHIEF
Julie Davis

ASSOCIATE PUBLISHER
Adam Arnold

PUBLISHER
Jason DeAngelis

NYAIGHT OF THE LIVING CAT vol. 2
© HAWKMAN／MECHA-ROOTS 2022
Originally published in Japan in 2022 by MAG Garden Corporation, TOKYO.
English translation rights arranged through TOHAN CORPORATION, Tokyo

Seven Seas press and purchase enquiries can be sent to Marketing Manager Lianne
Sentar at press@gomanga.com. Information regarding the distribution and purchase of
digital editions is available from Digital Manager CK Russell at digital@gomanga.com.

Seven Seas and the Seven Seas logo are trademarks of
Seven Seas Entertainment. All rights reserved.

ISBN: 978-1-63858-754-5
Printed in Canada
First Printing: January 2023
10 9 8 7 6 5 4 3 2 1

▨▨▨▨ READING DIRECTIONS ▨▨▨▨

This book reads from *right to left*,
Japanese style. If this is your first time
reading manga, you start reading from
the top right panel on each page and
take it from there. If you get lost, just
follow the numbered diagram here.
It may seem backwards at first,
but you'll get the hang of it! Have fun!!

Follow us online: www.SevenSeasEntertainment.com